CRIMINAL JUSTICE AND THE PURSUIT OF TRUTH

Tim Hillier and Gavin Dingwall

BRISTOL
UNIVERSITY
PRESS

First published in Great Britain in 2023 by

Bristol University Press
University of Bristol
1-9 Old Park Hill
Bristol
BS2 8BB
UK
t: +44 (0)117 374 6645
e: bup-info@bristol.ac.uk

Details of international sales and distribution partners are available at bristoluniversitypress.co.uk

British Library Cataloguing in Publication Data
A catalogue record for this book is available from the British Library

ISBN 978-1-5292-0318-9 hardcover
ISBN 978-1-5292-0323-3 paperback
ISBN 978-1-5292-0319-6 ePub
ISBN 978-1-5292-0320-2 ePdf

Cover design: Andrew Corbett
Front cover image: Unsplash/Ben Neale

Bristol University Press uses environmentally responsible print partners.

Printed in Great Britain by CMP, Poole

Contents

Preface

Why write a book about the search for truth in the criminal justice process? Surely it is the purpose of any criminal justice system to arrive at the truth? Surely any defensible process must ensure that innocent people are not convicted and punished for a crime that they did not commit and that conviction and punishment are reserved for those who offend? There is, though, an implicit – and potentially dangerous – assumption that our criminal justice process, or indeed any other, can fulfil this task. If procedural reforms are suggested, they should – one hopes – be driven and judged against whether they would expedite truth-finding. To this end, one of the critical tasks that this book attempts to perform is to explore ways in which current procedure could be improved either to minimize the risk that innocent people are convicted or, on occasion, to increase the likelihood that those who offend are convicted. This, though, is only part of the purpose of the book.

A second aim is to recognize openly that the search for truth can conflict with other legitimate values and purposes. Take the example of an illegal search that yields incriminating evidence. Prioritizing truth would favour using such evidence to aid conviction, assuming that society benefits from the conviction and punishment of criminals, a notion some challenge. Yet, ignoring the context in which evidence was obtained threatens other values important to society. Individuals have human rights protections, notably in this context the right to a fair trial. These rights would be of little value if someone whose rights were infringed had no recourse. Excluding improperly obtained evidence may on occasion result in a factually guilty person being acquitted, but perhaps the need to preserve the integrity of the fact-finding process justifies this outcome. Truth may not always trump all other concerns, even if, as here, there is a potentially undesirable trade-off.

Our final broad theme is to question whether traditional criminal justice processes are equipped to discern the truth surrounding a criminal event. Perhaps society is simply expecting too much. Most crimes are not solved. As will be documented, the system does not operate in the manner often assumed; most suspects confess and most defendants plead guilty, meaning that the emblematic contested trial is a rare event. Alternative models of justice are gaining traction (see Chapter 9). One of the claims made is that these processes are more conciliatory and that an accepted truth is more likely to emerge from a shared understanding and from a joint narrative than from pitting two diametrically opposed accounts before a neutral factfinder. Our suggestion is that in order to assess the virtues of both traditional and alternative conceptions of criminal justice, and to assess their relative abilities to distinguish truth from falsehood, fundamental questions have to be asked about why society seeks to punish wrongdoers. The search for truth is linked intrinsically to the process of blame identification, and blame identification matters because it profoundly affects the person to whom culpability is attributed, especially in criminal cases.

A brief outline of the book is offered here to assist the reader. The contemporary trial is seen as the most appropriate forum for determining the facts surrounding a crime and, critically, whether the defendant bears responsibility. Chapter 1 starts by situating the trial in historical context and reviews earlier means of ascertaining liability. Many of the processes described appear absurd (and often barbaric) to contemporary eyes, but, historically, there was an acceptance that the methods had probative value. There was also a belief in absolute truth, which these techniques would expose. However, the chapter reveals truth to be conceptually complex and contested. Attention will also be given to lying, showing that falsity does not necessitate bad faith. This finding is vital to later chapters as it shows that erroneous conclusions can be drawn despite all parties acting in good faith and believing in the veracity of their accounts.

Crimes seldom come to official attention unless an allegation is made by a member of the public. The ways in which allegations are made and are responded to are considered in Chapter 2. Given the centrality to the criminal justice process, this is an under-explored research area. The need for such research is particularly compelling as society comes to terms with the way in which allegations of child sexual abuse were dismissed historically. Official reviews have shown that the police in particular failed to assess the evidence that they were presented with (many victims did not originally report the offending, probably in part because they thought that their evidence would not be believed). Nevertheless, false allegations are sometimes made and a balance has to be struck between encouraging victims to report crimes and subjecting their evidence to scrutiny so that miscarriages of justice are avoided.

An allegation may lead to an arrest. Some suspects vehemently deny the alleged wrongdoing, but others admit guilt at this stage. Assuming that the confessor is factually guilty, this outcome can be viewed as highly desirable: truth has emerged without the expense and the trauma of a trial. Experience shows, though, that not all apparent confessions are safe. Chapter 3 starts by reviewing the psychological literature that seeks to explain why individuals may admit to crimes for which they are not responsible. Some cases can be attributed to oppressive law enforcement, yet in other cases people have confessed in the absence of any coercion. This is a particular concern in English law as confession evidence does not need to be corroborated. There have been many cases where defendants have sought to retract confessions at trial, arguing that the means by which they were obtained render them suspect. The relevant law is analyzed to see whether the primary determining factor is the veracity of the confession or a broader concern about the rights of suspects in the criminal justice process.

Chapter 4 turns to witness reliability. Juries attach great weight to testimony and yet witnesses' accounts can be highly unreliable. An initial concern is that demeanour may give an unjustified impression of accuracy. The law also limits the situations where witnesses can present hearsay evidence – on the basis that it cannot be adequately tested – and the chapter reviews the exceptions to this rule and asks whether they compromise establishing the truth. Identification evidence is notoriously fallible and, it has been suggested, leads to a high proportion of miscarriages of justice. This links more generally into issues of memory; of how facts are processed at times of stress, and of how they are subsequently recalled in another stressful environment.

An area where the search for truth is pitted against other vital objectives relates to the use that can be made of probative evidence that has been illegally or unfairly obtained. If the focus was solely on fact-finding, Chapter 5 would be short as there would be a compelling basis for admitting such evidence. Yet no legal system adopts such an approach. The need to deter malpractice by law enforcement agencies, allied to the desire to maintain broader systemic integrity, has led some jurisdictions to exclude illegally obtained evidence automatically even if it would prove guilt. This 'fruits of the poison tree' doctrine is associated most strongly with the United States and the development of this position is contrasted with England and Wales where the courts are afforded broad discretion to determine whether unfairly obtained evidence should be excluded. Case law shows that exclusion is exceptional. What this means for the current discussion is that probative evidence can be used more readily in England and Wales than in many comparable jurisdictions.

Chapter 6 explores trial narrative. Prosecutors are charged with determining whether there is a realistic chance that the evidence will lead to the suspect's conviction. The evidence has to provide a compelling story because people make sense of the world and of events through narrative. Police and prosecutors are therefore engaged in a process of case construction while the advocate's skill is in presenting the evidence in a way that is coherent and compelling. The centrality of storytelling challenges notions of the trial as a rational and scientific process and the implications of this to the search for truth are analyzed.

In a contested trial, the defence has the opportunity to submit a counter narrative. These alternative narratives are considered in Chapter 7. The counter narrative is often simple: 'I do not bear responsibility and the evidence that you seek to use against me is insufficient to prove that I do'. Indeed, the defence is under no obligation to respond to the prosecution's case. But there are rules surrounding what evidence the defence can use when presenting their narrative. The most important rules relate to past conduct on the part of witnesses – particularly with regards to complainants in sexual offence cases – and where a defendant seeks to introduce evidence of their own good character. The danger is that the significant prejudicial effect of such evidence outweighs its (at best) marginal probative value. Here a decision has been taken not to entrust the jury with all of the available evidence. This suggests that fact-finding is sometimes best served if the evidence is filtered before being considered by the factfinder. Does this cast doubt on a jury's ability to weigh up the evidence and then determine the truth?

Accounts of the criminal process often stop after conviction and it is easy to see why conviction can be portrayed as a finding not only of guilt but also of circumstance. The sentencing exercise, though, remains heavily dependent on the truth, or at least it should, and the reasons why are articulated in Chapter 8. Two themes in particular are developed. Acceptance of guilt, in the form of a guilty plea, is far more common than contested trials but, in practice, can entail plea negotiation. Someone may admit guilt to an offence that fails to reflect the reality of what occurred; usually what is not reflected is the gravity of the offending conduct. There are evident concerns that an inducement based on a significant sentence discount may lead someone who is factually innocent to plead guilty. A miscarriage of justice, though, may also follow if someone receives a disproportionately lenient sentence based on a misrepresentation of the circumstances of the offence. A secondary point relates to the use of sentencing guidelines, which courts in England and Wales must follow unless it is contrary to the interests of justice. What the guidelines often do is select facts that should have relevance when determining the appropriate sentence and then prescribe the effect that the presence (or absence) of these facts should have. In other words, determinations of factual significance have already been made.

As has already been mentioned, one of the themes of this book is whether current criminal justice institutions and processes are the optimal means of establishing truth. The chapters mentioned up until now highlight various concerns. The adversarial trial (though seldom employed in practice) rests on the idea that weak evidence can be exposed when subjected either to a more compelling counter narrative or to persuasive critique by a skilled advocate. This orthodoxy has become increasingly challenged. Scholars and activists have identified various alleged flaws with 'old' justice paradigms and have devised alternative models that, among other claims, are purported to improve the likelihood of the truth emerging. There are marked distinctions between alternative models, but most adopt what can broadly be classified as a 'restorative justice' approach. Chapter 9 investigates the theoretical basis for the claims made by reformers and reviews the empirical evidence that tends to support the view that both victims and offenders find the process valuable. One of the reasons why, it is argued, is that stakeholders share a desire to explain the event and this has the potential to lead to consensus and settlement.

Chapter 10 draws out some fundamental themes in the book and points to the limitations of the current criminal justice system, not only in terms of establishing truth but also in terms of realizing significant social benefit. Three areas of focus are taken to assess the current system's ability to find the truth. First, we consider the extent to which the criminal process adopts a person, rather than a system, approach to bad events with a focus on identifying individuals to blame rather than addressing the wider problems resulting from crime. Second, we consider the position of children within the criminal process. Discussions about the overriding purpose of the criminal process tend to concentrate on the system pertaining to adult offenders and ignore or marginalize the less visible juvenile justice system. Juvenile justice perhaps highlights many aspects of the relationship between truth and criminal justice in general. Third, we conclude by considering other possible approaches to criminal justice and the extent to which the current system's preoccupation with a narrow historical truth undermines the wider pursuit of justice for all. The pursuit of truth is used as a means of identifying those deserving of punishment, even though the many harms of punishment are as well documented as the limited effect punishment has in reducing crime. Society must resist the default position that current criminal justice paradigms are optimal either in terms of truth-finding or in terms of responding to criminal harm.

Our sincere thanks are due to a number of people who have assisted us in various ways throughout the writing of this book. We are grateful to Bristol University Press for their enthusiasm for the project and for their assistance and skill in producing such an attractive book. Policy Press, an imprint of Bristol University Press, published our previous work *Blamestorming, Blamemongers and Scapegoats: Allocating Blame in the Criminal Justice Process* (Dingwall and Hillier, 2016) and our experience was such that we had no hesitation in approaching Bristol University Press again with the proposal for this book. Professor Dave Walsh, a colleague in the School of Law at De Montfort University, guided our thinking about confession evidence and brought a number of psychological studies to our attention. Danielle Bates and Jessica Gallagher provided outstanding research assistance. Any writer fortunate enough to have worked with able and enthusiastic research assistants will appreciate the value that they bring to a project. Finally, our family and friends have once again taken a keen interest in the book and have supported us as we worked on it (particularly during the COVID-19 lockdown restrictions in 2020). It is to them that we dedicate it.

Tim Hillier and Gavin Dingwall
Leicestershire, November 2020

1

The Criminal Process and the Pursuit of Truth

'Clive has dedicated his 35 year career to unearthing the truth.' So begins the preface to the autobiography of Clive Driscoll, a former Detective Chief Inspector with the Metropolitan Police (Driscoll, 2015). Driscoll is probably best known for leading the investigation that resulted in the conviction of two of the men responsible for the death of Stephen Lawrence. Criminal investigations and the entire criminal process culminating in the criminal trial are regularly characterized as a pursuit of the truth:

> Underlying the question of guilt or innocence is an objective truth: the defendant, in fact, did or did not commit the acts constituting the crime charged. From the time an accused is first suspected to the time the decision on guilt or innocence is made, our criminal justice system is designed to enable the trier of fact to discover the truth according to law. (*Burlington* v *Missouri* 451 US 430 (1981))

In *Jones* v *National Coal Board* [1957] 2 QB 55 Denning LJ (as he then was) identified that the judicial role 'above all, is to find out the truth' (p 63). The same point was made by the US Supreme Court in *Tehan* v *United States ex rel. Shott* 382 US 406 (1966): 'The basic purpose of a trial is the determination of the truth' (p 416). It was reiterated by Marvin E. Frankel, who sat as a judge of the US District Court for the Southern District of New York between 1965 and 1978 and was a key figure in the development of sentencing guidelines in the United States, who wrote: 'Trials occur because there are questions of fact. In principle, the paramount objective is the truth' (Frankel, 1975, p 1033).

In *Jones* v *National Coal Board* [1957] 2 QB 55 Denning LJ contrasted the adversarial system developed by common law countries with the inquisitorial system: 'In the system of trial which we have evolved in this country, the judge sits to hear and determine the issues raised by the parties, not to conduct an investigation or examination on behalf of society at large, as happens, we believe, in some foreign countries' (p 63). The case concerned a claim brought by the widow of a coal miner killed in a mining accident. Today the case might well have given rise to a criminal prosecution for corporate manslaughter but the law at the time meant that the widow had to seek compensation under section 49 of the Coal Mines Act 1911 and in an action for negligence. Mr Jones had been killed underground as a result of a roof fall that occurred at a location where another roof fall had occurred only weeks earlier. Liability hinged on the question of whether or not adequate roof supports had been put in place following the first fall: liability depended on a determination of the facts surrounding the accident. In the words of one of the leading texts on the law of evidence: 'When a court of law sets out to decide whether a contested event took place as party A asserts or, to the contrary, in the way that party B contends, the court is trying to get at the truth of the matter in dispute' (Roberts and Zuckerman, 2010, p 3).

Tracing the history of the jury trial, Harvard Professor of Law, James Bradley Thayer, wrote in 1890–91:

> [Let] us ask what it is that juries, inquests, assizes, were created for ... They were wanted, in a pending legal controversy, where the parties were at issue on some question of fact, to say what the fact was, and the name for this thing was *rei veritas* [the truth of the thing]. (Thayer, 1890–91, p 148)

Thayer states that many questions of fact are decided by the courts themselves: 'A stream of questions as to the reality, the *rei veritas*, the fact, of what was alleged before them, was constantly pouring in'. He gives the example of a 14th-century case where a prisoner confessed but, when brought before the court, claimed that the confession had been obtained under duress by his jailer. In order to evaluate the claim, the justice sent for several other prisoners and the jailer and, after questioning them in the presence of the prisoner, concluded that the claim was false (1890–91, p 148). For Thayer, the courts have always appeared to have been concerned with establishing 'facts' and he explicitly uses 'fact' as 'indicating things, events, actions, conditions, as happening, existing, really taking place' (1890–91, p 151). It follows that:

> The question of whether a thing be a fact or not, is the question of whether it is, whether it exists, whether it be true. All inquiries into the truth, the reality, the actuality of things are inquiries into the fact about them. Nothing is a question of fact which is not a question of the existence, reality, truth of something, of the *rei veritas*. (Thayer, 1890–91, p 152)

More recently, some writers have questioned whether the search for truth remains the sole purpose of the criminal justice process. Campbell et al (2019, p 27) have argued that, as well as the search for truth, notions of fairness are central to the criminal justice process and are particularly important at trial. In an extensive study of the trial, Duff et al wrote:

> Trials, it might be argued, aim to establish the truth. They aim to establish whether the defendant committed the offences with which they have been charged as defined by the criminal law, whether they are entitled to any defence, and to determine whether they can be punished. Trials are thus of purely instrumental value: they serve the more fundamental interest that the state has in establishing who we can justly punish for their crimes. (Duff et al, 2007, p 4)

Duff et al proceed then to question whether truth-finding is the sole aim:

> First, although almost everyone will agree that trials have epistemically ambitions (even if some are sceptical about whether those ambitions can be fulfilled), a question remains about what the trial's epistemically aim is or should be. Is truth the ultimate aim sought, or is truth part of some more ambitious aim that the trial might have? Is the aim merely to establish the truth of a fact or set of facts about the defendant, as the standard story suggests? Or does a criminal conviction have normative significance, such that it can be justified only if the court can be normatively committed to the verdict? (Duff et al, 2007, p 6)

Despite this more recent questioning, the *standard story* continues to frame the dominant narrative: the primary purpose of the criminal justice process generally and the criminal trial in particular is the pursuit and capture of an objective truth – did the defendant do it? Underlying this is the notion that there is a single, objectively verifiable truth. This chapter will explore conceptions of truth, drawing on the philosophical and epistemological literature. It will also provide an introduction to psychological and neurological accounts of truth, giving particular attention to the problems posed by 'false memory'.

The evolution of the modern criminal process

According to Pollock and Maitland in the 12th or 13th century: '[The] language of the law ... had no word equivalent to our *trial*. We have not to speak of trial; we have to speak of proof. The old modes of proof might be reduced to two, ordeals and oaths; both were appeals to the supernatural' (Pollock and Maitland, 1895, p 330). The two main forms of ordeal were fire and water. Ordeal by fire involved the accused carrying a red-hot bar of iron; if the wound healed cleanly within three days, they were considered innocent, while a lack of healing denoted guilt. Ordeal by water saw the accused plunged into a pool of water, on a rope with a knot in it; if the accused sank to the depth of the knot, they were deemed to be innocent and pulled free, while floating was taken as a sign of guilt. There was criticism of the use of ordeals but Pollock and Maitland reported that both were 'freely used' in the 12th century. A major turning point was the Fourth Lateran Council of 1215, where Pope Innocent III prohibited the clergy from taking part in such ordeals (McAuley, 2006). The secular authorities quickly followed and Pollock and Maitland (1895) could find no instances of ordeal in England after the death of King John in 1216.

The oath required the accused to swear away the charge, normally supported by the oaths of 'oath helpers'. Initially, such oath helpers were kinspeople of the accused but 'in the course of time the law no longer required kinsmen, and we see a rationalistic tendency which would convert the oath helpers into impartial witnesses to character' (Pollock and Maitland, 1895, p 330). Those who swore falsely would ultimately face the wrath of God and run the risk of subsequent conviction for perjury. The formalities required for taking the oath were such that some accused preferred to take their chances with the red-hot iron (Pollock and Maitland, 1895, p 330).

As criticism of ordeal and oath increased, the trial, in a form recognizable today, began to replace them. Professor Thayer located the origins of the modern English trial at the Norman invasion:

> When the Normans came into England they brought with them, not only a far more vigorous and searching kingly power than had been known there, but also a certain product of the exercise of this power by the Frankish kings and the Norman dukes; namely, the use of the inquisition in public administration, ie, the practice of ascertaining facts by summoning together by public authority a number of people most likely, as being neighbors, to know and tell the truth, and calling for their answer under oath. (Thayer, 1890–91, p 152)

According to Pollock and Maitland, it was at this point that the adversarial and inquisitorial approaches to criminal justice emerged (Pollock and Maitland, 1895, p 333).

The oath

Use of the ordeal may have disappeared from criminal justice by the 13th century but the oath, albeit in a modified form, has continued to have significance in the modern trial. A major study of the oath and its development was undertaken by Helen Silving (1959a).

> The familiar oath of the present-day courtroom has been traced to a prereligious, indeed, pre-animistic period of culture. Supernatural beings were unknown, and man believed that he possessed magic power which could produce any desired result. A vehicle of this power was the curse, which could kill as effectively as physical force. It worked through the magic inherent in the word or the magic act ... The oath was a self-curse, uttered in conditional form, operating irrevocably upon occurrence of the condition. Thus the self-curse could be utilized as a means of guaranteeing that a promise would be performed. (Silving, 1959a, p 1330)

Failure to perform the promise would result either in the sanction specified in the oath or in the more generic penalty for perjury. In Roman and Greek civilization it was thought that Jupiter/Zeus visited perjurers with lightning.

The origins of the modern courtroom oath are traced back to the book of Genesis and the oaths demanded by Abraham and Isaac. In both instances, the oath was taken on male genitalia (Genesis

24: 2–9; Genesis 47: 29). However, as Silving points out: 'All advanced monotheistic religions have been disturbed by these peculiarly primitive features of the oath' (1959a, p 1331). As a result, the oath has become combined with an affirmation of faith. Until comparatively recently there was little connection between the oath and the truth. As we have already seen, false oaths could be decisive of facts. Any sanction for perjury was a matter for God.

Silving suggests that this is linked to earlier notions of truth and a lack of distinction between morality and fear of disadvantage or harm: 'To [the ancient Semites] success was virtue and failure was vice. "Truth" was not – as it is in the ideal of modern man – accordance with objective facts, but was successful assertion of one's cause' (1959a, p 1334). Truth comes to denote an expression of power and this explains the fact, alluded to in Pollock and Maitland (1895), that joining a group of oath takers was about expressing solidarity and power: 'The original judicial oath was not incidental to testimonial evidence. Rather the reverse was the case; witnesses supported the oath. Indeed, testimony did not originally constitute an independent means of proof. It was but a means of fortifying the litigants' oath' (Silving, 1959a, p 1337).

The oath was not without its critics. Aristotle characterized the oath as 'an unproved statement supported by an appeal to the gods' (quoted in Silving, 1959a, p 1337). In the Sermon on the Mount, Jesus said:

> Again, you have heard that it was said to the people long ago, 'Do not break your oath, but fulfill to the Lord the vows you have made.' But I tell you, do not swear an oath at all: either by heaven, for it is God's throne; or by the earth, for it is his footstool; or by Jerusalem, for it is the city of the Great King. And do not swear by your head, for you cannot make even one hair white or black. All you need to say is simply 'Yes' or 'No'; anything beyond this comes from the evil. (Matthew 5: 31–7)

The oath became more popular, as we have already seen, following the decline in the use of ordeal as a method of settling disputes. The oath started to transform into a vow to tell the truth and theologians began to argue that it was not oaths per se that were wrong, only false oaths. The oath remained an issue of controversy throughout the Middle Ages:

> In his Summa Theologica, St. Thomas Aquinas argued that he who takes the oath is not obligated to 'tell the whole truth.' He may remain silent, for there is a difference

between silence and falsehood. But where there has been *infamia*, or express evidence of guilt, and he is asked to confess, he must not conceal the truth. (Silving, 1959a, p 1346)

And:

[In] 1698, upon order of Pope Innocent XII, Franciscus Memmius made a thorough inquiry into the question of the 'expediency of abrogating the custom of requiring accused persons, prior to interrogation, to take an oath to tell the truth.' He arrived at the conclusion that the custom should be abolished, since it was 'violent and unjust.' (Silving, 1959a, p 1346)

The doubt about the efficacy of oaths (particularly those taken by the accused) continued during the 18th century. In chapter 18 of his *Essay on Crimes and Punishments*, Cesare Beccaria wrote:

There is a palpable contradiction, between the laws and the natural sentiments of mankind in the case of oaths, which are administered to a criminal to make him speak the truth, when the contrary is his greatest interest ... oaths become, by degrees, a mere formality, and all sentiments of religion, perhaps the only motive of honesty in the greatest part of mankind, are destroyed. (Beccaria, 1769)

Influenced by Beccaria, one of the early reforms following the French Revolution was the abolition of the accused's oath. In 1795, the revolutionary government proposed the complete abolition of the oath and its replacement with a simple promise by witnesses 'to tell the truth'.

The oath had also been criticized by the philosophers. Johann Gottlieb Fichte, developing the ideas of Immanuel Kant, wrote: '[What] is there supposed to be in an oath calculated to restrain a man, who will publicly assert a falsehood, from making a false assertion under oath?' (Fichte, 1869, p 283). He concluded that the oath should never be administered and that there would be no need for oaths in a properly organized state.

Helen Silving identified a number of states that had considered abolishing the oath but the conclusion drawn was always that the oath affords 'a particular safeguard to truth finding' and that 'the State should not forego utilizing this means of influencing the witness' (Silving, 1959a, p 1359). In English law, the accused could not give evidence under oath until the Criminal Evidence Act 1898, but that did not stop more general criticism of the use of the oath in judicial proceedings. Foremost among the critics was Jeremy Bentham, who published a paper on the subject in 1817. Bentham's opening words contain the essential paradox of the oath:

> By the term oath, taken in its largest sense, is universally understood, a ceremony composed of words and gestures, by means of which the Almighty is engaged eventually to inflict on the taker of the oath, or swearer, as he is called, punishment, in quantity and quality, liquidated, or more commonly unliquidated, in the event of his doing something which he, the swearer, at the same time and thereby engages not to do, or omitting to do something which he in like manner engages to do. (Bentham, 1817, p 191)

Silving concluded her review of the oath by supporting calls for its abolition. Although the focus here has been on the oath, similar arguments apply to the affirmation. Silving argued:

> The desirability of abolition is corroborated by a modern re-evaluation of the rules of self-incrimination and confession, to which the oath is closely related. Essentially a self-curse, the oath is an anticipatory self-condemnation or self-incrimination, carrying a promise of confession. Thus, many of the arguments against compulsory self-incrimination and confession seem applicable to a compulsory oath ... Our law presupposes man to be a perfectly rational being, who weighs profit against loss with the precision of a calculating machine and, at the same time, is the most lenient judge of his own sins. Law presumes that man will always wish to testify in his own behalf when he is innocent and that he will never, except on rational grounds, or under external coercion, make a false confession. Therefore, we bar coerced confessions and compulsory self-accusation, while according 'voluntary' confessions and declarations against interest high probative value ... Psychoanalysis has shown, however, that man is not an entirely rational being, and that his sense of guilt

8

does not operate in an unambiguous fashion ... He may expressly, or by implication, 'adjudge' himself guilty of the crime of which he stands accused, and which he did not commit, in order to atone for an entirely different crime, a 'crime' of childhood. And because this sense of guilt is often intense, he may be the severest judge of his present acts. Thus, far from invariably justifying his action as the reasonable man is believed to do, man sometimes tends to incriminate himself. (Silving, 1959b, p 1573)

The topics of confessions and self-incrimination are discussed in Chapter 3.

Oaths were discussed in *Attorney General* v *Bradlaugh* (1885) 14 QBD 667. The case concerned Charles Bradlaugh, founder of the National Secular Society, who had been elected to Parliament but refused to take the oath of allegiance under the Parliamentary Oaths Act 1866 on the basis that he did not believe in any God. In giving judgment, the Court of Appeal discussed oaths more generally. In the earlier case of *Omichund* v *Barker* (1745), 1 Atk 21 Willes CJ had stated:

> I am of opinion that such infidels as believe in a God, and that He will punish them if they swear falsely, may and ought to be admitted as witnesses in this, though a Christian country. And on the other hand I am clearly of opinion that such infidels, (if any such there be), who either do not believe in a God or if they do, do not think that he will either reward or punish them in this world or the next, cannot be witnesses in any case nor under any circumstances.

The Court of Appeal also considered Phillipps on Evidence where it was stated that:

> It is not sufficient that the witness believes himself bound to speak the truth from a regard to character, or to the common interests of society, or from a fear of the punishment which the law inflicts upon persons guilty of perjury. That is not sufficient. The question is, whether he can take an oath. The question is, not whether he is bound in honour; it is whether he is bound by an oath. (*Attorney General* v *Bradlaugh* (1885) 14 QBD 667)

That position was confirmed by the Court of Appeal, which rejected Bradlaugh's appeal. Although Quakers and Moravians were allowed to affirm as a result of section 1 of the Quakers and Moravians Act 1833, their objection was to the blasphemous nature of the oath rather than a lack of fear of divine reward or punishment. The Oaths Act 1978 does allow those who do not believe in God to affirm but it remains the case that, subject to very few exceptions, no evidence is admissible in court unless given upon oath or affirmation. It is a contempt of court for a witness to refuse to affirm or be sworn. In the overwhelming majority of cases, therefore, witness testimony is given on oath or solemn affirmation. The extent to which that results in the court hearing 'the truth, the whole truth, and nothing but the truth' (Ormerod and Perry, 2018, part F4.32) will form the main topic of this book.

The nature of truth

In Dorothy L. Sayers' *Busman's Honeymoon*, Lord Peter Wimsey is apprised of the elusive nature of truth:

> Reckon there's several kinds of truth, my lord. There's truth as far as you knows it; and there's truth as far as you're asked for it. But that don't represent the whole truth – not necessarily. (Sayers, 1937, p 126)

In an article published in *The Nation* in January 1992, Steven Tesich, the Serbian-American playwright and screenwriter, wrote about 'Watergate Syndrome' and how the result of the Watergate scandal was a collective 'shying away' from the truth: 'We came to equate truth with bad news and we didn't want bad news anymore, no matter how true or vital to our health as a nation'. Tesich traced political developments through the 1980s and early 1990s and concluded that: 'In a very fundamental way, we as a people have freely decided that we want to live in some post-truth world' (Tesich, 1992, p 13). Tesich's piece was sandwiched between articles on agricultural workers in California and the threat to Pacific salmon and seemed unlikely to remain in public consciousness for very long. Yet the concept of a 'post-truth world' had a resonance to such an extent that the *Oxford English Dictionary* credits Tesich's article as being the first use of 'post-truth', which was the 2016 International Word of the Year. The front cover of *TIME* magazine on 23 March 2017 starkly asked: 'Is Truth Dead?' – echoing another famous *TIME* magazine cover from 8 April 1966, which asked: 'Is God Dead?'. The concepts of 'fake news' and 'post-truth society' seem to suggest that the distinction between what is and what is not true has become blurred.

Following that March 2017 edition of *TIME*, Duquesne University School of Law hosted the symposium 'Shall These Bones Live? Resurrecting Truth in American Law and Public Discourse' on 16 and 17 November 2017. In the foreword to the special symposium edition of the *Duquesne Law Review*, Professor Wilson Huhn wrote: 'The law school hosted this conference … at a moment of crisis in our society – a crisis of faith – a crisis of confidence in our ability to seek and know the truth' (Huhn, 2018, p 1). For Huhn, truth is at the centre of the civilizing endeavour. In respect of criminal justice:

> Only when investigators are devoted to uncovering what really occurred; when prosecutors diligently seek to prosecute wrongdoers; when defense attorneys are obedient to their duty not to partake in the misprision of evidence or suborn perjury; when witnesses tell the truth, the whole truth, and nothing but the truth; when juries evaluate the trust-worthiness of evidence in a fair and objective manner; when trial and appellate judges administer justice without respect to persons, and do equal right to the poor and to the rich, and faithfully and impartially discharge and perform all the duties incumbent upon them – only then can we have faith that our courts will punish the guilty and absolve the innocent. (Huhn, 2018, p 4)

The standard account of criminal justice therefore relies on the courts reaching a 'true' verdict in order that society can have faith that only the guilty are punished and the innocent will be absolved.

Truth has been a central issue for philosophy throughout its history, unsurprisingly given its centrality to our view of the world. Capturing a clear and certain view of truth remains, however, a challenge. Many continue to ask, as Pontius Pilate did, 'Truth? What is That?' (John 18: 37).

Perhaps the most established answer is to be found in the correspondence theory of truth, which posits that a belief or statement is true if there exists an appropriate entity – a fact – to which it corresponds. If there is no such entity, the belief or statement is false. The correspondence theory of truth can be traced back to the works of Aristotle and Plato. For Aristotle: 'To say of what is that it is not, or of what is not that it is, is false, while to say of what is that it is, and of what is not that it is not, is true' (Metaphysics, Book IV, Part 7). Later, Thomas Aquinas would argue that '[truth] is the equation of thing and intellect' and '[a] judgment is said to be true when it conforms to the external reality' (De Veritate, Q 1, A 1–3).

At the start of the 20th century, there was a reaction against philosophical idealism and realist theories gained prominence. Foremost among the English language philosophers at the time were G. E. Moore and Bertrand Russell. Both initially rejected a correspondence theory of truth as being a source of idealism. Instead, they initially developed an identity theory: a true proposition is identical to the facts. This was similar to the correspondence theory, which provides that what we believe or say is true if it corresponds to the way things actually are – to the facts. By the end of the first decade of the 20th century, Moore and Russell had come to reject this identity theory and embraced the correspondence theory of truth: a belief is true if there exists an appropriate entity – an ontological fact – to which it corresponds. If there is no such entity, the belief is false.

The main positive argument given by advocates of the correspondence theory of truth is its obviousness. In the 17th century, Descartes had stated: 'I have never had any doubts about truth, because it seems a notion so transcendentally clear that nobody can be ignorant of it … the word "truth", in the strict sense, denotes the conformity of thought with its object' (Descartes, 1639, AT II 597). Even philosophers whose overall views may well lead one to expect otherwise tend to agree. Kant stated that '[the] nominal definition of truth, that it is the agreement of [a cognition] with its object, is assumed as granted' (Kant, 1787, B82). A similar point was made by William James: 'Truth, as any dictionary will tell you, is a property of certain of our ideas. It means their "agreement", as falsity means their disagreement, with "reality"' (James, 1907, p 96). Indeed, the Oxford English Dictionary tells us: 'Truth, n Conformity with fact; agreement with reality'.

According to Maurice Cornford, truth is the correspondence between ideas and objective reality and such correspondence is often only partial and incomplete. It is possible for some propositions to be absolutely true and Cornford gives the example of the proposition asserting that William the Conqueror invaded England in the year 1066:

> But most statements which we make cannot be said in
> this way to be absolutely true … they are partial, relative,

approximate truths. This characteristic of truth – that it is for the most part partial and not absolute, approximate and not exact, provisional and not final – is very well known to science. (Cornford, 1976, p 136)

In 2013, to celebrate its 125th anniversary, the Aristotelian Society held a series of online conferences, the first of which was on the subject of truth. The conference proceedings were published and included papers from the back catalogue and commentaries by contemporary philosophers. In 1950, a famous debate on the nature and definition of truth had taken place at the Society between John Langshaw Austin and Peter Frederick Strawson and the debate was revived at the 2013 virtual conference.

In his 1950 paper, Austin posed some initial questions of truth and our perceptions of it:

What is it that we say is true or is false? Or, how does the phrase 'is true' occur in English sentences? The answers appear at first multifarious. We say (or are said to say) that beliefs are true, that descriptions or accounts are true, that propositions or assertions or statements are true, and that words or sentences are true: and this is to mention only a selection of the more obvious candidates. Again, we say (or are said to say) 'It is true that the cat is on the mat,' or 'It is true to say that the cat is on the mat,' or '"The cat is on the mat" is true.' We also remark on occasion, when someone else has said something, 'Very true' or 'That's true' or 'True enough'. (Austin, 1950, p 30)

For Austin, a statement is true when it corresponds to the facts; more specifically, he argued:

A statement is said to be true when the historic state of affairs to which it is correlated by the demonstrative conventions (the one to which it 'refers') is of a type with which the sentence used in making it is correlated by the descriptive conventions … When a statement is true, there is, of course, a state of affairs which makes it true and which is toto mundo distinct from the true statement about it: but equally of course, we can only describe that state of affairs in words (either the same or, with luck, others). (Austin, 1950, pp 31–2)

In his later book, *How to Do Things with Words*, Austin examined further the nature of truth and the extent to which true/false represents a real dichotomy:

> It is essential to realise that 'true' and 'false', like 'free' and 'unfree', do not stand for anything simple at all; but only for a general dimension of being a right or proper thing to say as opposed to a wrong thing, in these circumstances, to this audience, for these purposes and with these intentions. (Austin, 1962, p 144)

For Austin, therefore, truth is a continuum. Like Cornford, Austin rejected the straightforward true/false dichotomy of correspondence theory. In his commentary to Austin's 1950 paper, Charles Travis asks:

> Should the description, 'The street is lined with eating establishments', eg, given of a street full of soup kitchens interspersed with gin mills affording the odd free pickled egg, count as a just enough account of how things were to merit the title 'true'?—a question whose answer is more than likely to depend on the circumstances in which the description was, or would be, given. (Travis, 2013, p 30)

Travis's response relied heavily on a redundancy theory of truth first introduced to the Aristotelian Society by Frank Plumpton Ramsay in 1927. Ramsay, a mathematician, argued that stating a fact is true is no more than stating a fact:

> Truth and falsity are ascribed primarily to propositions. The proposition to which they are ascribed may be either explicitly given or described. Suppose first that it is explicitly given; then it is evident that 'it is true that Caesar was murdered' means no more than that Caesar was murdered, and 'it is false that Caesar was murdered' means that Caesar was not murdered. They are phrases which we sometimes use for emphasis or for stylistic reasons, or to indicate the position occupied by the statement in our argument. So also we can say 'it is a fact that he was murdered' or 'that he was murdered is contrary to fact. (Ramsay, 1927; reprinted in Travis, 2013, p 9)

Subsequent chapters examine the extent to which it is possible to discern a clear view of truth from the criminal process; a process that appears to position truth and the search for truth centre stage.

Lying

The nature of truth has been a central question for philosophers, but less attention has been accorded to falsity. Sissela Bok, who has written one of the very few philosophical books on lying, remarked on the fact that while the index of the eight-volume 1967 *Encyclopedia of Philosophy* contained more than 100 references to truth, there was not a single one to lying or deception (Bok, 1999). Bok wrote the first edition of *Lying* in the aftermath of Vietnam and Watergate and in the context of a growing public mistrust of politicians. Her words are particularly relevant and apposite in a world dominated by the global spread of COVID-19. Bok considers the justifications given for lying, the moral issues raised and the variety of types of lies told.

Much philosophical discussion of falsity and deception sets out from Kant's unambiguous position that rejects any justification of lying:

> Truthfulness in statements which cannot be avoided is the formal duty of an individual to everyone, however great may be the disadvantage accruing to himself or another ... To be truthful (honest) in all declarations, therefore, is a sacred and absolutely commanding decree of reason, limited by no expediency. (Kant, translated by Beck, 1949, p 346)

The duty to tell the truth at all times stemmed from Kant's categorical imperative, the absolute and unconditional requirement that must be obeyed at all times and in all circumstances: 'Act only according to that maxim whereby you can, at the same time, will that it should become a universal law' (translated by Ellington, 1993, p 30). Kant's rejection of the concept of a 'benevolent lie' has been the subject of much criticism and debate. His essay on the supposed 'right to lie' was a response to the Franco-Swiss writer, Benjamin Constant, who had argued:

> The moral principle, 'It is the duty to tell the truth,' would make any society impossible if it were taken singly and unconditionally. We have proof of this in the very direct consequences of which a German philosopher has drawn from this principle. The philosopher goes so far as to

assert that it would be a crime to lie to a murderer who has asked whether our friend who is pursued by him had taken refuge in our house ... It is a duty to tell the truth. The concept of duty is inseparable from the concept of right ... To tell the truth is thus a duty: but it is a duty only in respect to one who has a right to the truth. But no one has a right to a truth which injures others. (Constant, 1797, pp 123–4)

Kant dismisses the expression 'a right to the truth' as one without meaning. The question of whether it is right to lie to a murderer has been reframed and reset in countless philosophy classes over time and the central ethical issue remains unresolved. It retains an important significance for criminal justice both in respect to the right not to incriminate oneself and also in relation to false allegations and confessions, which are discussed in the following chapters. Chapter 4 also discusses the ability to detect lies.

Truth and the criminal process

It seems generally accepted that a criminal trial is a search for the truth: to establish beyond a reasonable doubt the guilt (or otherwise) of the accused:

> Truth, while no guarantee of justice, is an essential precondition for it. Public legitimacy, as much as justice, demands accuracy in verdicts. A criminal justice system that was frequently seen to convict the innocent and to acquit the guilty would fail to win the respect of, and obedience from, those it governed. It thus seems fair to say that, whatever else it is, a criminal trial is first and foremost an epistemic engine, a tool for ferreting out the truth from what will often initially be a confusing array of clues and indicators. To say that we are committed to error reduction in trials is just another way of saying that we are earnest about seeking the truth. If that is so, then it is entirely fitting to ask whether the procedures and rules that govern a trial are genuinely truth-conducive. (Laudan, 2006, p 2)

It may be unarguable that 'public legitimacy' requires 'accuracy in verdicts' and yet, as this book seeks to demonstrate, there are serious doubts as to whether the search for the truth is in reality the main focus of the criminal process. The focus on the criminal trial obscures an important aspect of the whole endeavour of criminal justice:

> The criminal process is presented sometimes as if it were a vital tool of crime control, but the majority of crime never comes to the attention of the police or other enforcement agencies, and even when offences are brought to official attention they do not always elicit a formal response. It is estimated that less than half of crimes are reported to the police and, of those, between four-fifths and two-thirds are recorded: and these figures vary depending on the offence type ... Moreover, even when crime is reported to and recorded by the police, the police will not be able to identify a suspect in the vast majority of cases. In the year ending March 2018, police forces closed almost half (48 per cent) of offences with no suspect identified, a similar proportion to the previous year. (Campbell et al, 2019, p 2)

In the year ended March 2019, nearly six million offences were recorded by the police (and other agencies) in England and Wales. Less than 8 per cent of those offences resulted in a charge or summons. For certain groups of offences, the proportion charged or summonsed is even lower: for sexual offences generally the proportion is less than 4 per cent and for rape it is less than 2 per cent. The offences for which the highest proportion are charged or summonsed are those involving possession of weapons where the charging/summonsing rate is just over a third (Home Office, 2020a). According to the Crime Survey for England and Wales, there were an estimated 11.2 million offences in the year ended March 2019 (Office for National Statistics, 2019a). In the same period, 59,728 defendants were tried in the Crown Court (Office for National Statistics, 2019a). It is clear, therefore, that only a very small proportion of crimes result in trial and conviction. From this perspective, the search for truth does not seem so thorough and consideration of which cases result in trial and conviction may become increasingly relevant to 'public legitimacy'. The methodology of the criminal trial is also of relevance:

> We need hardly say that we have no wish to lessen the fairness of criminal trials. But it must be clear what fairness means in this connection. It means, or ought to mean, that the law should be such as will secure as far as possible

that the result of the trial is the right one. (Criminal Law
Revision Committee, 1972, para 62)

The 'rules of the game' are discussed further in Chapters 4 and 5.

Modern law recognizes that sometimes courts at first instance may be in error in identifying the truth and there is therefore a well-developed system of appeal. This has not always been the case. In the 13th century, the only way of challenging a court finding was by instituting separate criminal proceedings against the judge or jury, usually in the form of an accusation of perjury (Holdsworth, 1922, p 214). According to Holdsworth, not until the 14th century was a distinction made between challenges to the judgment and accusations against the judge or jury. Challenges to the judgment could be made on the basis that there was some clear error on the record of the case and the Court of King's Bench had jurisdiction to hear such cases and, if appropriate, correct the record. At this time, 'the common law knew nothing of an appeal by re-hearing of the case' (Holdsworth, 1922, p 214). Until 1704, the writ of error could only be issued at the discretion of the Crown (*The Rioters' Case* (1683) 1 Vern 175). In *Paty's Case* (1704) 2 Salkeld 503, the Court of King's Bench held by a majority of 10 to 12 that it was not in the Crown's power to deny a writ of error. In fact, the writ of error was little used and alternative methods to deal with factual errors at first trial were found.

In civil cases, by the 14th century both the Court of Common Pleas and the Court of King's Bench had granted new trials but the same could not be said of criminal trials. Holdsworth pointed out that it was settled by the 17th century that there could be no new trial following an acquittal (Holdsworth, 1922, p 216) and he quotes Lord Coleridge C J who said that '[the] practice of the courts has been settled for centuries, and is that in all cases of a criminal kind where a prisoner or defendant is in danger of imprisonment, no new trial will be granted if the prisoner or defendant, having stood in that danger, has been acquitted' (*R v Duncan* (1881) 7 QBD 198). Until the 17th century, the position was the same in relation to convictions.

2

Allegations

The continuing preoccupation with historical child sexual abuse cases has focused attention on a number of associated issues. An issue central to this book and the focus of this chapter is the nature of allegations/ false allegations. In looking into the way in which allegations of sexual abuse are dealt with, the chapter will explore the nature, importance and significance of allegations in the criminal justice process and the ways in which 'credibility' and 'truth' are examined and evidenced.

The power of allegations

On 22 July 2019, Carl Beech was found guilty by a jury at Newcastle Crown Court of 12 counts of perverting the course of justice and one count of fraud. Mr Justice Goss sentenced Beech to a total of 18 years' imprisonment (*R* v *Beech*, Sentencing Remarks, Unreported, Newcastle Crown Court, 26 July 2019). Between December 2012 and March 2016, Carl Beech (referred to as 'Nick') had made a series of allegations of murder and child sexual abuse against a number of public figures. These included some particularly serious allegations about the abuse of boys on the Dolphin Square estate in Pimlico in London. The names of several of the prominent individuals against whom allegations were made were reported in the press. They included the former Conservative Home Secretary, Lord Brittan, the former Chief of the Defence Staff, Field Marshall Lord Bramall, the former Prime Minister, Edward Heath, and the former Labour MP, Greville Janner (*Daily Telegraph*, 2015).

Beech had first contacted the police with allegations of child sexual abuse in the autumn of 2012 after the broadcast of a documentary about the life of the media personality, Jimmy Savile, and the launch of Operation Yewtree. Partly as a result of Beech's allegations, the

Metropolitan Police launched Operation Midland in November 2014. In March 2016, Operation Midland was ended with no charges being brought (*The Guardian*, 2016). In February 2016, following concerns expressed about the nature of both the allegations and the Metropolitan Police inquiries, the then Metropolitan Police Commissioner, Sir Bernard Hogan Howe, asked a retired High Court Judge, Sir Richard Henriques, to conduct a review into the actions of the Metropolitan Police Service in relation to these allegations.

Meanwhile, also in the autumn of 2012, the MP for West Bromwich East, Tom Watson, had been contacted by a former police officer, Peter McKelvie, about allegations of a senior paedophile ring that had existed in the early 1990s and been the subject of an official cover-up. Watson had previously come to prominent public attention for his role in exposing the use of phone hacking by a number of national newspapers. He therefore had a reputation as someone who was not afraid to take on the establishment and was perhaps a natural choice of contact for McKelvie. On 24 October 2012, Watson raised the issue in Parliament and called on the police to re-open investigations (*Hansard*, 2012; *The Guardian*, 2012). Partly as a result of these allegations (so as well as those raised by Beech), the Metropolitan Police launched Operation Midland in November 2014.

Before the end of 2012, Tom Watson had been contacted by 'Nick'/ Carl Beech. His allegations were consistent with what Watson had already heard from McKelvie:

> A middle-aged man known as 'Nick', who says he was repeatedly abused and raped by a network of VIPs and politicians, [had] told the police that he witnessed the murder of three other victims − one boy strangled by a Tory MP during an orgy, another killed in the presence of a Conservative minister, and a third deliberately run over by a car. Watson doesn't yet know whether or not this is true. 'But there is no doubt in my mind that sexual abuse by powerful figures took place.' Did they include politicians? 'There is no doubt in my mind that at least one politician abused kids.' And there was a cover-up? 'Well …' He hesitates for a moment. 'Something went on.' (Aitkenhead, 2014)

On 29 October 2011, Sir James Wilson Vincent Savile died at his home in Leeds. On 9 November 2011, thousands of mourners lined the streets of Leeds as the cortege passed *en route* to a requiem mass in

Leeds Cathedral. The death and funeral were widely reported and the many obituaries that appeared were, in the main, celebratory about Savile's life. Dame Janet Smith concluded: 'In death, as in life, Savile had a seal of approval and, even if the obituaries were not uniformly reverential, their overall tenor was that Savile was almost (but not quite) a national treasure' (Dame Janet Smith Review, 2016, para 1.1).

During Savile's life there had been rumours about sexual misconduct and he had been investigated by the police on several occasions but no further action had resulted from those investigations. Such rumours had circulated within the media but, as Dame Janet Smith's inquiry found, Savile readily threatened litigation to protect his reputation: '[T]he newspapers were wary of him and took care not to publish anything they could not fully justify' (Dame Janet Smith Review, 2016, para 4.22).

During his life, the rumours about Jimmy Savile remained just that. There were no public allegations made against Savile and the possible truth of the rumours remained largely untested. Whether this was because of Savile's powerful friends and the threat of litigation, the lack of even 'a scintilla of evidence' against him or the 'perfectly credible explanation of why rumour links him to young girls' was not investigated.

Things changed rapidly following Savile's death. With the threat of litigation gone, the rumours about his behaviour began to gain traction. Immediately following Savile's death in October 2011, journalists from BBC's *Newsnight* programme began investigations into Savile's past. They ascertained that Savile had been interviewed in 2007 under caution by Surrey police in connection with allegations of indecent assault carried out at Duncroft Approved School for Girls in Staines in the early 1970s. At the time, the Crown Prosecution Service decided there was insufficient evidence to take any further action. The *Newsnight* team interviewed former pupils at Duncroft but in December 2011 the *Newsnight* editor, Peter Rippon, told the team to cease the investigation on the basis that there was insufficient evidence to proceed with it.

The *Newsnight* investigative team had consisted of Meirion Jones, Liz MacKean and Hannah Livingstone. Jones's aunt, Margaret Jones, had been the headmistress at Duncroft School in the 1970s. Meirion Jones had visited his aunt a number of times at the school and claimed to have seen Savile there on six occasions between 1970 and 1976. Jones claimed that Savile had taken a group of pupils out in his Rolls Royce (The Pollard Review, 2012, para 3.1.3). Jones told Nick Pollard, who had been appointed on 16 October 2012 as chair of an independent review commissioned by the BBC to look into the *Newsnight* investigation, that such events had given him a personal interest in investigating Savile.

In early 2011, Jones had come across an online account of sexual assaults by a 'JS' at Duncroft School. The account appeared consistent with other accounts on Friends Reunited. In July 2011, Jones discussed the story with Mark Williams-Thomas, a former detective with Surrey Police, who agreed to investigate the possible involvement of Savile in the assaults and whether any police investigation had taken place. In the same month, Jones also discussed the story with Liz MacKean. The death of Savile on 29 October 2011 was, according to Jones 'the cue for me to begin my investigation in earnest' (The Pollard Review, 2012, para 3.1.6). Jones met with Peter Rippon on 31 October 2011 to discuss the possibility of an investigative piece on Savile. According to the Pollard Review there are conflicting accounts of that meeting. Jones claimed that Rippon greeted the idea enthusiastically, while Rippon recalled he had been 'quite lukewarm' about the story (The Pollard Review, 2012, para 3.1.7). Pollard found that the evidence suggested that Rippon fluctuated in his attitude to the story (The Pollard Review, 2012, para 3.1.7).

As the investigation progressed during early November 2011, Livingstone and MacKean found contact information for 60 former residents of Duncroft School, of whom five reported that they had been abused by Savile at the school and another reported that they had been abused by Savile at Stoke Mandeville Hospital (The Pollard Review, 2012, para 3.1.14). One of the former residents revealed that Surrey Police had investigated complaints against Savile but that she had received a letter from the police indicating that they had decided not to pursue them on account of Savile's age (The Pollard Review, 2012, para 3.1.16). This information gave weight to the story and a date for transmission of the report was set for 7 December 2011, but a last-minute editorial decision was made not to broadcast.

The BBC's decision not to proceed with the investigation then became a story in itself. On 8 January 2012, the *Sunday Mirror* ran the story under the headline 'BBC axe investigation into Sir Jimmy Savile and the schoolgirls'. It claimed that the investigation 'had been due on screen only days before a BBC1 Christmas special celebrating the star's work' (Owens, 2012). Allegations of a cover-up continued during 2012. At the same time, Mark Williams-Thomas continued his investigations.

On 3 October 2012, ITV broadcast a documentary called *Exposure: The Other Side of Jimmy Savile* (ITV, 2012a). According to a spokesperson for ITV, the documentary was 'the result of an in-depth investigation into long-standing allegations of serious and widespread sexual misconduct by Sir Jimmy Savile' (Higgens, 2012). The documentary was presented by Mark Williams-Thomas. It contained interviews with women who claimed they had been abused by Savile. In the documentary, the founder of Childline, Esther Rantzen, was shown the interviews by Williams-Thomas and commented that "[there] were always rumours that [Savile] behaved very inappropriately sexually with children".

Following the broadcasting of the documentary, others came forward to make allegations against Savile. On 21 November 2012, ITV broadcast a further documentary called *Exposure Update: The Jimmy Savile Investigation* (ITV, 2012b). In the period immediately following the programme, more people came forward with allegations of abuse. There was also considerable criticism of the BBC, both for cancelling the original documentary in 2011 and for ignoring allegations made about Savile during his time working at the BBC.

On 16 October 2012, the BBC set up two separate enquiries: one was headed by Dame Janet Smith to review the culture and practices of the BBC during the time Savile had worked there; the other was headed by Nick Pollard, a former television executive, to investigate the decision to cancel broadcast of the *Newsnight* report about Savile.

The day after the broadcasting of the first ITV documentary, the Metropolitan Police announced that its Child Abuse Investigation Command would begin an 'assessment' of the allegations made against Savile (BBC News, 2012). Later in the same month, the Metropolitan Police together with the National Society for the Prevention of Cruelty to Children (NSPCC) set up an inquiry to be known as Operation Yewtree. By the time the inquiry closed in December 2012, it had heard from 569 alleged victims of abuse. The findings were published as *Giving Victims a Voice* in January 2013 (NSPCC, 2013).

The gateway to the criminal justice system

> The police may be the normal gateway to the criminal justice process, but it is a gate that they open relatively seldom. (Bowling et al, 2019, p 261)

In the year ended December 2019, the police recorded just over five million criminal offences. Of those, only 7.1 per cent (355,930) resulted in a charge or summons; in 42 per cent of cases, investigations were concluded with no suspect identified; and a third of cases were discontinued because of perceived evidential difficulties (Home Office, 2020a). The overall figures mask considerable variation between types of offences: the charge/summons rate for possession of weapons offences is 35.1 per cent, while the rate for sexual offences is 3.3 per cent (the rate for rape is 1.5 per cent) (Home Office, 2020a). As of 30 September 2019, there were 124,784 police officers in England and Wales. With an estimated total population of 59.5 million, that equates to one police officer for every 476 citizens. It also means that there are just over 40 recorded offences for every officer – which equates to less than one per week.

Given the foregoing figures, it is perhaps unsurprising that the majority of criminal trials are initiated by contact made with the police by members of the public. Such contact is made for a variety of reasons, many of them not crime related. In 2015, the College of Policing provided an analysis of all emergency calls made to the police and found that 83 per cent of them were unrelated to crime (College of Policing, 2012 p 9). More recently, HM Inspectorate of Constabulary and Fire & Rescue Services reported:

> Incidents reported to the police relate to issues including public safety and welfare, crime, anti-social behaviour and transport. There are many ways that incidents can be reported to the police: victims, witnesses or other third parties can tell a police officer, PCSO [Police Community Support Officer] or member of staff either on the street or at the front counter of a police station; victims, witnesses or other third parties can telephone incidents to police control rooms; victims, witnesses or other third parties may report an incident online; the police might discover the crime themselves; or other agencies such as social services may refer them. It is also possible that other agencies will refer an incident that is clearly a crime. (Justice Inspectorates, 2020, para 1)

Calls to the police for help only involve clear references to crime in a minority of cases, although the exact proportion varies between places, over time and according to different definitions and research methodologies. Nonetheless, most policing does not involve use of law enforcement powers. As Bowling et al point out:

> Altogether the police are marginal to the control of crime and the maintenance of order, and always have been. Only a tiny fraction of crimes come to their attention or are

recorded by them, and the overwhelming majority of these are not cleared up (apart from serious violent offences such as homicide). (Bowling et al, 2019, p 261)

Thus, whether or not an investigation takes place will very often depend on the nature of the allegations made. After reviewing the relevant literature, Bowling et al report:

> Studies of detective work show that only a relatively small number of major incident enquiries fit the model of 'classical' detection ... Most crimes are cleared up almost immediately, as a result of the offender still being at the scene when the police arrive or being named or fully and accurately described by victim or witnesses (Steer 1980). Thus, only a small proportion of crimes are cleared up by investigative techniques bearing any resemblance to either the 'classical' or the 'bureaucratic' modes beloved by fiction. Most solved cases are essentially self-clearing. This does not mean that detectives are useless or inefficient (Morris and Heal 1981: 33; see also Maguire 2008: 440–1). There is also, of course, the relatively small but significant category of cases where the perpetrator is not initially known ('whodunits' in detectives' jargon) but which are nonetheless successfully cleared up by methods including the 'classical' and 'bureaucratic' modes and the construction and exploration of possible narratives explaining the crime (Innes 2003, 2007). However, the pressure on detectives to achieve more 'primary' clear ups (not based on post-arrest or sentence interviewing) has led to increasing use of innovative methods which may themselves be ethically, legally, and practically problematic. (Bowling et al, 2019, p 114)

The innovative methods referred to include target setting and greater use of crime management models:

> The need to grade reported cases more formally according to their prospects of solvability became apparent during the 1980s as crime levels grew and so did the pressure on the police to enhance their appearance of efficiency, effectiveness, and economy. But first attempts to screen out cases according to explicit criteria of formality attracted

condemnation when they were revealed to the public. However, as New Public Management (NPM), target specification, and monitoring intensified in the 1990s, more formalized systems came to be adopted, culminating in the 2000s when a formal operating system, the Volume Crime Management Model (VCMM) became standard, meaning that only leads with a reasonable chance of resulting in a positive outcome (i.e. arrest, prosecution) are followed up (O'Neill, 2018). (Bowling et al, 2019, p 113)

According to the Association of Chief Police Officers, volume crime is any 'crime which, through its sheer volume, has a significant impact on the community and the ability of the local police to tackle it. Volume crime often includes priority crimes such as street robbery, burglary and vehicle-related criminality, but can also apply to criminal damage or assaults' (ACPO, 2009, p 8).

The College of Policing provides further guidance for police officers in its Authorised Professional Practice briefings. These provide guidance on a wide range of police activity, including the conduct of investigations. Its introduction to investigation states: 'It is the duty of prosecutors to make sure that the right person is prosecuted for the right offence, and to bring offenders to justice. Casework decisions made fairly, impartially and with integrity help to deliver justice for victims, witnesses, defendants and the public' (College of Policing, 2020).

The need for greater efficiency and effectiveness has, it is argued, led to the nature and number of allegations having a greater significance in terms of the decision to continue or discontinue an investigation.

Moral panics and signal crimes

According to the introduction to the third edition of Stanley Cohen's *Folk Devils and Moral Panics* (Cohen, 2011), the objects of panic belong to seven clusters of social identity:

- young, working-class, violent males;
- school violence;
- 'wrong drugs: used by wrong people at wrong places';
- child abuse;
- sex and violence and the adverse effects of the media;
- welfare cheats;
- refugees and asylum seekers.

Cohen then explains the term 'moral panic':

> Societies appear to be subject, every now and then, to periods of moral panic. A condition, episode, person or group of persons emerges to become defined as a threat to societal values and interests; its nature is presented in a stylized and stereotypical fashion by the mass media; the moral barricades are manned by editors, bishops, politicians and other right thinking people; socially accredited experts pronounce their diagnoses and solutions; ways of coping are evolved or (more often) resorted to; the condition then disappears, submerges or deteriorates and becomes more visible ... Sometimes the panic passes over and is forgotten, except in folklore or collective memory; at other times it has more serious and long lasting repercussions and might produce such changes as those in legal and social policy or even in the way society conceives of itself. (Cohen, 2011, p 1)

According to Watney (1987, p 41), moral panics 'mark the site of permanent ideological struggle over the meanings of signs'. Allegations are made in a particular social context and their effect, their importance and the manner in which they are received will be influenced by prevailing moral panics. Martin Innes makes a similar point from the opposite direction in his *Signal Crimes: Crime, Disorder and Control.* Innes defines 'signal' as:

> [A] sign that has an effect. Signals are present when, in moving information from a transmitter to a receiver, some change is induced in the state of the latter. Conceptualized in this way, the notion that some crimes act as signals focuses upon how they communicate information about the prevalence and distribution of risks and threats across social space. They conduct and channel processes of social reaction towards some issues, and away from others. (Innes, 2014, p 1)

He continues:

> These signalling processes can be observed in public reactions to a large number of crimes over the years. For

example, when the deceased body of Rachel Nickell was found on Wimbledon Common in South West London, it rapidly acquired the properties of a powerful signal crime. Intense media and public interest in the murder was triggered by a confluence of factors. First there was the uniquely harrowing circumstances in which she was found, with her two year old son found clinging to his mother's blood soaked body saying 'wake up mummy'. This was augmented by the fact that the victim was extremely photogenic, which provided the tabloid and broadcast media in particular, with an iconic image that could be repeatedly attached to their reporting. In this sense, it was an archetypal signal crime. It was eminently visualizable, with the capacity to connotatively depict the presence of danger, invoking consequences for how many people thought and felt about their safety.

But as the police investigation and subsequent court case progressed a second, very different 'signal' emerged. Very early on in their enquiries police had identified Colin Stagg as a potential suspect and he was prosecuted and convicted on the basis of the evidence that they generated. However, following 14 months in custody, after which his conviction was overturned upon appeal because of serious doubts about the integrity of aspects of the police investigation and its evidence, a negative control signal was triggered, causing damage to public trust and confidence in the police. It was not until 16 years after the original murder that Robert Napper was convicted of manslaughter on the grounds of diminished responsibility. (Innes, 2014, p 3)

Both moral panics and signal crimes will, it is argued, have a major influence on allegations of criminal activity and subsequent investigation of that activity. The immediate risk from this is that following signals and responding to panics are likely to be inconsistent with the search for an objective truth.

In a comparison of the response to child trafficking and abuse in the 19th and 21st centuries, Cree et al provide two examples of how '[m]oral panics do harm in the "real" world, victimising some and demonising others, while at the same time championing moral entrepreneurs and masking the underlying issues that are at stake' (Cree et al, 2014, p 432).

In the 19th century, the focus of concern had been prostitution and particularly the involvement of children. In 1880, Josephine Butler protested against the 'sexual servitude of young girls', claiming that girls as young as 12 were being incarcerated in (regulated) Belgian brothels (Mumm, 2006). In 1881, a Select Committee of the House of Lords was set up 'to inquire into the law for the protection of young girls from artifices to induce them to lead a corrupt life, and into the means of amending the same'. The Committee found that 'juvenile prostitution, from an almost incredible early age, exists to an appalling extent in England generally, and especially in London' (Report from the Select Committee on the Contagious Diseases Acts, House of Commons, 1882). Interestingly, the House of Commons Select Committee, which at the same time had been considering the Contagious Diseases Act 1864, found that in the areas controlled by the legislation there had been 'a great and continuous decrease in the number of juvenile prostitutes in the subjected districts'. The committee saw much merit in the maintenance of the legislation but it failed to diminish the opposition to the law (Walkowitz, 1980).

Cree et al draw parallels with the situation in the 1880s and the current panic about child trafficking. In situations of moral panic it becomes increasingly difficult to establish an objective truth.

The Independent Inquiry into Child Sexual Abuse

In response to the growing number of allegations of historical sexual abuse and continuing claims of official cover-ups, on 7 July 2014, the then Home Secretary, Theresa May, announced the establishment of 'an independent inquiry panel of experts in the law and child protection to consider whether public bodies and other non-state institutions have taken seriously their duty of care to protect children from sexual abuse' (May, 2014). The inquiry panel was to be non-statutory but the Home Secretary gave assurances that it would be given full access to government papers and would be free to call witnesses as it required.

On 8 July 2014, it was announced that Baroness Butler-Sloss, former President of the Family Division, would chair the panel. Butler-Sloss was the sister of Sir Michael Havers, who had been Attorney General during the period when the abuse and cover-ups were alleged to have taken place. As a result, a number of MPs and child abuse groups expressed concerns about the appointment and Baroness Butler-Sloss stepped down on 14 July.

She was succeeded by Fiona Woolf CBE, at the time Lord Mayor of London, who was appointed chair of the panel on 5 September (BBC,

2014a). On 1 July 2014, Simon Danczuk MP had told MPs that a dossier containing allegations of child sexual abuse had been presented to the then Home Secretary, Leon Brittan, in the late 1980s (BBC News, 2014a). The implication was that Leon Brittan had been involved in a cover-up of the allegations. There were also rumours circulating about the former Home Secretary's own personal conduct. The fact that Fiona Woolf had had previous social contact with Lord and Lady Brittan led to complaints about her appointment. On 31 October, a number of victims' groups met with the Home Secretary and following the meeting Fiona Woolf stood down as chair (BBC News, 2014b).

The terms of reference for the panel were published on 4 October and on 4 February 2015 the Home Secretary announced that Justice Lowell Goddard, a judge of the High Court of New Zealand, would chair the inquiry. The non-statutory inquiry would be dissolved to be replaced by a new, statutory inquiry under the Inquiries Act 2005 (May, 2015). In carrying out its task, the Independent Inquiry into Child Sexual Abuse (IICSA) would: 'Consider the experience of survivors of child sexual abuse; providing opportunities for them to bear witness to the Inquiry, having regard to the need to provide appropriate support in doing so' (IICSA, 2015).

IICSA promised to liaise with similar inquiries elsewhere and specifically mentioned the Australian Royal Commission into Institutional Child Sexual Abuse, the Independent Jersey Care Inquiry, the Historical Institutional Abuse Inquiry in Northern Ireland, and the Scottish Inquiry into Historical Abuse of Children in Care. IICSA also promised to work closely with the National Police Chiefs Council's Operation Hydrant, which was described as a 'coordination hub established in June 2014 to deliver the national policing response, oversight, and coordination of non-recent child sexual abuse investigations concerning persons of public prominence, or in relation to those offences which took place within institutional settings' (NSPCC, 2020). In 2016, Justice Lowell Goddard was succeeded as chair by Professor Alexis Jay, OBE. The inquiry continues to hear evidence and publish findings, the most recent being *"People Don't Talk About It"* – a report on child sexual abuse within minority ethnic communities (IICSA, 2020).

The website of the Inquiry provides some background:

> The information and statistics currently available do not give a full account of the scale of child abuse across England and Wales, but estimates suggest that one child in every 20 in the United Kingdom has been sexually abused. In

2014, police statistics show that there were over 28,000 recorded sexual offences where the victim was aged under 16. There are likely to have been many more offences that were not reported to the police. As in Australia, Northern Ireland, Jersey and Scotland, the level of public concern has resulted in calls for an overarching inquiry to look at the big picture, to learn the lessons of the past, to take stock of child protection procedures that are currently in operation, and to set a new course for the future. In conducting its work, the Inquiry is liaising with the Australian Royal Commission into Institutional Child Sexual Abuse, with the Independent Jersey Care Inquiry, with the Historical Institutional Abuse Inquiry in Northern Ireland, and with the Scottish Inquiry into Historical Abuse of Children in Care. Together the inquiries have much to learn from each other. The Inquiry is also liaising with Operation Hydrant, the national police investigation into more than 1400 investigations of non-recent sexual abuse of children. (IICSA, 2020)

The one in 20 estimate of the numbers of children sexually abused can be compared with the Crime Survey for England and Wales (CSEW) estimates in 2019: 'One in five adults aged between 18 and 74 years experienced at least one form of child abuse, whether emotional abuse, physical abuse, sexual abuse, or witnessing domestic violence or abuse, before the age of 16 years (8.5 million people)' (Office for National Statistics, 2020). The CSEW estimated that 7.5 per cent of adults aged 18 to 74 years experienced sexual abuse before the age of 16 years (3.1 million people): approximately one in 14 adults (Office for National Statistics, 2020).

In the year ended March 2019, the police recorded 60,685 child sexual abuse incidents. In 2019, the National Association for People Abused in Childhood (NAPAC) answered 8,658 calls on their support line and replied to hundreds of emails from people looking for support. There were 62,840 further attempts to call NAPAC's support line during this period (National Association for People Abused in Childhood, 2020). In the year 2018/19, Childline dealt with 8,841 contacts relating to child sexual abuse (Childline, 2019, p 9).

The first time the CSEW included questions asking adults whether they had been abused as children was in 2015–16 (Office for National Statistics, 2016). The survey found that the proportions of adults reporting experience of childhood abuse increased with age:

> For example, adults aged 16 to 24 and 25 to 34 reported lower levels of any sexual assault (3% and 5%) than those aged 45 to 54 and 55 to 59 (both 9%). It is difficult to determine whether this indicates a reduction in the prevalence of child abuse in more recent years or whether it is due to survivors being more willing to disclose past abuse the further in time they are away from the experience. (Office for National Statistics, 2016, p 3)

A possible third explanation for the variation in reporting rates is not mentioned: as we will see in Chapter 4, memories are not like old photographs or video recordings. They develop and change over time. An alternative explanation to the two offered by the CSEW is that, over time, memories become less accurate and more susceptible to outside influences.

Discussions about the true extent of crime have always been contentious. Ever since the first official criminal statistics were published in the 19th century, concern has been expressed that the official figures reveal only a proportion of total crime committed. It was partly to address this problem that the British Crime Survey (now CSEW) was introduced in 1984. Arriving at a 'true' figure for the level of child abuse that occurs is therefore extremely problematic. In the context of criminal justice there is a danger that judgments about the veracity and credibility of allegations may become influenced by the perceived scale of the 'problem'.

In November 2015, IICSA launched the Truth Project. Modelled on similar schemes elsewhere, the project was established to allow 'victims and survivors of child sexual abuse to share their experiences with the Inquiry' (IICSA, 2020). The underlying purpose was to 'ensure that the voices of victims and survivors are heard' (IICSA, 2020). The Truth Project is open to anyone who, as a child:

- was sexually abused by a person in an institution; or
- first came into contact with the person that sexually abused them in an institution; or
- reported the child sexual abuse to a person in authority and the report was ignored or not acted upon appropriately; or
- was sexually abused and someone in an institution could have known about the abuse but ignored it or did not act upon it appropriately. (King and Brähler, 2019, p 7).

The overarching research questions for the Truth Project (King and Brähler, 2019, p 9) are:

- What have victims and survivors shared about their experiences of child sexual abuse and the institutional contexts in which it occurred and was responded to?
- What similarities and differences are there in victims' and survivors' experiences of sexual abuse across time periods, groups and institutions?

Information can be supplied in writing, in person or by phone and: 'All experiences are shared in an informal, non-legal and confidential manner (with some exceptions when absolutely necessary to keep individuals safe)' (King and Brähler, 2019, p 9). The Truth Project adopts a trauma-informed approach, underpinned by five key principles:

- recognizing that the experience of child sexual abuse is subjective and individuals should be respected;
- being aware that trust is not to be taken for granted, but fostered;
- empowering victims and survivors in their interactions with the Inquiry;
- prioritizing the safety and wellbeing of victims and survivors and working to prevent re-traumatization;
- acknowledging the impact of child sexual abuse and institutional failures, therefore, looking out for staff wellbeing (King and Brähler, 2019, p 9).

The information obtained is then anonymized and is considered by the IICSA panel 'when reaching their conclusions and making recommendations for the future' (IICSA, 2020). Up to March 2020, IICSA had received 4,738 'total experiences', including 3,646 'victims and survivors' who had shared their experiences with the Truth Project (IICSA, 2020). A total of 26,656 people had contacted the Inquiry (IICSA, 2020).

The approach of the Truth Project poses some interesting questions for criminal justice and the significance to be attached to allegations. The trauma-based approach, which recognizes that experience of crime is subjective, sits uncomfortably with a criminal process searching for an objective truth. The choice of name for the Truth Project was influenced by the establishment of similar truth commissions elsewhere but the effect of the title cannot be underestimated: it seems legitimate to assume that a Truth Project is searching for the truth. We look at truth commissions in more detail in Chapter 9.

Victims, survivors or complainants?

One aspect of the child abuse discourse is the naming of interested parties. The legal system has traditionally dealt with suspects, defendants, the accused, complainants and witnesses. The terms are neutral so as not to contaminate the fact-finding process of the trial. In recent years, partly as a result of the development of a trauma-based approach, there has been increasing use of the terms 'victims' and 'survivors' as synonyms for complainants and witnesses. This is particularly true in the areas of child abuse, domestic abuse and human trafficking.

The issue is discussed at some length in the Independent Review of the Metropolitan Police Service's handling of non-recent sexual offence investigations alleged against persons of public prominence which was chaired by Sir Richard Henriques (Henriques Review, 2016). Sir Richard contrasts the approach taken by the Rt. Hon Dame Elish Anglioni DBE QC, chair of the Independent Review into the Investigation and Prosecution of Rape in London, which was commissioned by the Metropolitan Police in 2014, with that of Operation Hydrant Senior Investigating Officer Guidance written by the Chief Constable of Norfolk, Simon Bailey. Throughout her report, Dame Elish Anglioni refers to a person making an allegation of rape as a 'complainant'. The same term is used in the joint Metropolitan Police and Crown Prosecution Service response to her report. Simon Bailey's guidance for Senior Investigating Officers uses the term 'victim'.

Sir Richard Henriques is quite clear on the appropriate term:

> All 'complainants' are not 'victims'. Some complaints are false and thus those 'complainants' are not 'victims'. Throughout the judicial process the word 'complainant' is deployed up to the moment of conviction whereafter a 'complainant' is properly referred to as a 'victim'. Since the entire judicial process, up to that point, is engaged in determining whether or not a 'complainant' is indeed a 'victim', such an approach cannot be questioned. No Crown Court judge will permit a 'complainant' to be referred to as a 'victim' prior to conviction. Since the investigative process is similarly engaged in ascertaining facts which will, if proven, establish guilt, the use of the word 'victim' at the commencement of an investigation is simply inaccurate and should cease. (Henriques Review, 2016, para 1.12)

He continues: 'It should be sufficient to say, at this stage, that since the whole of the investigative process is engaged in the task of collating evidence to determine whether a complaint is true or false, any device which seeks to ignore or minimise that possibility should be put aside' (Henriques Review, 2016, para 1.14). He also refers to the stated policy of the College of Policing in 2016 that '[at] the point when someone makes an allegation of crime, the police should believe the account given and a crime report should be completed' (Henriques Review, 2016, para 1.21). Henriques' concern here is the effect of such a belief on the burden of proof:

> In many allegations of non-recent sexual abuse, the only pieces of evidence are the complaint and the suspect's response. Is the investigating officer required to believe the complainant and then suddenly become objective and impartial as he interviews the suspect? Surely objectivity and impartiality should prevail throughout the whole process. (Henriques Review, 2016, para 1.25)

Furthermore:

> Since a complainant may or may not be telling the truth, the present policy [of believing the complainant] causes those not telling the truth to be artificially believed and, thus, liars and fantasists, and those genuinely mistaken, are given a free run both unquestioned and unchallenged. The obligation to believe at the outset can and does obstruct the asking of relevant and probing questions designed to elicit the truth. The asking of such questions can be achieved in a sympathetic, kindly and professional manner. Criminal investigation should include the process of investigating from the outset and not waiting for some evidence to the contrary to turn up. (Henriques Review, 2016, para 1.28)

On the basis of the foregoing, Henriques recommends that the practice of believing the victim should be discontinued: 'It should be the duty of an officer interviewing a complainant to investigate the facts objectively and impartially and with an open mind from the outset of the investigation' (Henriques Review, 2016, recommendation 2). He therefore recommends that: 'In future, the public should be told that "if you make a complaint we will treat it very seriously and investigate it thoroughly without fear or favour"' (Henriques Review, 2016, recommendation 3).

The views of Sir Richard Henriques have not attracted universal support. In an article published in the *Criminal Law Review* in 2014, the former Director of Public Prosecutions, Sir Keir Starmer, invoked the human rights of the victim:

> In England and Wales we have been confronting some uncomfortable truths about the way in which our criminal justice system protects children who have been sexually abused. What we have uncovered is that we have been proceeding on the basis of certain deep rooted assumptions about victim behaviours, which, frankly, do not withstand scrutiny ... Over time, the effect has been to distance those most in need from the protection of the criminal law; the very opposite of effective and accessible criminal law arrangements. As we scratch away here, we uncover some very profound issues going to the very heart of our criminal justice system. Not least because in many respects all that the police and prosecutors were doing in concluding that these vulnerable victims were not credible was second guessing the way in which they would be treated in court ... What is required is an 'attitude shift' across the criminal justice system. The old tests of credibility have to go and they have to be replaced with a more sophisticated approach that starts with *the assumption that the victim is telling the truth* and seeks to build a case and make links between different allegations. (Starmer, 2014, p 86, emphasis in original)

Following the initial publication of the Henriques Report in 2016, the College of Policing commissioned a review of the recommendations, headed by Assistant Commissioner, Rob Beckley (College of Policing, 2018). In relation to terminology, there was support for retaining the term 'victim' but there was a recommendation that materials by the College of Policing and the National Police Chiefs Council should describe 'the differing interpretations and sensitivities, thus guiding investigators to be prepared to adapt their choice of wording according to the audience and context' (College of Policing, 2018, para 4.7). In relation to believing the victim, the recommendation was that:

The College of Policing and NPCC [National Police Chiefs Council] should approach the Home Office to amend the crime recording counting rules to remove the words 'The intention that victims are believed' to 'The intention is that victims can be confident they will be listened to and their crime taken seriously'. If accepted the College of Policing APP [Authorised Professional Practice] and training materials should be reviewed to support this approach. (College of Policing, 2018, para 8.10)

Changes were made to the Home Office Counting Rules for Recording Crime in September 2019 and they now state:

The Standard directs a victim focused approach to crime recording. The intention is that victims are believed and benefit from statutory entitlements under the Code of Practice for Victims of Crime (CPVC). This seeks to ensure that those reporting crimes will be treated with empathy and their allegations will be taken seriously. Any investigation which follows is then taken forward with an open mind to establish the truth. (Home Office, 2020b, para 2)

The College of Policing's Authorised Professional Practice (APP) for Investigations now provides a definition of both 'victim' and 'witness' taken from *Black's Law Dictionary* (College of Policing, 2020). Investigators are required to treat 'witnesses' with dignity and respect.

False allegations

On 20 December 2013, David John Bryant was convicted at the Crown Court at Bournemouth of an offence of buggery (*R v Bryant* [2016] EWCA Crim 1245). He was subsequently sentenced to six years' imprisonment. On 3 April 2014, following an Attorney General's reference, Bryant's sentence was increased to eight years and six months by the Court of Appeal. In the criminal trial the prosecution relied on the evidence provided by the complainant (or 'victim'), Danny Day. Day alleged that in 1976, when he was 14 years old, he had been befriended by Bryant. On a number of occasions he had visited Bryant at the fire station in Christchurch, Dorset, where Bryant was a part-time firefighter. On the last occasion he visited he alleged he was held down and sexually assaulted by Bryant and another man. Day did not report the incident at the time although he had told a school friend.

In 2012, Day had returned to the Christchurch area to discover that Bryant was a respected local citizen and reported the 1976 incident to the police. Bryant was interviewed and admitted that he had been a part-time firefighter at the relevant time and that he had met Day. He denied the allegation of buggery. There was no other evidence so the trial became a question of which person the jury believed. They believed Day, as had the police.

Following Bryant's conviction, Day then brought civil proceedings, claiming damages against Bryant. In the course of those proceedings, Day was required to disclose his medical history. That history disclosed that Day had a history of lying and cheating and was suspected of having an underlying personality disorder. The Court of Appeal was satisfied that, had the jury had the benefit of the evidence, they would not have convicted Bryant and his conviction was quashed.

False allegations are not unknown. What *is* unknown is the proportion of allegations that are false. The idealized form of the criminal justice process will test allegations and subject them to forensic examination. The reality is rarely as scientific. Cases will often come down to a choice between two possible versions of the truth. It can be very difficult to disprove a false allegation. Had Danny Day not sought damages, it is possible that Bryant would still be a convicted sex offender.

In a discussion of false allegations in rape trials, Candida Saunders wrote:

> Examining the available research, however, quickly reveals that the prevalence of false allegations of rape is far from empirically settled (see also Rumney 2006; Ministry of Justice 2010; Home Office 2010). As recent incisive reviews have highlighted, false allegations have been found to represent 1.5 per cent of rape cases, 90 per cent of rape cases and virtually every other figure in between (Rumney 2006; Lisak et al. 2010). (Saunders, 2012, p 1153)

Sir Richard Henriques refers to Simon Bailey's estimate:

> I was concerned at the suggestion made by Chief Constable Bailey that 0.1% of all complaints may be false. That assessment, admittedly 'off the cuff', bore no relation to my own experience over a lifetime in the Courts nor to my assessment of several complaints during this review. In fact, nobody knows, nor can ever know, the extent of false complaints. It is critical, however, that those charged

with the responsibility of investigating crime, or instructing others in that process, have in mind the real, as opposed to the remote, possibility that a complaint may be false. (Henriques Review, 2016, para 36)

Beliefs about the proportion of allegations that are false will affect assessments of witness credibility. In the past, certain categories of complainants have faced a high degree of scepticism when reporting criminal offences. In *The Great Children's Home Panic*, Richard Webster wrote:

It was in California in the 1970s and 1980s that a new culture of child protection gradually emerged ... One of the distinctive features was the manner in which it set out to combat the systematic disbelief with which allegations of sexual abuse were all too frequently met. The development was in many ways both necessary and overdue. But the rigid ideology which lay behind this view meant that in too many cases, an attitude of systematic disbelief was replaced not by an open minded willingness to investigate, but by a systematic credulity. (Webster, 1998, pp 36–7)

The quotation from Webster appears in the study of false allegations in sexual and child abuse cases by Ros Burnett and others:

Because sexual abuse is typically unwitnessed and leaves no physical marker, responses to claims made are dependent on believing that the reported abuse has occurred and on believing the accounts of complainants. This is therefore an area in which the criminal justice system is particularly liable to make errors of judgement, and in which prior assumptions and mindset will influence outcomes. Where there is scope for doubt, and choice, in the absence of decisive information, it is inevitable that personal passions, groupthink, and cognitive biases will come into play ... Slowly over the last few decades, but with crescendo over the last few years, a major shift has taken place in responding to sexual crime. That shift ... is from systematic disbelief to systematic credulity. As a backlash to an era during which the accused was given the benefit of the doubt, the 'default belief' now is that the accused is guilty. In the absence of objective biometric evidence, judgements become more an act of faith and choosing to err on the side of the perceived greater injustice. (Burnett, 2016, p 5)

Discussion of false allegations has tended to focus on sexual and child abuse cases but the possibility of false allegations is not confined to such categories. Any allegation of a crime may be true, partly true or false. A false allegation may be made knowingly and deliberately or it may be made in the genuine, but erroneous, belief that something happened. In Chapter 4 we look in more detail at false memories and their relationship to truth. In the idealized criminal process, the allegation will often start the investigation but it will then be examined and tested so as to establish 'truths' that are 'beyond reasonable doubt'. In many cases that does not happen. In other cases the allegation can lead to a confession. In the next chapter we shall consider the place of the confession in the criminal justice process.

3

Confessions

> Frequently regarded as the most unequivocal evidence of
> guilt, a confession relieves doubts in the minds of judges and
> jurors more than any other evidence. In criminal law, the
> confession evidence is considered to be the most damaging
> form of evidence produced at trial and a prosecutor's most
> potent weapon. (Conti, 1999, p 14)

Some individuals express an overwhelming need to admit to their
misconduct. Others have little choice but to do so when faced with
overwhelming incriminating evidence. In both cases, the truth can be
arrived at in an expedient manner and with minimal involvement from
the criminal justice system – most suspects who confess to the police
will not seek to retract their confession later but will admit guilt again
prior to the trial by entering a plea of guilty. Assuming factual accuracy
and a lack of coercion, a confession can be viewed as an optimum
criminal justice outcome. Prosecutors are not faced with the task of
determining whether the evidence suggests that conviction is a realistic
prospect or in the public interest. Trial uncertainty is avoided. Limited
state resources can be diverted to other cases, with the possibility that
the additional resource secures the conviction of other offenders. The
benefits of a confession go beyond the financial as victims, witnesses
and defendants are spared the inconvenience and distress of attending
court. All of these benefits are considerable.

Confessions are an incredibly powerful indicator of guilt in the eyes
of jurors (Kassim, 1997; Watson et al, 2010; Garrett, 2011). Why
someone may admit criminality is therefore important. Gudjonsson

distinguishes between three general factors that explain why individuals make confessions:

> [Suspects] confess due to a combination of factors, rather than to one factor alone. Three general factors appear to be relevant, in varying degree, to most suspects. These relate to an *internal* pressure (e.g. feelings of remorse, the need to talk about the offence), *external* pressure (e.g. fear of confinement, police persuasiveness), and perception of *proof* (e.g. the suspects' perceptions of the strength of the evidence against them). The single strongest incentive to confess relates to the strength of the evidence against suspects. (Gudjonsson, 2003, p 157, emphasis in original)

The fact that the case against someone appears strong intuitively would appear to be a prime motivator but Walsh and Bull (2012) found in an empirical study of false welfare claimants that the weight of evidence alone was not an influential factor in determining why someone confessed. It is also worth reflecting on why people *do not* confess to committing an offence in circumstances when denial seems implausible. Here Gudjonsson (2003, p 116) identifies five possibilities:

- fear of legal sanctions;
- concern about one's reputation;
- not wanting to admit to oneself what one has done;
- not wanting one's family and friends to know;
- fear of retaliation.

Though the benefits of confessions are obvious, so too are the dangers of relying solely or too heavily on confession evidence: put starkly, people have confessed to crimes that they did not commit. A series of appellate court decisions have documented situations where innocent people have confessed to crimes following police conduct that could variously be described as improper, duplicitous or oppressive. Robust procedural protection is essential if we are to be confident that 'confessions' are indeed confessions (see Chapter 10). Miscarriages of justice, though, can arise when there is no state malpractice whatsoever. Research shows that some individuals voluntarily and readily 'confess' to crimes they did not commit when no pressure is applied and all procedural rules have been complied with. Legal protection should not then depend on whether there was bad practice on the part of the authorities if the aim is to reduce the possibility of miscarriages of justice.

This chapter will start with an important question of definition. What exactly amounts to a confession? It will then turn to why someone may confess to a crime they were not responsible for. This will necessitate a review of some of the key psychological explanations. After that, the way in which the law protects those who confess will be considered. The cases all involve people who admitted guilt to the police and then sought to retract the confession at their trial on the basis that it was obtained unfairly or illegally. The concluding section will address the overarching relationship between the admissibility of confession evidence and the search for truth in criminal justice. It will become apparent that values relating to the probity of the criminal justice process can trump truth-finding, at least at times. An argument will be advanced that the two are not wholly distinct. Excluding evidence in one case – even if it does indeed show guilt – can raise the possibility of unearthing the truth in later cases. However, it will be conceded that judicial interpretation does undermine this argument as senior judges in England and Wales have restricted the circumstances where confession evidence can be excluded to a limited number of cases where grave injustice can be found. The first question, though, is definitional. What amounts to a confession?

Definitions of guilt: confessing and accepting responsibility

In English law, a confession encompasses 'any statement wholly or partly adverse to the person who made it, whether made to a person in authority or not and whether made in words or otherwise' (Police and Criminal Evidence Act 1984, section 82(1)). In definitional terms, this is far wider in scope than the popular image of a suspect admitting an offence to the police during a formal interview. An informal admittance to a friend, for example, would clearly suffice. Nonetheless, some definitional questions remain. In *R v Hasan* [2005] UKHL 22, the House of Lords ruled on the following question:

> Whether a 'confession' in section 76 of the Police and Criminal Evidence Act 1984 includes a statement intended by the maker to be exculpatory or neutral and which appears to be so on its face, but which becomes damaging to him at the trial because, for example, its contents can

then be shown to be evasive or false or inconsistent with the maker's evidence on oath.

The initial question is temporal: does a statement have to be adverse at the time that it was made or can its inculpatory nature emerge during the course of the trial? There are various ways in which a seemingly innocuous statement could become detrimental or damning. One such way is where the contents of the statement are shown to be false; the unravelling of a statement at trial is hardly an unusual occurrence. Evasiveness and inconsistency while giving evidence in court may not prove that the statement was false but it may well impact on the factfinder's assessment – and probably adversely. The relevance of the legal definition, as will be discussed later, concerns the means by which a statement can be excluded at trial. As well as a generic discretionary ground to exclude evidence on the grounds of 'unfairness' (Police and Criminal Evidence Act 1984, section 78; see further Chapter 5), there are additional specific grounds for excluding confession evidence (section 76(2)). The definitional question, therefore, carries legal significance as it determines the possible grounds for excluding a statement. The House of Lords held that:

> [Section] 76(1), read with section 82(1), requires the court to interpret a statement in the light of the circumstances when it was made. A purely exculpatory statement (e.g. 'I was not there') is not within the scope of section 76(1). It is not a confession within the meaning of section 76. (*R v Hasan* [2005] UKHL 22, at [58])

The definition of 'confession' used in this chapter follows this ruling and is therefore limited to statements that are inculpatory when made. Neutral statements that later prove harmful at trial do not fall within this definition although, under English law, they may be held inadmissible if obtained unfairly (Police and Criminal Evidence Act 1984, section 78). Similarly, our working definition does not require the statement to be oral or written, nor need the statement to have been made to someone acting in authority.

'Confessions' do not prove guilt. In this chapter, the context should make it obvious when a confession refers to a statement, made voluntarily or not, where there is no proof of guilt or where, exceptionally, the evidence shows that the individual did not or could not commit the crime in question. The word 'confession' will also be used where there is evidence of factual guilt (possibly compelling evidence) but where there is doubt that the statement was given voluntarily. Regardless of context, in the rest of this chapter the word 'confession' will not be placed in inverted commas nor will the verb 'to confess'. Clearly, the potential that innocent people confess to crimes that they did not commit is a central concern to any criminal justice system. For the purposes of this book, we need to review carefully the psychological reasons that may lead people to do so, as well as whether the legal protections are adequate. The next section looks at why people may falsely confess.

Confessions by the factually innocent

Two infamous American cases illustrate how law enforcement agencies and the criminal justice system encounter false confessors. When the much-lauded and pioneering pilot Charles Lindbergh's infant son was kidnapped and killed in 1932, more than 200 people confessed to the crime. Richard Hauptmann, who was convicted of the offence and later executed, was not one of them. Elizabeth Short, a waitress and aspiring actress, was the victim of a horrific murder in 1947 and the case garnered mass attention due to the nature of her demise. The crime remains unsolved despite the fact that more than 500 people have now confessed to it (some of whom were born after the killing took place). The risk of a miscarriage of justice is particularly great as juries are seen to attach great weight to a confession – even if it is excluded at trial (Kassim, 2017) – although there is empirical evidence which suggests that juries are now more aware of the possibility that confession evidence may be false and are cognizant of the means that the police have used to obtain confessions (Mindthoff et al, 2018).

The extent to which the innocent plead guilty is, obviously, unknown. One supposes that false confessors will often subsequently plead guilty and the facts surrounding the case will never be scrutinized. Yet, the fact that assessing the extent of the problem empirically is impossible means that one must not draw the conclusion that it is rare. Rather, one has to recognize the phenomenon, try to understand it and determine what measures should be introduced to filter out confessions where there are grounds for suspicion. It will be shown later in this chapter that the primary legal challenge is how to respond to true confessions made in dubious circumstances. Here, though, the legal issue is simple: justice cannot be served if the innocent are convicted and punished. Truth is paramount. It should also be remembered that a false confession results in undeserved (though possibly wanted) punishment and the end of an investigation that might have identified the actual perpetrator, possibly before they offended again. False confessions may give the illusion that law enforcement agencies have acted effectively, but public confidence could rapidly evaporate when it emerges that a false confession was taken at face value or was obtained in breach of the law. Victims too would take little comfort in realizing that the person responsible was still at large.

A distinction can be drawn between three types of false confession: voluntary false confessions; coerced compliant false confessions; and (the most challenging to understand) coerced-internalized false confessions. Voluntary false confessions involve no police malpractice, while the circumstances surrounding the confession are paramount with regards to coerced compliant false confessions and coerced-internalized false confessions. Legally, the circumstances in which a confession was made matters more than factual accuracy: if the statement was made through oppression or the statement was made in consequence of anything said or done that is likely to make the confession unreliable, it must be excluded (The Police and Criminal Evidence Act 1984, section 76(2)). If it was obtained 'unfairly', the courts have a discretion to exclude (section 78). Disregarding accuracy in determining admissibility challenges the idea that the primary concern of the law of confessions is to avert miscarriages of justice and also suggests that there may be scant protection for those who make voluntary false confessions. More needs to be said about who pleads guilty to offences that they have not committed.

What characterizes innocent people who confess?

Remarkably little is known about false confessors. This is due to a number of factors. The most obvious is that someone who voluntarily admits to something that they did not do is unlikely to seek to retract the statement – unless fresh evidence later emerges (for example, corroborating evidence linking someone else to the crime) the miscarriage is unlikely to ever be detected. Other cases will never be known about because the police will effectively filter them out at an early stage if the claim seems fantastical. The most detailed study into the characteristics associated with false confession cases was undertaken by Drizin and Leo (2004), who reviewed 125 cases of proven false confessions in the United States between 1971 and 2002. Their key findings were as follows:

- Ninety-three per cent of the false confessions were made by men.
- Eighty-one per cent of the confessions were made in murder cases, 8 per cent in rape cases and 3 per cent in arson cases. However, this is misleading as all of the reported cases will be concerned with more serious offences.

- The most common reasons why the confession was found to be false were that the actual offender was identified (74 per cent of cases) and/ or that new scientific evidence was discovered (46 per cent of cases).
- Sixty-three per cent of false confessors were under the age of 25 and 32 per cent were under the age of 18.
- Ten per cent of those who made a false confession had a diagnosed mental illness.
- In about 30 per cent of cases, more than one confession to the same crime had been obtained, which, it was argued, suggests that one false confession is sometimes used to coerce others.

Understanding why innocent people admit 'guilt'

Psychologists suggest that there is no straightforward reason as to why people confess to crimes that they did not commit. As has been said, a widely used categorization differentiates between voluntary false confessions, coerced-compliant confessions and coerced-internalized confessions, though elements of each can be present in any given case (Scherr et al, 2020). Each will be considered in turn. Little will be said about coerced-compliant confessions as the reasons why someone may confess in these circumstances are readily apparent.

The first category – *voluntary false confessions* – can be defined as 'a self-incriminating statement that is purposefully offered in the absence of pressure by the police' (Conti, 1999, p 21). Someone may make such a statement for diverse reasons. The first – as was no doubt the case in the Lindbergh and Short murders – is a pathological need for recognition. A second cause may be that the person is confessing due to an underlying sense of guilt arising from another unrelated offence or event. In that sense, the confession constitutes a form of 'self-punishment'. Gudjonsson (2003) expands on both explanations. The actions of someone who confesses due to a desire for notoriety constitute a pathological attempt to enhance self-esteem due to feelings of inadequacy; most likely, this can be attributed to a personality disorder (Gudjonsson, 2003, p 197). Where the confession is made in an attempt to assuage a sense of guilt that is unrelated to the offence, the behaviour is most likely to be linked to depressive symptoms or illness (Gudjonsson, 2003, p 197).

Not all decisions to proffer a voluntary false confession are necessarily irrational. For example, someone may confess in order to protect a friend or family member (thereby almost certainly committing a criminal offence in the process). Someone who already has a criminal record might, for example, confess in order to stop a younger family member acquiring a criminal record that could hinder future opportunity. Conversely, someone may confess believing that a friend with previous convictions would likely receive a custodial term if convicted. A political career was ruined and two people received prison terms when Vicky Pryce wrongly claimed that she had been driving rather than her former husband, Chris Huhne, who would have received a driving ban had he been found guilty of speeding. Another rational explanation for falsely confessing would be to confess to a lesser offence in the hope that this would deflect attention away from a more serious offence for which the individual bore responsibility.

The second category of false confessions are classified as *coerced-compliant confessions*. Here the individual confesses due to the 'extreme measures of police interrogation' (Conti, 1999, p 22), despite knowing that they were not responsible. Psychologically, the explanation as to why people subjected to this conduct confess is obvious: 'coerced-compliant false confessions are explained by the innocent suspect's wish to escape an aversive situation and ensure a pleasant consequence' (Conti, 1999, p 23). The challenge in such cases is a legal one; at what point do police interrogation techniques become severe enough that an ensuing confession should be held inadmissible. This will be considered later in the chapter.

Coerced-internalized confessions – the third category of false confessions – are the most problematic to comprehend. Conti defines them thus: '[When] suspects who are innocent, but anxious, fatigued, pressured, or confused, and then subjected to highly suggestive methods of police interrogation, actually come to believe that they have committed the crime' (Conti, 1999, p 22). Again this presents a challenge for the law. People in police custody and those being interviewed in connection with an offence will often experience all of these sensations. This suggests that it is necessary for legal safeguards to be in place to ensure that methods of investigation are acceptable, given our knowledge that suggestive interrogation can lead innocent people to believe that they are responsible for the offence in question. What explains the process? Schacter and Singer (1962) formed a two-factor theory of emotion based on physiological arousal and cognitive processes. Those who are suggestible may cognitively perceive a physiological response as guilt and would then draw the erroneous conclusion that they are feeling guilty and that the explanation for this is that they must have been involved in the crime. This process highlights the need for additional protection for those who may be judged especially vulnerable to pressure in a police interview. Later in this chapter it will be shown how this has been recognized in English law. Ofsche (1989) identified seven types of interrogation techniques that seem to increase the risk of a coerced–internalized false confession:

- The interviewer states, confidently and repeatedly, that they believe that the suspect is guilty.
- People who contradict the interviewer's apparent belief in the suspect's guilt are isolated from the suspect. Similarly, evidence suggesting innocence is not revealed.
- The interrogation is lengthy and intensive.
- Claims that there is incontrovertible proof of guilt are made repeatedly.
- If the suspect has suffered past memory problems, they are reminded of this throughout. If there is no past history, it is suggested that the suspect may have a mental disorder, which would explain why they cannot recall committing the crime.
- The interviewer demands that the suspect accepts their account of events.
- The interviewer attempts to cause distress by emphasizing the potential consequences of continuing to deny responsibility for the offence.

Drizin and Colgan (2004) provide a real-life example of an internalized false confession where several of these aspects are apparent. Fourteen-year-old Michael Crowe denied strenuously that he had stabbed his sister Stephanie to death. After three interrogations, his story changed and he maintained: 'I'm not sure how I did it. All I know is that I did it' (Drizin and Colgan, 2004, p 141). During these three interrogations a number of false evidential claims were made: Crowe was told that his hair was found in his sister's grasp; that her blood was in his bedroom; that all of the ways to enter the house had been locked; and that he had failed a lie detector test. The interviewer then suggested to Crowe that he had a split personality and that 'good Michael' had blocked out what 'bad Michael' had done and that he should try to imagine how 'bad Michael' had killed his sister. A grave miscarriage of justice was only averted when someone with the victim's blood on his clothing was later arrested.

Confessions: from psychological vulnerability to legal protection

Where the evidence supports the facts that the individual did in fact commit the crime to which they confess, one would imagine that the prime function of the legal system should be to expedite the process.

Yet, even if there is no doubt that the person confessing committed the offence, there is an acceptance that the circumstances surrounding the making of the confession matter. On the one hand, this makes perfect sense – why have detailed procedural rules, if no penalty is attached to their breach? But, as with other forms of tainted evidence (see Chapter 5), other remedies are available (such as civil proceedings or police disciplinary actions) if the evidence proves detrimental to the person who made the confession.

Most people who confess do not seek to retract the statement that they made. However, on occasion defendants do try to argue that a confession (regardless of whether it is true or false) should be excluded at trial because of the circumstances when it was made. The argument is slightly different depending on whether the confession is true. If it is false, and the prosecution case is otherwise threadbare, the argument is that exclusion is necessary in order to stop an apparent miscarriage of justice. In this context, it is an argument of truth. If the confession appears to be true, which would generally be gauged with reference to the supporting evidence, the argument appears subtly different. A confession's 'value' to the prosecution largely depends on the other evidence. If there is a wealth of supporting evidence, a confession may add little more. The argument for exclusion here is one of fairness: the rules of procedure must be followed so as to allow a fair trial. In England and Wales there remains a common law duty to ensure a fair trial and that includes a right to exclude unfairly obtained evidence (*R* v *Sang* [1980] AC 402).

The common law duty now coexists with statutory provisions contained in the Police and Criminal Evidence Act 1984 (see further Bicak, 2001). This Act contains a discretionary power to exclude evidence that would have 'such an adverse effect on the fairness of the proceedings that the court ought not to admit it' (section 78). Chapter 5 reviews the use of this section to exclude unfairly obtained evidence that retains probative value more broadly. Many of the cases on section 78, however, relate to confession evidence and will be considered in this chapter. Section 76 contains additional, specific grounds for excluding confessions – regardless of whether they are true – and these need to be considered first:

> S 76(2) If, in any proceedings where the prosecution proposes to give in evidence a confession made by an accused person, it is represented to the court that the confession was or may have been obtained–
>   (a) by oppression of the person who made it; or

(b) in consequence of anything said or done which was likely, in the circumstances existing at the time, to render unreliable any confession which might be made by him in consequence thereof,

the court shall not allow the confession to be given in evidence against him except in so far as the prosecution proves to the court beyond reasonable doubt that the confession (not withstanding that it may be true) was not obtained as aforesaid.

Regardless of whether the confession may have been obtained in circumstances likely to render it unreliable or by oppression (or both), the Act is explicit that the truth of the confession is immaterial. The rationale cannot be to ensure that evidence of a probative nature comes before the court. Far more will be said about the purpose of exclusion later in the conclusion to this chapter. A second initial observation is that exclusion under section 76 is mandatory. This signals parliamentary intent but this has been weakened through judicial interpretation. Both section 76(2)(a) and section 76(2)(b) have been narrowly defined – to the extent that it is difficult to find appellate decisions where exclusion was deemed appropriate – and this has meant that, in practice, the discretionary ground for exclusion in section 78 has been more important. However, that does not mean that section 76(2) has little bearing on police practice as officers will be mindful that confessions made in contravention of the section will be excluded. Both grounds for exclusion in section 76(2) will now be considered in turn.

Oppression

The first ground for mandatory exclusion is where it is represented that the confession was or may have been obtained by oppression of the person who made it. Police interviews are for many suspects stress-inducing experiences, and this applies both to those who have committed the offence and to innocent suspects. There are risks of the police abusing the situation and/or suspects in order to make them more likely to confess – this may be in the genuine belief or indeed knowledge that the person committed the offence. This category of confession constitutes a coerced-compliant confession applying Conti's (1999) definitions.

At the same time, though, the police must be able to interview suspects and challenge their accounts and this may result in an atmosphere that some would find oppressive. There have been cases, as will be shown, where the police were not responsible for the pressure that led a suspect to confess but where the experience of being in custody would undoubtedly have been experienced as highly oppressive. The definition of 'oppression' is thus all-important.

Section 78(8) of the Police and Criminal Evidence Act 1984 provides a partial definition of oppression: it includes 'torture, inhuman or degrading treatment, and the use or threat of violence (whether or not amounting to torture)'. These practices are prohibited by Article 3 of the European Convention on Human Rights and the extensive case law – for example, *Ireland* v *UK* (1978) 2 EHRR 25, *Jalloh* v *Germany* (2006) 44 EHRR 32, *Kafkaris* v *Cyprus* (2008) 49 EHRR 35 and *MSS* v *Belgium and Greece* (2011) 53 EHRR 2 – on the interpretation of Article 3 in the European Court of Human Rights. This jurisprudence has influenced the domestic courts. In *El-Masri* v *Former Yugoslav Republic of Macedonia* (2012) 57 EHRR 25, the Grand Chamber held that:

> In order for ill-treatment to fall within the scope of [Article] 3 it must attain a minimum level of severity. The assessment of this minimum depends on all the circumstances of the case, such as the duration of the treatment, its physical or mental effects and, in some cases, the age, sex and state of health of the victim. Further factors include the purpose for which the treatment was inflicted together with the intention or motivation behind it. (at [196])

The value of the European Court of Human Rights cases, though, is limited in that the court was often responding to manifest and obvious instances of inhuman and degrading treatment. To take the facts of one of the most important Article 3 cases, in *Ireland* v *UK* (1978) 2 EHRR 25, British forces subjected suspected terrorists to 'wall-standing, hooding, subjection to noise, deprivation of sleep and deprivation of food and drink' (although this amounted to a breach of the individuals' Article 3 rights, none of these practices were held to amount to torture). Oppression has seldom been found in domestic cases. A notable exception was in *R* v *Paris* (1992) 97 Cr App R 99. The judgment articulates powerfully the degree of pressure that the police had put one of the co-accused under:

> The officers ... were not questioning him so much as shouting at him what they wanted him to say. Short of physical violence, it is hard to conceive of a more hostile

and intimidating approach by officers to a suspect. It is impossible to convey on the printed page the pace, force and menace of the officer's delivery. (at p 103)

The facts of R v *Fulling* [1987] QB 426 provide a useful illustration of conduct that was not found to be oppressive. While Fulling was in police custody, it was alleged that officers told her that her partner had been having an affair with a woman who was in an adjacent cell. She maintained that her confession was secured solely because of her wish to get out of the police station. It was argued on her behalf that the confession should be excluded as the police's conduct had been oppressive. The Court of Appeal held that the term 'oppression' should be given its dictionary meaning, which was taken as the 'exercise of authority or power in a burdensome, harsh, or wrongful manner; unjust or cruel treatment of subjects, inferiors, etc.; [and] the imposition of unreasonable or unjust burdens' (at p 432). On face value, the allegations made against the police would appear to satisfy this definition. The Court, however, was influenced by a quotation in the dictionary, which, in effect, introduced an exceptionally high threshold: '[there] is not a word in our language which expresses more detestable wickedness than oppression' (at p 432). 'Detestable wickedness' could admittedly be found more easily in R v *Paris* (1992) 97 Cr App R 99, but the effect of the ruling in R v *Fulling* is that oppression will only be found *in extremis*.

As confessions obtained through oppression must be excluded (Police and Criminal Evidence Act 1984, section 76(2)(a)), evidence that could be highly probative would be excluded and this may go against the grain of this book, which explores how the criminal justice system can best uncover truth. The authors will not dwell on this point because any legal system that sanctions the use of oppression – and specifically torture, or inhuman or degrading treatment – lacks moral legitimacy in our eyes (see Bufacchi and Arrigo, 2006; Twiss, 2007; Thaler, 2016). A vast literature exists about the 'legitimacy' of torture (for example, Franklin, 2009; Alhoff, 2012; Kramer, 2014). Some have attempted to put forward utilitarian arguments that torture may be acceptable if it leads to evidence that stops a greater harm from occurring – this is often referred to as the 'ticking bomb' argument. Our objection, though, remains absolute.

The fact that torture may lead to the truth on some occasions is a weak argument for sanctioning its use. Research shows that evidence obtained through torture is inherently unreliable (Franklin, 2009; Hajjar, 2009; Schiemann, 2012): even if someone finds the practice justifiable in some hypothetical scenario, they would need to concede that torture will often lead to evidence of dubious or no value. 'Ticking bomb' scenarios can easily be devised, particularly in the context of terrorism, that could later 'legitimate' a wider and more speculative use of torture in the hope of unearthing valuable evidence.

Unreliability

Unlike oppression, the second ground for exclusion is framed broadly, yet this has not resulted in extensive case law, which seems surprising given the number of factors that could render confession evidence unreliable. It is necessary to review such case law as exists in some detail as it sets out the parameters of the protection afforded to those who confess due to things said or done likely to render a confession made in those circumstances unreliable: if this protection is wanting, innocent individuals could well admit to things that they played no part in. This covers both coerced-compliant confessions and coerced-internalized confessions. A legalistic distinction is important here. Exclusion under section 76(2)(b) is mandatory. If exclusion fails on that ground, it remains possible that a court will still exclude a confession under section 78 (see later). This is a broader provision and thus affords more scope. However, at least theoretically, it is far preferable for protections against official malpractice to be mandatory rather than discretionary. The courts have, in a similar vein to section 76(2)(a), interpreted section 76(2)(b) very narrowly, with the practical effect that judicial discretion largely determines whether confessions obtained in dubious circumstances will be excluded.

Section 76(2)(b) states that a confession must be excluded if it was, or may have been, obtained 'in consequence of anything said or done which was likely, in the circumstances existing at the time, to render unreliable any confession which might have been made by him in consequence thereof'. In *R v J* [2003] EWCA Crim 3309, the Court of Appeal sought to clarify the section: '[what] the court is concerned with on admissibility is the reliability of the confession, given the circumstances in which it was obtained, and not its veracity' (at [44]). That might appear contradictory, and requires significant judicial mental dexterity, but the fact that the truth of the confession is immaterial bears repeating.

Nothing in the section states that the police (or another investigatory agency) must have done or said anything; the actor(s) responsible are not specified. However, in *R v Goldenberg* (1988) 88 Cr App R 285, it was established that someone other than the defendant has to say or do something that might make a subsequent confession unreliable. Goldenberg was suffering from heroin withdrawal symptoms in police custody and asked for the interview to take place, during which he confessed. He claimed subsequently that he had done so in order to get bail so that he could feed his addiction. This seems plausible and would cast doubt on the reliability of his confession. If the primary rationale for the mandatory exclusion of confession evidence is reliability, then there is a compelling case that the circumstances surrounding Goldenberg's confession should have led to exclusion and that the judicial interpretation of the provision was too narrow.

A contrast can be drawn with the factual scenario in *R v Wahab* [2002] EWCA Crim 1570, where the defendant's lawyer, following his client's instructions, approached the police to see if a favourable agreement could be reached. The confession may well have arisen as a consequence of an agreement struck between the lawyer and the police, but here the instigator was the defendant himself and, at the time, the circumstances were no different from those facing any suspect in detention. This is not to deny that most people in police custody feel intrinsic pressure, rather it is to draw a distinction between someone wanting to confess so that they can leave a police station and someone desperate to do so because they are suffering from heroin withdrawal.

Unfairness

Due to the restrictive approach taken with regards to section 76(2), recourse will usually have to be made to section 78 of the Police and Criminal Evidence Act 1984 when considering whether confession evidence is to be excluded. The section provides the following:

> In any proceedings the court may refuse to allow evidence on which the prosecution proposes to rely to be given if it appears to the court that, having regard to all the circumstances, including the circumstances in which the evidence was obtained, the admission of the evidence would have such an adverse effect on the fairness of the proceedings that the court ought not to admit it.

The section confers a wide discretion. Appellate courts have recognized this and have provided limited guidance to judges faced with making a decision on whether a confession should be admitted. This recognizes (correctly) that factual scenarios differ widely and that it is undesirable as a matter of policy to have routine appeals on narrow factual distinctions. The approach taken is articulated in *R v Jelen* (1989) Cr App R 456: 'The circumstances of each case are almost always different, and judges may well take different views in the proper exercise of their discretion even where the circumstances are similar. This is not an apt field for hard case law and well-founded distinctions between cases' (at p 465).

Challenging a judicial decision not to exclude is difficult as a consequence: the courts have adopted a test akin to *Wednesbury* unreasonableness, which, to paraphrase, would allow an appeal only if the initial decision were so 'unreasonable' that no reasonable judge acting reasonably could have arrived at it (*Thomson v R* [1998] 2 WLR 927). The courts, therefore, have interpreted the mandatory grounds for excluding a confession in section 76(2) narrowly while, at the same time, made it near-impossible to challenge a discretionary decision not to exclude taken by a trial judge. As a consequence, confessions, once made, are very difficult to retract, whether on the basis of oppression, unreliability or unfairness.

Some broad principles about the use of section 78 can nonetheless be discerned from the case law. The first is that minor infractions of criminal procedure will not suffice. Any breach must be significant and substantial. Some breaches evidently fall within this category even though there may have been no bad faith on the part of the police. Reading the section, a focus on the severity of the breach makes sense as no mention is made of the need for deliberate malpractice. Here a distinction can possibly be drawn between fairness to the accused and fairness to the trial. The two do not necessarily coincide. Admitting an unfairly obtained confession (or other prejudicial evidence) may harm the interests of the defendant but simultaneously have public benefit if it helps establish who is liable for a crime.

At the same time, the courts have stopped short of saying that the faith of the police is wholly irrelevant. Indeed, in borderline cases, it has been held that whether the police acted in bad faith is a relevant concern (*R v Walsh* (1989) 91 Cr App R 161). This suggests a holistic approach to assessing fairness even though the courts have stressed that disciplining the police is not a legitimate concern (*R v Mason* [1988] 1 WLR 139). Most of the reported cases concern alleged breaches of the Police and Criminal Evidence Act 1984 and the associated Codes of Practice. Both are highly detailed and this chapter cannot do anything other than outline in the broadest of terms how the courts have responded to breaches of four key protections when these have given rise to a confession: the absence of a caution; the absence of an appropriate adult; the denial of legal advice; and breaches of recording requirements.

Where 'there are grounds to suspect [an individual] of an offence [he] must be cautioned before any questions about an offence, or further questions if the answers provide the grounds for suspicion, are put to [him] if either the suspect's answers or silence ... may be given in evidence to a court in a prosecution' (Police and Criminal Evidence Act 1984, para 10.1, code C). *R v Kirk* [2000] 1WLR 567 illustrates that a failure to caution a suspect can lead to the exclusion of a confession under section 78. Initially, Kirk was arrested for the theft of a bag from an elderly woman and for assault. Her injuries were, though, more serious and she later died from complications associated with emergency surgery. At the point that the police questioned Kirk, they were aware of her death yet they failed to caution him in relation to manslaughter or robbery. The Court of Appeal stressed that a suspect must know 'at least in general terms the level of offence in respect of which he is suspected' (at p 572) as that might influence whether he chose to admit guilt. According to the Court in *R v Gill* [2003] EWCA Crim 2256, 'the principle purpose of [administering a caution] is to ensure, so far as possible, that interviewees do not make admissions unless they wish to do so and are aware of the consequences' (at [46]).

Appropriate adults must be present when 'a juvenile or person who is mentally disordered or otherwise mentally vulnerable' is to be 'interviewed regarding their involvement or suspected involvement in a criminal offence or offences, or asked to provide or sign a written statement under caution or record of interview' (Police and Criminal Evidence Act 1984, para 11.13, code C). Their role in ensuring both probity of process and countering the possibility of miscarriages of justice is obvious. The danger is illustrated in the leading case of *R v Aspinall* [1999] 2 Cr App R 115, where the suspect told a series of lies during an interview that took place without an appropriate adult. His appeal against conviction was granted, effectively on two linked grounds: the first, that an appropriate adult would have urged him to seek legal advice; and, the second, that an appropriate adult, or legal representative, would have stressed the importance of giving a truthful account to the police.

Section 58(1) of the Police and Criminal Evidence Act 1984 states that a 'person arrested and held in custody in a police station or other premises shall be entitled, if he so requests, to consult a solicitor privately at any time'. The law is detailed and there are notable exceptions, which space does not allow consideration of, but, generally, a suspect 'must be permitted to consult a solicitor as soon as is practicable' (section 58(4)) and someone who requests legal advice should not be interviewed by the police until they have received it (Police and Criminal Evidence Act 1984, para 6.6, code C). The courts have stressed that the right to legal advice constitutes 'one of the most important and fundamental rights of a citizen' (*R* v *Samuel* [1988] QB 615 at p 630). Breaches of this right are thus treated seriously but, even so, exclusion is not automatic, particularly if the court concludes that the presence of a solicitor would not have made a material difference because, for example, the suspect was well aware of his legal rights (*R* v *Alladice* (1988) 87 Cr App R 360) or would have made the confession in any event. *R* v *Samuel* [1988] QB 615 provides an illustration of a case where the refusal to allow legal representation led to the exclusion of a confession. Samuel's solicitor averred that, because of the severity of the crimes he was suspected of and the fact that he had maintained innocence in four interviews, he would have advised Samuel not to exercise his right to silence. As a consequence, there was a genuine possibility that the solicitor's absence might have affected Samuel's decision to confess.

The recording requirements in code F of the Police and Criminal Evidence Act 1984 are similarly detailed and, again, this paragraph provides only a basic overview as to how the courts deal with confessions made in circumstances where the requirements are not complied with. An interview is defined in code C, para 1 as questioning a person regarding his involvement or suspected involvement in a criminal offence or offences, for the purpose of eliciting evidence that may be given in court. The general requirement is that an accurate record of each interview with a suspect is taken regardless of whether the interview is held in a police station (Police and Criminal Evidence Act 1984, code C, para 11.7(a)). However, an audio recording is usually required if an interview takes place with someone suspected of an indictable offence in a police station (Police and Criminal Evidence Act 1984, code E, para 3.1). A failure to comply with the recording requirements is generally seen as sufficiently serious to warrant the exclusion of any confession made during the interview (*R* v *Keenan* [1990] 2 QB 54), but there have been exceptional cases where confessions have been held to be admissible despite flagrant procedural breaches, on the basis that the failure to record would not prejudice the defendant (for example, *R* v *Dunn* (1990) 91 Cr App R 237).

Confessions, truth and systemic probity

Whether or not a confession is admissible at trial is not determined by its factual accuracy. Broader notions of systemic probity largely decide whether a confession should be excluded. This has the effect of denying to the jury evidence that might be highly probative in determining the defendant's guilt. Yet, that account is too simplistic. Protecting those caught up in the criminal justice system, whether innocent or guilty, is wholly legitimate and this entails concentrating not on whether or not a confession was true but on the circumstances surrounding it being made. There is the potential, given this focus, for accurate confessions that would aid the conviction of the guilty to be excluded, with the consequence that some people who are factually responsible for crimes will escape conviction.

Few surely would advocate for the abandonment of any concern other than the truth. At the extreme, few would argue that confessions obtained through torture should be admitted, even if the confession turned out to be true. Domestic law leaves no doubt that evidence obtained in oppressive circumstances cannot be admitted (section 76(2)(a) of the Police and Criminal Evidence Act 1984). The courts, though, have tempered this rule of admissibility by holding that oppression must be defined in very strict terms. Confessions obtained in consequence of anything said or done that was likely to render such a confession unreliable must also be excluded (section 76(2)(b)). A narrow interpretation has been applied to this ground as well. This means that the final ground – unfairness – offers most scope for the exclusion of confession evidence. Judicial interpretation has resulted in a largely discretionary, as opposed to a mandatory, mechanism for excluding confessions at trial. The conceptual ambiguity of 'unfairness' (and its opposite – 'fairness') dictates a fact-sensitive case-by-case approach; appellate courts have avoided providing meaningful guidance for fear of restricting the reasoning that judges must engage in.

While it cannot be known what factors a court will find relevant or determinative in deciding whether a confession was obtained in circumstances that would make its admissibility unfair (unless these are specified in a written judgment), the veracity of the statement should have no bearing. There is no way of knowing whether the fact that there is additional incriminating evidence supporting a confession does in fact influence judicial thinking. Nonetheless, in a book concerned with truth as a value in the criminal justice process, this policy decision to deem truth an irrelevant concern demands explanation. After all, howsoever obtained, confessions may retain probative value.

For analytical purposes, the models of criminal justice that will be discussed in more depth in Chapter 10 provide focus. Disregarding factually accurate confessions is problematic from a crime control perspective. If the overarching goal of crime control is to expedite the processing of guilty individuals through the justice system, then facilitating the use of confessions is inherently beneficial. Rewarding someone who confesses guilt at an early stage and subsequently admits the charge(s) prior to trial (see Chapter 8) with a (potentially significant) sentencing discount makes sense. This is an inducement. However: (a) someone may well welcome the opportunity to admit responsibility and avoid trial; (b) the prejudicial evidence linking the suspect to the offence(s) may be such that no meaningful defence is available, in which case determining an appropriate penalty becomes the concern; and (c) this is all tempered by the fact that a suspect is not required to confess even if the evidence against them is overwhelming and even if their legal advisers have pointed out the likely ramifications. Any legal system prioritizing crime control as a value would then seek to encourage the making of confessions and limit the grounds for excluding confession evidence at trial. The expansive definition of confession in the Police and Criminal Evidence Act 1984 certainly helps address the first concern; any full or partial admittance broadly speaking constitutes a confession that is admissible against the defendant at trial. It can also be argued that the *interpretation* of the safeguards contained in the Act makes the subsequent exclusion of a confession extremely unlikely, despite seemingly strict statutory rules of admissibility. The manner in which this has been achieved is that the mandatory grounds for exclusion (section 76(2)) have been interpreted in such a restrictive manner that exclusion is usually considered on a discretionary basis (section 78), with minimal guidance from appellate judgments. Reviewing the case law reveals that exclusion will be rare and reserved for the most serious procedural breaches.

Crime control models of justice do not, of course, jettison all procedural protection. Rather, there is a presumption that probative evidence should only be excluded in exceptional cases, and confession evidence can often be classified as highly probative. There might, under a crime control model, be an expectation that establishing the truth would be the key determinant of admissibility – and, if not, that truth would certainly inform the decision. This would, in turn, suggest that there would be a presumption that a truthful confession would be admissible at trial. Miscarriages of justice are to be avoided under all models of criminal justice. Crime control is not served if an innocent person is convicted and punished for a crime that they did not commit. The aim is to expedite the truth-finding process, not to bypass it.

The conception of a miscarriage of justice is wider under a crime control model. There is a tacit belief that the system has failed if an offender is not prosecuted, convicted and punished. This reasoning is obvious but not without problems. Truth becomes the sole measure of success; however, it should not be the only means of assessing the success of an outcome. To take an example, in England and Wales, a decision to prosecute depends not only on whether there is sufficient evidence for a realistic chance of conviction – a question of whether guilt can be established on the basis of the available evidence – but also on whether prosecution is judged to be in the public interest. The implication is clear: there are situations where someone should not be prosecuted even if the evidence points firmly towards guilt. An example of where this might occur would be where the value of the goods stolen was minimal and the offender was of advanced age. Would a decision to prosecute in these circumstances amount to a miscarriage of justice? Or, if truth is our only measure of success, would a decision not to prosecute constitute a miscarriage of justice? These are not insignificant questions, particularly when discussing crime control objectives where the parameters of a miscarriage of justice appear wider. There is also a practical matter: what of scenarios where an individual confesses due to the weight of evidence or feelings of remorse but a decision is nonetheless taken not to prosecute? Public interest dictates that some reliable confessions will be excluded because a decision is taken not to proceed with the case or to caution the offender instead. Even with judicial reticence to exclude confessions, decisions are being taken on public interest grounds to terminate prosecutions where the evidence suggests that conviction was likely and in some cases where guilt was admitted.

Due process safeguards can be found throughout the Police and Criminal Evidence Act 1984 and the accompanying Codes of Practice. Parliament's intent was obvious. The law is detailed but the central premise is clear: 'truthful' confessions must be excluded if they were, or might have been, obtained in specified ways. Confession evidence carries such a prejudicial effect that stringent safeguards are necessary to reduce the possibility that the confession was obtained through oppression, unfairness or anything said or done that may render it unreliable. There is an awareness of the risks of coerced-compliant confessions and of coerced-internalized confessions. So, why this desire to exclude truthful confessions? One answer might be to deter the police from engaging in unacceptable practice. The courts, though, have rejected this as an explicit rationale (*R* v *Delaney* (1988) 88 Cr App R 338). Exclusion nonetheless has the potential to act as a disincentive to investigative malpractice. This focus on procedural propriety legitimates exclusion where the evidence proves guilt on the basis that rules of procedure serve a purpose. If that is the case, there needs to be a consequence for non-compliance. There is also a recognition that excluding some truthful confessions is a means of protecting those who confess in situations where the veracity of the confession is less certain.

One due process approach that the law in England and Wales has avoided is a requirement that a conviction cannot be based on uncorroborated confession evidence. This provides an obvious safeguard against false confessions (whether voluntarily made or not), although such a policy would make the task of the prosecutor more challenging. It would, however, offer some protection to those who make voluntary false confessions who are currently not protected in English law. The risk that innocent individuals may confess was documented earlier in the chapter but the preference in policy terms is to provide procedural protections concerning the circumstances in which a confession was made rather than a requirement for additional evidence that may, in combination, establish guilt. All of this depends on how these statutory protections are interpreted by the judiciary and one must caution against undue optimism that the Police and Criminal Evidence Act 1984 and accompanying Codes of Practice provide robust due process guarantees in practice.

The historical context is important in understanding the approach taken in the Police and Criminal Evidence Act 1984. A spate of high-profile miscarriages of justice in the early 1980s raised fundamental concerns about police probity and the ability of the legal system to respond. Several of these cases involved confession evidence obtained after violence or threatened violence. Taken together, the cases exposed brutality and treatment that led to patently wrongful convictions. These were all cases of coerced-compliant false confessions. Urgent and comprehensive legal reform was necessary. The detail in the Police and Criminal Evidence Act 1984 and its accompanying Codes of Practice are the direct response.

Police practice has changed as a result and the scope for miscarriages of justice based on confession evidence has been diminished (Moston and Stephenson, 1993) (although it has not been eradicated). Concentrating solely on the truthfulness of a confession would have been a mistake, for it could legitimate the malpractice that existed (to an unknown extent) prior to the Police and Criminal Evidence Act

1984, hence the focus on the context in which a confession was made. Excluding reliable confessions obtained in breach of the Act may have an additional utilitarian benefit in that it may improve future practice and reduce the potential for people to be convicted on the basis of false confessions. Admittedly, this aim may be somewhat illusory due to the way in which the judiciary have interpreted the Act. Moreover, it assumes that law enforcement agencies take a keen interest in the law reports. Were they to do so, they may take comfort from the manner in which the mandatory grounds for exclusion (section 76(2)) have been interpreted. The upshot of this is that excluding a confession is likely to have a minimal effect on future police conduct. The Police and Criminal Evidence Act 1984 may well have espoused due process rights as a reaction to high-profile miscarriages of justice that involved coerced confessions. It is suggested that, in interpreting these provisions, the courts have steered a line which means that only the most manifest breaches will result in confession evidence being excluded, as the cases discussed earlier in this chapter illustrate. Despite parliamentary intent, crime control values would appear to drive practice. Confessions will seldom be excluded, save in the most extreme circumstances. This may not offer the systemic protection envisaged but does allow factfinders to make determinations of guilt based on all the available evidence, including adverse admissions that the defendant now wishes to retract.

4

Witness Testimony

Before a prosecution is brought, the Crown Prosecution Service (CPS) needs to be satisfied that there is sufficient evidence to provide a realistic prospect of securing a conviction against the suspect(s). In assessing the evidence, the CPS needs to consider the admissibility of the evidence and this is considered in more detail in Chapter 5. It must also consider the reliability and credibility of the evidence. In order to do so, it must consider whether there are any reasons to question the accuracy and integrity of the evidence. Very often this will involve making judgments on the veracity, integrity and credibility of witnesses who may be called upon to give their testimony in court. Andrew Choo sets out the traditional view on how the criminal trial can make assessments of witness reliability:

> Any statement may be unreliable because of defects in the perception, memory, sincerity, or ability to narrate clearly, of the maker of the statement. Suppose that a witness, W, states in his or her testimony that 'The car I saw driving away was red'. This statement may be unreliable because (1) W may have perceived the car to be red when it was in reality of some other colour; (2) W may have genuinely forgotten that the car was of some other colour; (3) W may be lying; or (4) W may be trying to say that the car was of some other colour, but be lacking in the ability to narrate this clearly. In this situation, because the statement has been made in court by the person who witnessed the event, it will have been possible to observe his or her demeanour at the time of making the statement. Further, the statement is likely to have been a sworn statement. Finally, it would be possible to subject the witness to 'contemporaneous'

cross-examination in relation to the statement. Such cross-examination would, it is said, assist in exposing any defects in the witness's perception, memory, sincerity, or clarity of narration. (Choo, 2018, p 264)

Oaths and sworn statements were discussed in Chapter 1.

An increasing body of psychological research has cast doubt on the efficacy of the application of common sense and experience in assessing witness veracity, integrity and credibility. This chapter is concerned with the extent to which factfinders at trial are able to make accurate judgments about witness veracity, integrity and credibility on the basis of their demeanour and the extent to which the trial can reveal defects in perception, memory, sincerity or clarity of narration. The chapter will consider a number of key issues that raise questions about the extent to which courts can and should rely on witnesses always to tell the truth, the whole truth and nothing but the truth.

Witness demeanour, credibility and the ability to detect lies

In March 2020, the UK went into lockdown in response to the rapid spread of COVID-19 infections. All but essential travel was stopped and people were encouraged to work from home. On 23 March 2020, the Lord Chief Justice, Lord Burnett of Maldon, announced the pausing of all jury trials. As far as hearings in the magistrates' courts were concerned, Lord Burnett announced that 'all hearings that can lawfully take place remotely should do so if the facilities exist' (Courts and Tribunals Judiciary, 2020). One of the immediate issues raised in relation to remote hearings was witness demeanour. In May 2016, the Judicial College published the first *Crown Court Compendium*. Intended as a guide for Crown Court judges, the Compendium provides guidance on jury and trial management, summing up and sentencing. The most recent edition was edited by six circuit judges, a recorder and the former Criminal Law Commissioner, Professor David Ormerod QC (Judicial College, 2018). The Compendium makes six references to 'demeanour':

• At paragraph 23, the guidance for members of the jury is that they 'may take such notes as they find helpful. However, it would be better not to take so many notes that they are unable to observe the manner/demeanour of the witnesses as they give their evidence' (Judicial College, 2018, section 3.1).

- Where witnesses give evidence via video, caution should be shown in deciding whether to allow the jury to see a transcript of the video evidence and the jury must 'take care to watch the video as it is shown, so that they can assess the manner/demeanour of the witness when giving evidence' (Judicial College, 2018, para 3.28).
- Where hearsay evidence (discussed in the next section) is admitted, judges should give the jury a warning about the limitations of such evidence. One of the three stated limitations is 'the inability of the jury to assess the demeanour of the witness' (Judicial College, 2018. section 14, para 2): 'The jury need to be directed that hearsay evidence may suffer from the following limitations when compared with evidence given on oath by a witness at trial. There has usually been no opportunity to see the demeanour of the person who made the statement' (Judicial College, 2018).
- In relation to sexual offences, the Compendium quotes from the 2010 *Benchbook*, approved by the Court of Appeal in *R v Miller* [2010] EWCA Crim 1578: 'The experience of judges who try sexual offences is that an image of stereotypical behaviour and *demeanour* by a victim or the perpetrator of a non-consensual offence such as rape held by some members of the public can be misleading and capable of leading to injustice. That experience has been gained by judges, expert in the field, presiding over many such trials during which guilt has been established but in which the behaviour and *demeanour* of complainants and defendants, both during the incident giving rise to the charge and in evidence, has been widely variable. Judges have, as a result of their experience, in recent years adopted the course of cautioning juries against applying stereotypical images of how an alleged victim or an alleged perpetrator of a sexual offence ought to have behaved at the time, or ought to appear while giving evidence, and to judge the evidence on its intrinsic merits. This is not to invite juries to suspend their own judgement but to approach the evidence without prejudice' (Judicial College, 2018, para 20.1, emphasis added).

The Compendium appears to have a slightly confused attitude to demeanour. On the one hand, juries should be encouraged to focus on demeanour and not become too distracted by note-taking; they should take care to watch video evidence, the better to assess manner and demeanour; and they are told that one of the reasons for not trusting hearsay evidence is that you are not able to judge the demeanour of the original statement maker. On the other hand, juries should be careful to avoid applying stereotypical images of how alleged victims or perpetrators should appear when giving evidence.

In *Clarke v Edinburgh and District Tramways Co.* (1919) SC (HL) 35, Lord Shaw of Dunfermline, in discussing why appeal courts should be reluctant to overturn the findings of facts of courts at first instance, remarked:

> [Witnesses] without any conscious bias towards a conclusion may have in their demeanour, in their manner, in their hesitation, in the nuance of their expressions, in even the turns of the eyelid, left an impression upon the man who saw and heard them which can never be reproduced in the printed page. (at p 36)

That view was confirmed in the case of *Owners of Steamship Hontestroom v Owners of Steamship Sagaporack* [1947] AC 37, when Lord Sumner said that:

> [Not] to have seen the witnesses puts appellate judges in a permanent position of disadvantage as against the trial judge, and, unless it can be shown that he has failed to use or has palpably misused his advantage, the higher Court ought not to take the responsibility of reversing conclusions so arrived at, merely on the result of their own comparisons and criticisms of the witnesses and of their own view of the probabilities of the case. (at p 47)

The remark was quoted by Lord Justice Leggatt in *SS (Sri Lanka), R (On the Application Of) v The Secretary of State for the Home Department* [2018] EWCA Civ 1391. Lord Justice Leggatt indicated that things had changed since 1947 and that 'it has increasingly been recognized that it is usually unreliable and often dangerous to draw a conclusion from a witness's demeanour as to the likelihood that the witness is telling the truth' (at para 36). A few sentences later, however, he observed:

> [This] is not to say that judges (or jurors) lack the ability to tell whether witnesses are lying ... Still less does it follow that there is no value in oral evidence. But research confirms that people do not in fact generally rely on demeanour to detect deception but on the fact that liars are more likely to tell stories that are illogical, implausible, internally

inconsistent and contain fewer details than persons telling the truth. (at para 40)

In *R v D (R)* [2014] 1 LRC 629, the Crown Court sitting at Blackfriars had to consider the issue of whether a defendant should be required to remove her burka and niqab. Judge Peter Murphy ruled that the defendant could wear her burka during proceedings but would have to remove it for the purpose of identification and when giving evidence. The decision was, in part, justified on the basis that:

> It was unfair to ask a witness to give evidence against, or a juror to pass judgment on, a defendant who could not be seen. It was unfair to expect a juror to evaluate evidence given by or about a person who could not be seen, deprived of an essential tool for doing so, namely, being able to observe her demeanour when questioned and her reaction to other evidence as it was given. (at para 59)

Research by Paul Ekman and Maureen O'Sullivan (1991; Ekman et al, 1999) suggests that some highly trained individuals have some ability to detect lies but most people, including police officers, judges and psychiatrists score no better than chance in deciding whether someone is telling the truth or not. Charles F. Bond, Jr. and Bella M. DePaulo (2006) carried out a meta-analysis of research into deception detection accuracy. In their conclusion they ask the question:

> How successful are people at duping others? How often do people detect others' deception attempts? To address these questions, psychologists arrange for people to make truthful and deceptive statements and for others to classify these statements as truths or lies. Across hundreds of experiments, typical rates of lie–truth discrimination are slightly above 50%. For the grand mean, 54% is a reasonable estimate. (at p 230)

Although the focus here has been on demeanour, many also claim that inconsistencies can indicate deception. Again, the scientific evidence casts doubt on the commonly held view that inconsistent stories prove lying. Indeed, Granhag and Stromwall (2001) suggest that, in some circumstances, repetition of a rehearsed false story can produce more consistency than *ad hoc* reconstruction from memory.

Despite scientific evidence pointing to the fact that demeanour and a lack of story consistency are not always reliable guides, lay people and experts continue to assess validity and veracity on those factors. The Independent Asylum Commission's review of the UK asylum system quoted from a psychotherapist:

> One woman told me that she had been raped in the Democratic Republic of Congo, first by the chief of prison and then in descending order of the hierarchy, ending with the cleaner. She told me this only after 10 or more counselling sessions and then with great shame. Her demeanour was consistent with the trauma and I believe her. (Independent Asylum Commission, 2008, p 74)

UK national guidelines on the assessment of asylum claims state that 'discrepancies, exaggerated accounts, and the addition of new claims of mistreatment may affect credibility' (Immigration and Nationality Directorate, 1998). Assessing credibility on the basis of 'experience and common sense' will inevitably involve the use of personal experience and can often amount to little more than the question 'what would I, or people I know, do in this situation?' (Graycar, 1991).

Although there are outliers and people who have a particular skill in detecting deception, the majority fare little better at deciding whether someone is lying than they would if they spun a coin. Such a conclusion casts doubt on the ability of the criminal trial, with its reliance on witness testimony, to arrive at the truth.

Hearsay evidence

The concept of 'hearsay' is deeply rooted in the history of criminal trials. As Lord Thomas CJ explained in *R* v *Horncastle* [2009] EWCA Crim 964:

> [The] law of England and Wales has ... always insisted that it is ordinarily essential that evidence of the truth of a matter be given in person by a witness who speaks from his own observation or knowledge. It uses the legal expression 'hearsay' to describe evidence which is not so given, but rather is given second hand, whether related by a person to whom the absent witness has spoken, contained in a written statement of the absent witness,

given in the form of a document or record created by
him, or otherwise ... (at p 970)

In the same case in the Supreme Court, Lord Phillips explained that:

There were two principal reasons for excluding hearsay
evidence. The first was that it was potentially unreliable. It
might even be fabricated by the witness giving evidence
of what he alleged he had been told by another. Quite
apart from this, the weight to be given to such evidence
was less easy to appraise than that of evidence delivered by
a witness face to face with the defendant and subject to
testing by cross-examination. (R v Horncastle [2009] UKSC
14, at p 21)

In R v Riat [2012] EWCA Crim 1509, Hughes LJ remarked:

[Hearsay] is necessarily second-hand and for that reason
very often second-best. Because it is second-hand, it is that
much more difficult to test and assess. The jury frequently
never sees the person whose word is being relied upon. Even
if there is a video recording of the witness' interview, that
person cannot be asked a single exploratory or challenging
question about what is said. From the point of view of a
defendant, the loss of the ability to confront one's accusers is
an important disadvantage. Those very real risks of hearsay
evidence, which underlay the common law rule generally
excluding it, remain critical to its management. Sometimes
it is necessary in the interests of justice for it to be admitted.
It may not suffer from the risks of unreliability which often
attend such evidence, or its reliability can realistically be
assessed. Equally, however, sometimes it is necessary in the
interests of justice either that it should not be admitted at
all, or that a trial depending upon it should not be allowed
to proceed to the jury because any conviction would not
be safe. (at para 3)

In day-to-day life we make considerable use of hearsay and use direct
and indirect information interchangeably: we pass on 'facts' to others
based on the 'facts' others have told us. The passing off of indirect
evidence as direct evidence underpins much social interaction. Yet
in the court setting, because jurors need to see the person giving

evidence, hearsay is to be avoided. Interestingly, *Blackstone's Criminal Practice* (2020, para F16.4) states: 'The dangers of reliance on hearsay are lessened where the fact-finder is a judge'.

Section 114 of the Criminal Justice Act 2003 provides four exceptions to the rule against hearsay:

(1) In criminal proceedings a statement not made in oral evidence in the proceedings is admissible as evidence of any matter stated if, but only if—
   a) any provision of this chapter or any other statutory provision makes it admissible,
   b) any rule of law preserved by section 118 makes it admissible,
   c) all parties to the proceedings agree to it being admissible, or
   d) the court is satisfied that it is in the interests of justice for it to be admissible.

Section 118 preserves common law exceptions to the hearsay rule in relation to certain public documents and information. In deciding whether or not it is in the interests of justice to admit hearsay evidence, guidance is provided by section 114(2):

(2) In deciding whether a statement not made in oral evidence should be admitted under subsection (1)(d), the court must have regard to the following factors (and to any others it considers relevant)—

   a) how much probative value the statement has (assuming it to be true) in relation to a matter in issue in the proceedings, or how valuable it is for the understanding of other evidence in the case;
   b) what other evidence has been, or can be, given on the matter or evidence mentioned in paragraph (a);
   c) how important the matter or evidence mentioned in paragraph (a) is in the context of the case as a whole;
   d) the circumstances in which the statement was made;
   e) how reliable the maker of the statement appears to be;
   f) how reliable the evidence of the making of the statement appears to be;
   g) whether oral evidence of the matter stated can be given and, if not, why it cannot;
   h) the amount of difficulty involved in challenging the statement;
   i) the extent to which that difficulty would be likely to prejudice the party facing it.

The Court of Appeal made it clear in *R v Taylor* (2006) EWCA Crim 260 that a court did not need to consider each and every factor on the list in deciding the interests of justice.

Over the years, there has been an increase in the amount of hearsay evidence that is admitted in criminal proceedings. There has been some concern that relaxing the rule against hearsay may contravene Article 6(3)(d) of the European Convention on Human Rights, which provides, *inter alia*, that everyone charged with a criminal offence has the right 'to examine or have examined witnesses against him'. In *Al-Khawaja and Tahery v UK* (2011) 54 EHRR 23:

> [Where] a hearsay statement is the sole or decisive evidence against a defendant, its admission as evidence will not automatically result in a breach of [A]rt 6(1). At the same time where a conviction is based solely or decisively on the evidence of absent witnesses, the Court must subject the proceedings to the most searching scrutiny. Because of the dangers of the admission of such evidence, it would constitute a very important factor to balance in the scales, ... and one which would require sufficient counterbalancing factors, including the existence of strong procedural safeguards. The question in each case is whether there are sufficient counterbalancing factors in place, including measures that permit a fair and proper assessment of the reliability of that evidence to take place. This would permit a conviction to be based on such evidence only if it is sufficiently reliable given its importance in the case. (at para 147)

In Chapter 5 we explore further the sometimes conflicting aims of ensuring a just and fair trial and obtaining the truth. The two aims are neatly summed up in rule 102 of the Federal Rules of Evidence, which expresses the overarching purpose of rules of evidence: 'These rules should be construed so as to administer every proceeding fairly, eliminate unjustifiable expense and delay, and promote the development of evidence law, to the end of ascertaining the truth and securing a just determination'. Judged from a truth-finding perspective, the arguments against hearsay evidence may appear to lack substance, particularly given the scientific evidence that casts doubt on the supposed factfinding benefits of the physical presence of a witness in court. Ensuring a fair trial, and that justice is seen to be done, would appear to demand the existence of strong procedural safeguards and the avoidance, in as much as possible, of absent witnesses.

Identification evidence

> Eyewitness testimony is likely to be believed by jurors, especially when it is offered with a high level of confidence, even though the accuracy of an eyewitness and the confidence of that witness may not be related to one another at all. All the evidence points rather strikingly to the conclusion that there is almost nothing more convincing than a live human being who takes the stand, points a finger at the defendant, and says 'That's the one'. (Loftus, 1979, p 19)

On 22 August 2011, the *New York Times* reported that: 'Every year, more than 75,000 eyewitnesses identify suspects in criminal investigations. Those identifications are wrong about a third of the time, a pile of studies suggest'. (Liptak, 2011) According to the Innocence Project (2020), 367 convicted people have been exonerated following DNA testing since the first such exoneration in 1989. Of those, 69 per cent involved eyewitness misidentification.

In autumn 2013, the Laura and John Arnold Foundation asked the National Academy of Sciences (NAS) to assess the state of research on eyewitness identification and, when appropriate, make recommendations. In 2014, *Identifying the Culprit: Assessing Eyewitness Identification* was published (National Research Council, 2014). The summary set out the key issue: 'Eyewitnesses play an important role in criminal cases when they can identify culprits. Yet it is well known that eyewitnesses make mistakes and that their memories can be affected by various factors including the very law enforcement procedures designed to test their memories' (National Research Council, 2014, p 1). The report then provided a comprehensive review of the current state of scientific understanding of eyewitness identification and the factors leading to misidentification, and made a number of recommendations for the criminal justice system. In compiling the report, the committee of the NAS heard from leading experts, practitioners and stakeholders.

A survey of US prosecutors by Goldstein et al (1989) estimated that eyewitness cases constituted about 3 per cent of all felony cases. Applied to England and Wales, that would equate to about 150,000 potential eyewitness cases. 'Accurate eyewitness identification requires that a witness to a crime correctly sense, perceive, and remember objects and events that occurred and recall them later. The veracity of the witness' identification thus depends on the limits of sensation, perception, and memory' (National Research Council, 2014, p 45). The report uses a scenario to frame the current state of knowledge:

> While returning home late, you hear a muffled scream from around the street corner. Seconds later, you come face-to-face with a man turning the corner and moving swiftly past you. Instantaneously, properties of the scene are conveyed to you through patterns of light cast on the backs of your eyes and sensed by photoreceptors in your retina. Only a fraction of the information sensed is selected for further processing; ...
>
> Your percepts are initially encoded in short-term working memory, where content is limited and labile. ... but with time and recognition of the importance of the experience, your percepts are consolidated into long-term memory. Long-term memories are maintained in storage but subject to ongoing updates and modifications resulting from new experiences and perhaps distortions caused by sustained levels of stress. (National Research Council, 2014, p 46)

Visual and auditory sensations can be affected and distorted by noise. Attention can be hijacked by competing factors. A focus on conversation may result in a witness failing to notice changes to appearance. A commonly used psychological experiment involves a conversation between a participant and the experimenter. At some point the experimenter disappears from the participant's view and is replaced by someone with a different appearance. More than half of participants fail to notice the change and will deny a change has taken place when subsequently questioned. Attentional hijacking is particularly likely in highly charged emotional situations where the observer is subject to fear and arousal. Visual sensation occurs as light hits the retinal cells; perception is the process whereby the brain interprets those sensations: 'Perception does not reflect the sensory world passively, as camera film detects patterns of light' (National Research Council, 2014, p 55). Perception is a constructive process and involves:

• integrating and segmenting attended attributes of the visual image into objects;

- complementing and interpreting the product with expectations derived from memory of prior experiences with the world; and
- assigning meaning and emotional valence by reference to prior knowledge of function and value (National Research Council, 2014, p 56).

Perception can also be affected by sensory noise and can be distorted through memory recall. 'Evidence indicates that the structure of object memory is also categorical, suggesting that perceived objects are encoded in memory as a category type, often without specific detail' (National Research Council, 2014, p 58). The memory's use of categories can particularly affect our ability to identify someone of a different ethnicity to our own. Sporer has suggested that we all have a decreased ability to identify people from other groups of any kind. There is also a body of evidence that confirms that we are generally overconfident in our ability to identify others (Shaw, 2016).

The National Research Council report concluded by identifying:

> Restrictions on what can be seen under specific environmental and behavioral conditions (eg, as poor illumination, limited viewing duration, viewing angle), factors that impede the ability to attend to critically informative features of a visual scene (eg, the deleterious effect of an attention-grabbing element, such as a weapon, on the ability to correctly perceive the features of the assailant's face), distortions of perceptual experience derived from expectations, and ways in which emotion and stress enhance or suppress specific perceptual experiences. Memory is often far from a faithful record of what was perceived through the sense of sight: its contents can be forgotten or contaminated at multiple stages, it can be biased by the very practices designed to elicit recall, and it is heavily swayed by emotional states associated with witnessed events and their recall. From this analysis, the committee must conclude that there are insurmountable limits on vision and memory imposed by our biological nature and the properties of the world we inhabit. With this knowledge, it is possible to more fully appreciate the value and risks associated with eyewitness reports and accordingly advise those who collect, handle, defend, consider, and adjudicate such reports. (National Research Council, 2014, pp 69–70)

Many of the problems identified with eyewitness testimony apply at least equally to earwitness testimony. It seems clear that an over-reliance on witness testimony may jeopardize the discovery of the truth. More than 100 years ago, Hugo Münsterberg, one of the founding figures of applied psychology, suggested that criminal trials should make greater use of psychologists in order to understand better the nature of witness testimony. Ultimately, the truth of witness testimony is dependent on the truth of memory.

Memories

> Last summer I had to face a jury as witness in a trial. While I was with my family at the seashore my city house had been burglarised and I was called upon to give an account of my findings against the culprit whom they had caught with a part of the booty. I reported under oath that the burglars had entered through a cellar window, and then described what rooms they had visited. To prove, in answer to a direct question, that they had been there at night, I told that I had found drops of candle wax on the second floor. To show that they intended to return, I reported that they had left a large mantel clock, packed in wrapping paper, on the dining-room table. Finally, as to the amount of clothes which they had taken, I asserted that the burglars did not get more than a specified list which I had given the police.
>
> Only a few days later I found that every one of these statements was wrong. How did all those mistakes occur? ... in spite of my best intentions, in spite of good memory and calm mood, a whole series of confusions, of illusions, of forgetting, of wrong conclusions, and of yielding to suggestions were mingled with what I had to report under oath, and my only consolation is the fact that in a thousand courts at a thousand places all over the world, witnesses every day affirm by oath in exactly the same way much worse mixtures of truth and untruth, combinations of memory and of illusion, of knowledge and of suggestion, of experience and wrong conclusions. (Münsterberg, 1908, pp 39–44)

Hugo Münsterberg was born in Prussia in 1863 and attended the University of Leipzig in the 1880s, where he met one of the founding figures of psychology, William Wundt, and became his research assistant. He subsequently moved to the United States following an invitation from William James, where he became a Professor of Psychology at Harvard University. Münsterberg became President of the American Psychological Association in 1898 and as noted earlier was one of the founders of applied psychology. In 1908, he published *On the Witness Stand: Essays on Psychology and Crime* (Münsterberg , 1908), which was a collection of previously published work on the psychological factors affecting a criminal trial. In the introductory chapter, he outlines the emergence and rapid growth of psychology as an academic discipline but expresses surprise at its hitherto lack of practical application:

> Considering that perception and memory, feeling and emotion, attention and volition, and so on, are the chief factors of our daily life, entering into every one of our enjoyments and duties, experiences and professions, it seems astonishing that no path led from the seclusion of the psychological workshop to the market-place of the world. (Münsterberg, 1908, p 7)

He called for an independent applied psychology 'which stands related to the ordinary experimental psychology as engineering to physics' (Münsterberg, 1908, p 9):

> The time for such Applied Psychology is surely near, and work has been started from most various sides. Those fields of practical life which come first in question may be said to be education, medicine, art, economics, and law ...
>
> The lawyer and the judge and the juryman are sure that they do not need the experimental psychologist. They do not wish to see that in this field pre-eminently applied experimental psychology has made strong strides, led by Binet, Stern, Lipmann, Jung, Wertheimer, Gross, Sommer, Aschaffenburg, and other scholars. They go on thinking that their legal instinct and their common sense supplies them with all that is needed and somewhat more; and if the time is ever to come when even the jurist is to show some concession to the spirit of modern psychology, public opinion will have to exert some pressure. Just in the line of the law it therefore seems necessary not to rely simply on the technical statements of scholarly treatises, but to carry the discussion in the most popular form possible before the

wider tribunal of the general reader. (Münsterberg, 1908, pp 9–11)

It was with such an intention, of applying psychology to the world of law and lawyers, that Münsterberg published *On the Witness Stand*. He acknowledged that law and psychology came into context in many areas but the essay's primary focus was the mind of the witness: 'my only purpose is to turn the attention of serious men to an absurdly neglected field which demands the full attention of the social community' (1908, p 12).

Münsterberg references the work of the French psychologist, Alfred Binet. Binet had a particular interest in the links between psychology and law, having originally qualified as a lawyer in Paris in 1878. He practised at the Paris bar for six years but became disenchanted with the profession and instead turned his attention to the study of neurology and then psychology. In 1894, he became the director of the Laboratory of Experimental Psychology at the Sorbonne. He became particularly interested in child development and, together with Theodore Simon, developed the concept of 'mental age' and a scientific means of assessing it – what was to become known as the Binet–Simon Scale. In the course of his study of child development, Binet carried out numerous experiments, including a number investigating the role of suggestibility in visual memory. From these initial experiments, Binet carried out a number of experiments on eyewitness testimony. He sought to study suggestibility as a normal social and cognitive process. Within this framework, he conducted new experiments, the findings of which were published in 'On suggestibility' (Binet, 1900), which established the influence of comments or orders (suggestions) of the experimenter on the acts of remembering in subjects studied both individually and in groups.

Interest in memory research declined following the First World War and it was not until the 1970s that psychologists turned their attention again to the function and operation of memory. A leading figure in the research has been Elizabeth Loftus. In 1973, Loftus was appointed Assistant Professor at the University of Washington where she began an empirical study of eyewitness testimony and the role of memory. In 1974, together with John C. Palmer, she published 'Reconstruction of Automobile Destruction: An Example of the Interaction Between Language and Memory' (Loftus and Palmer, 1974). The article discussed an experiment in which participants were shown films of car collisions and then asked questions about events occurring in the films:

The question, 'About how fast were the cars going when they smashed into each other?' elicited higher estimates of speed than questions which used the verbs collided, bumped, contacted, or hit in place of smashed. On a retest one week later, those subjects who received the verb smashed were more likely to say 'yes' to the question, 'Did you see any broken glass?', even though broken glass was not present in the film. These results are consistent with the view that the questions asked subsequent to an event can cause a reconstruction in one's memory of that event. (Loftus and Palmer, 1974, p 585)

Further research by Loftus demonstrated the extent to which memories could be manipulated and altered by subsequent information/ misinformation. As a result of the research by Loftus, others became interested in memory. Wells (1978) made the direct connection between memory research and criminal justice with the publication of an article entitled 'Applied Eyewitness-Testimony Research: System Variables and Estimator Variables'. He drew a distinction between variables that are under the control of the criminal justice system (system variables) and those that are not (estimator variables). Estimator variables include the range of factors related to the criminal event, witness and perpetrator. Wells labelled them 'estimator variables' because their effect could only be estimated after the event. The focus of the criminal justice system over the past 40 years has been on system variables. Changes have been made to many areas of the investigation process, including how identification parades are conducted and interviewing techniques. Yet the danger of such reforms is that they can create an impression that by reducing system variables, estimator variables are automatically and simultaneously reduced.

In 2019, Elizabeth Loftus published an article to mark the 30th anniversary of the journal *Applied Cognitive Psychology* (Loftus, 2019). It gave her a chance to review the key issues and disagreements raised in memory and eyewitness research during her career. She listed four: the misinformation debate; eyewitness identification line-ups and confidence levels; expert testimony; and memory wars.

Witness misinformation is clearly critical to the criminal justice project. Loftus identified the central questions:

Does the misinformation impair the original memory by altering the traces that were once formed? Does the misinformation leave the original information intact, but perhaps impair the ability to retrieve it? This question about the permanence of our memories, once stored, is perhaps one of the most fundamental questions about the nature of memory …

Whatever process is going on, the end result can be a highly confident witness testifying in a persuasive manner at trial about a detail that is completely false. It is something the legal system needs to worry about right now, whereas the memory scientists, interested in theory, duke it out in the pages of academic journals. (Loftus, 2019, p 499)

The key debate in relation to identification line-ups is the level of confidence shown by a witness and the relationship of that confidence to accuracy. Loftus quotes from one of her earlier works:

[There] are many studies showing that the more confident a person is in a response the greater the likelihood that the response is accurate … some studies have shown no relationship at all between confidence and accuracy. … [sometimes] people can be more confident about their wrong answers than their right ones. I concluded with pessimism: 'To be cautious, one should not take high confidence as any absolute guarantee of anything'. (Loftus, 1979, p 101)

The danger is that factfinders at the criminal trial are influenced by a witness's confident demeanour and are more likely to find a confident witness to be credible, even if they are confidently wrong. More recent research has tended to show that if conditions are good, the relationship between confidence and accuracy can be quite strong but confidence can be very malleable. In the period between initial identification and the court hearing, a witness may well grow in confidence, thus rendering the confidence level 'a misleading cue as to the likely accuracy of the report' (Loftus, 2019, p 500). For that reason, it is more important to report the level of witness confidence at the time of the identification, together with the conditions present.

In the United States, a series of well-publicized miscarriages of justice led to an increasing use of expert witnesses in criminal trials. Their primary role was to explain aspects of the science behind eyewitness testimony. This increased use of experts was partly a result of the recommendations of the National Research Council's (2014) report. In England and Wales, with far fewer publicized miscarriages of justice, there has not been the same drive to include expert witnesses and as a result some of the misconceptions about memory and identification continue to obscure the factfinding process.

The fourth area of debate Loftus identifies is false memory. She provided expert evidence in the murder trial of George Franklin in 1990. Franklin's only accuser was his daughter, who claimed to have witnessed the murder and also to have been subject to a series of assaults by her father. She had repressed the memories for 20 years but claimed that they had started to return to her with a great degree of clarity. The 1990s saw a growth in therapeutic techniques and the recovery of repressed memories. Loftus was keen to investigate the phenomenon and undertook a series of experiments to ascertain whether it was possible to create false memories in participants. Her experiments showed that such a thing was possible and further research by Loftus and many others seemed to confirm the possibility of false memories that would be indistinguishable, to the person remembering, from true memories. Particularly in the area of historic sexual abuse, the issue of false and recovered memories is particularly problematic for criminal justice. The adversarial system typically tests the reliability of witnesses through the use of cross-examination. The process is designed to enable a distinction to be made between truth and non-truth. Yet those who are honestly mistaken as to memory may well present evidence as 'truth'.

Furthermore, research on attitudes to memory discloses that many people (including criminal investigators, and others involved in the criminal justice system) have inaccurate beliefs about how memory works. Forgetting and distorted memories can be wrongly classified as deceitful behaviour, and mistaken views about the nature of memory may affect factfinders' ability to assess credibility. In a large survey conducted by Simons and Chabris (2011), a range of incorrect memory beliefs were revealed. Nearly two thirds of respondents believed memory operated like a video camera and witness confidence was perceived by many as directly linked to witness veracity.

The combination of fallible human memory together with a lack of public awareness of the functioning of memory and perception has the potential to undermine the pursuit of the truth. In the United States, a combination of both factors has led to some well-publicized miscarriages of justice. The Innocence Project, which seeks to campaign to improve the criminal justice system, highlights a number of contributing factors to the high number of wrongful convictions. False confessions are included but the major cause is witness related.

5

Truth and the Probity
of Evidence-Gathering

Procedural rules prescribe the ways in which law enforcement agencies can obtain evidence that can be used in a subsequent prosecution. Inevitably, these rules are sometimes broken. Sometimes, though, the evidence found remains highly probative and potentially indicative of guilt. This presents an evident dilemma. If establishing truth is paramount, excluding relevant evidence is counterproductive. Worse, it would appear that such a stance would increase the potential for a wrongful conclusion to be drawn, which could result in a miscarriage of justice, even though this is more likely to be an undeserved acquittal than a suspect conviction. However, all rules of procedure have a purpose. They have been drafted so as to ensure (at least theoretically) that individuals are not put in situations where they have to provide samples, be searched or allow law enforcement officers to search their property without good cause. A lax approach when the rules are breached would provide little incentive for compliance on the part of law enforcement personnel. The issue may not appear so pressing if, say, an illegal search reveals that the suspect was handling stolen goods. But a failure to provide an effective remedy also has the potential to facilitate (as opposed to legitimate) unlawful searches that yield nothing. How such evidence is treated poses a challenge: there is an obvious temptation to admit that which might aid a deserved finding of guilt, but with a reservation that, in so doing, the state would benefit from breaking the law.

This chapter will start with an account of the English common law position, which generally holds that illegally, improperly or unfairly obtained evidence remains admissible at trial, save in exceptional cases. Section 78 of the Police and Criminal Evidence Act 1984 now governs the admissibility of illegally or unfairly obtained evidence and this forms the focus of the next section. The Police and Criminal Evidence Act 1984 departs from the common law in that courts must consider the circumstances in which evidence was obtained when determining whether admitting the evidence would render the proceedings unfair. A recent appeal case, *R* v *Twigg* [2019] EWCA Crim 1553, will be used to illustrate how a blatant procedural breach (though taken in good faith), which yielded highly incriminating evidence, was dealt with by the Court of Appeal. The judgment made brief mention of the European Convention on Human Rights. The chapter will then consider whether the Convention provides a remedy to victims of unlawful searches or other breaches of criminal procedure that result in incriminating evidence being found. Case law will be reviewed, which establishes that there is no automatic exclusionary rule (*Schenk* v *Switzerland* (1988) 13 EHRR 242; *El Haski* v *Belgium* (2013) 56 EHRR 31).

If the overarching aim of the criminal process is to arrive at the truth – and thereby to hold the guilty to account – the approach in England and Wales and in the European Court of Human Rights has to be correct. However, this begs the question of whether there is any value in having detailed laws of procedure if a breach incurs no penalty. Should the judicial function not include ensuring that pre-trial procedural rules are complied with? The traditional position in the United States, which is covered in the penultimate section, recognizes this and holds that procedural breaches should lead to automatic exclusion at trial (*Weeks* v *United States*, 232 US 383 (1914); *Mapp* v *Ohio*, 367 US 643 (1961); *Costello* v *United States*, 365 US 265 (1961)). The consequence can be stated thus: some guilty individuals are not prosecuted or are acquitted because of a lack of admissible, as opposed to probative, evidence.

Both stances make immediate sense, and can appear compelling. Our conclusion returns to the fundamental question: should procedural malpractice determine the admissibility of probative evidence illegally or unfairly obtained? And, if exclusion is warranted in such cases, why is the discovery of truth not the primary concern? Three claims – systemic unfairness, human rights protection and deterrence – will be tested and, while each is a legitimate value in criminal process, it will be argued that an approach that prioritizes the overall fairness of a trial, and which recognizes that the means by which evidence is obtained is relevant, is most appropriate. In some situations, a grave breach of the law should render the proceedings unfair. In other cases, though, exclusion would be disproportionate if the breach was minor and the prosecution case remained compelling.

The admissibility of illegally or unfairly obtained evidence in common law

Detailed rules, found mainly in the Police and Criminal Evidence Act 1984 and associated Schedules, specify how different types of evidence can be obtained in England and Wales. In part, the Act codified existing law, but most of the content was specific, precise and novel. The detail was necessary for various reasons, particularly because scientific advances had increased the means by which probative evidence could be found and a series of miscarriage of justice cases had exposed the danger of common law protection. Despite the scientific advances that have been made, it is striking that many of the contested cases still relate to the most rudimentary techniques of evidence-gathering such as the search of property. The Act also states what should happen in the event that the rules are not followed; this will be discussed in the next section. First, consideration will be given to the common law approach that pre-dates the 1984 Act so that the evolution of English law can be discerned.

Early case law established that, if evidence had probative value, the way in which it was obtained was of no relevance to its admissibility. In *Kuruma* v *The Queen* [1955] AC 197, the evidence incriminating the accused was found as the result of an illegal search. According to Lord Goddard CJ:

> [The] test to be applied in considering whether evidence is admissible is whether it is relevant to the matters in issue. If it is, it is admissible and the court is not concerned with how the evidence was obtained. While this proposition may not have been stated in so many words in any English case there are decisions which support it, and in their Lordships' opinion it is plainly right in principle. (at p 203)

Despite the unequivocal tone, Lord Goddard believed that it would still be appropriate to exclude improperly obtained evidence on occasion:

> No doubt in a criminal case the judge always has a discretion to disallow evidence if the strict rules of admissibility would operate unfairly against an accused ... If, for instance, some

admission of some piece of evidence, e.g. a document, had been obtained from a defendant by a trick, no doubt the judge might properly rule it out. (at p 204)

The House of Lords in *R* v *Sang* [1980] AC 402 upheld the general principle but did not refer to a residual discretion to exclude improperly obtained evidence:

> The fairness of a trial according to law is not all one-sided; it requires that those who are undoubtedly guilty should be convicted as well as that those about whose guilt there is any reasonable doubt should be acquitted. However much the judge may dislike the way in which a particular piece of evidence was obtained before proceedings were commenced, if it is admissible evidence probative of the accused's guilt it is no part of his judicial function to exclude it for this reason. (*R* v *Sang* [1980] AC 402, at p 437, per Lord Diplock)

One of the claims that has been made is that an exclusionary rule is necessary to deter malpractice by law enforcement agencies (see later). Lord Diplock rejected this reasoning and recognized that victims had other remedies:

> [The] function of the judge at a criminal trial as respects the admission of evidence is to ensure that the accused has a fair trial according to law. It is no part of a judge's function to exercise disciplinary powers over the police or prosecution as respects the way in which evidence to be used is obtained by them. If it was obtained illegally there will be a remedy in civil law; if it was obtained legally but in breach of the rules of conduct for the police, this is a matter for the appropriate disciplinary authority to deal with. What the judge at the trial is concerned with is not how the evidence sought to be adduced by the prosecution had been obtained, but with how it is used by the prosecution at trial. (*R* v *Sang* [1980] AC 402, at p 436)

The common law position, therefore, was concerned above all with whether the evidence had a bearing on the accused's guilt. Excluding evidence to deter illegal law enforcement was not part of the court's function – civil remedies were available and over-zealous officers risked disciplinary proceedings. However, neither of these leading authorities went as far as saying that illegally or unfairly obtained evidence should always be admitted if it had probative value. Both cases established that judges retained a discretion to exclude probative evidence if 'it would operate unfairly on an accused' (*Kuruma* v *The Queen* [1955] AC 197, at p 204). The example provided by Lord Goddard was where the evidence was obtained by trickery, although it is difficult to see how that is any more unfair on the accused than an illegal search. If trickery is particularly objectionable, it would appear that the officer's personal culpability is of relevance. As we shall see, other legal systems where illegally obtained evidence is presumptively excluded have also debated the relevance of the officer's blameworthiness and increasingly taken a view that it is potentially determinative of whether the evidence will be excluded. Regardless of whether an officer's culpability influences an exceptional decision to exclude or an exceptional decision to admit, the probative value of the evidence is not the concern. However, given the general tenor of the extracts from the judgments, it is obvious that, under the common law, judges would be expected to admit illegally or unfairly obtained evidence save in exceptional circumstances.

The Police and Criminal Evidence Act 1984

The extent of the judicial discretion to exclude unlawfully obtained evidence in England and Wales was made explicit in the Police and Criminal Evidence Act 1984. Section 78(1) provides the following:

> In any proceedings the court may refuse to allow evidence on which the prosecution proposes to rely to be given if it appears to the court that, having regard to all the circumstances, *including the circumstances in which the evidence was obtained*, the admission of the evidence would have such an adverse effect on the fairness of the proceedings that the court ought not to admit it. (emphasis added)

This represents a departure from the common law as the judge is directed to consider the way in which the evidence was obtained when determining whether the proceedings against the accused are fair. One might question whether this really amounts to a *discretionary* power to exclude. As was recognized in *R* v *Chalkley* [1998] QB 848, once a judge has determined that admitting the evidence would have such an adverse effect on the fairness of the proceedings that it ought not to be admitted, they have no discretion to admit the evidence. Determining whether the fairness of proceedings would be compromised if the evidence was admitted requires the judge to review the totality of the available evidence and the manner in which it was obtained. The essence of section 78 is 'fairness' – a broad and vague philosophical and legal concept – and so it is perhaps unsurprising that a considerable number of convictions that rested on ill-gotten evidence have been appealed. The trial judge's decision that admitting the evidence would not compromise the fairness of the trial almost certainly increased the likelihood of conviction but one must guard against drawing the conclusion that there is a direct causal link. Often the contested evidence forms but part of the prosecution case.

R v Twigg [2019] EWCA Crim 1553 provides a useful, and fairly typical, example of how section 78 operates in practice. The appellant had been convicted of causing death by careless driving while over the specified limit for a drug, contrary to section 3A(1)(ba) of the Road Traffic Act 1988. The trial judge admitted blood samples that were taken in breach of the procedures prescribed in the Road Traffic Act 1988. Twigg's story had changed. He told officers shortly after the collision that he had not smoked cannabis for months, but then admitted to smoking cannabis earlier in the day. A sample was taken and it found traces of cannabis that placed Twigg in excess of the specified limit. However, the procedure for taking the sample had not been followed. The healthcare professional who took the sample said that she would only have taken the sample if the police had requested it, as the law requires. Conversely, the police officer said that he would only have requested a sample if the healthcare professional said it was necessary. Both statements are consistent with section 7(3)(c) of the Road Traffic Act 1988, which stipulates that a police officer making a request must have been advised by a registered healthcare professional that the condition of the person required to provide a specimen might be due to drug use. Here, the healthcare professional had not reported any concerns of drug or alcohol use to the officer before the officer requested that the sample was taken. Should the positive sample have been excluded by the trial judge given there was a clear breach of procedure?

Twigg's honesty, or, more accurately dishonesty, informed the trial judge's decision to admit the evidence:

> The judge said that, whilst the Appellant presented as alert and coherent to the healthcare professional, this was after nearly an hour's delay, caused because the appellant had absconded from the scene. The healthcare professional had

asked the Appellant if he had taken any drugs. He lied. He could have told the truth. Had he answered honestly then it was highly likely that the healthcare professional would have reviewed her opinion about whether he was affected by cannabis. (at [22])

As well as Twigg's lie, other evidence suggested that his driving may have been affected by drugs at the time of the accident. The arresting officer smelt cannabis at his house and, when the officer asked whether he had smoked anything, he had replied 'not recently'. Having taken into account the totality of the evidence, the judge concluded that admitting the blood sample would not impinge on the fairness of the trial and that it would be appropriate to allow the prosecution to adduce it. Twigg's appeal was dismissed. Lord Justice Singh detailed all of the prosecution evidence, including Twigg's dishonesty (at para [73]), in arriving at this conclusion: there were grounds for assuming that he had taken drugs prior to the accident based on his response to the arresting officer and the officer's testimony that he had smelt cannabis at Twigg's house; and his contradictory accounts undermined his story. Lord Justice Singh concluded that the fairness of the proceedings was not compromised by admitting the evidence, even though the drug sample was improperly obtained.

Human rights protection

Reference was made in *R* v *Twigg* [2019] EWCA Crim 1553 to the protection afforded by the European Convention on Human Rights. Article 6 protects an individual's right to a fair trial:

> In the determination of his civil rights and obligations or of any criminal charge against him, everyone is entitled to a fair and public hearing within a reasonable time by an independent and impartial tribunal established by law. Judgment shall be pronounced publicly but the press and public may be excluded from all or part of the trial in the interests of morals, public order or national security in a democratic society, where the interests of juveniles or the protection of the private life of the parties so require, or to the extent strictly necessary in the opinion of the court in special circumstances where publicity would prejudice the interests of justice.

It can be seen that no specific reference is made to whether the use of improperly, unlawfully or illegally obtained evidence compromises an individual's right to a fair trial. Therefore, it fails to answer the question of whether improperly, unlawfully or illegally obtained evidence must be excluded regardless of its probative worth. In the UK, primary and subordinate legislation (including the Police and Criminal Evidence Act 1984) must be interpreted in a way compatible with rights set out in the European Convention on Human Rights 'so far as it is possible to do so' (Human Rights Act 1998, section 3(1)). This applies to legislation, such as the Police and Criminal Evidence Act 1984, enacted prior to the Human Rights Act 1998 coming into force. Section 3 of the Human Rights Act 1998 does not allow courts to make new laws; any interpretation must be consistent with existing law so far as possible. Section 3(2) also states that the interpretative power granted does not affect the validity, operation or enforcement of any Act. In that situation, a declaration of incompatibility would be made under section 4 of the Act.

Jurisprudence from the European Court of Human Rights has established that member states are not required to have an automatic exclusionary rule to comply with their Article 6 obligations. *Schenk v Switzerland* (1988) 13 EHRR 242 illustrates the approach taken by the Court. Schenk had been charged with hiring someone to kill his wife and the evidence adduced at trial included unlawfully obtained recordings of a telephone call. His appeal to the European Court of Human Rights failed, as the majority held that the Swiss proceedings had not infringed his right to a fair trial. Two factors were critical to the majority ruling: the recording formed only part of the prosecution case (at para [48]); and Schenk had been given the opportunity to challenge the recording's admissibility at his trial (at para [47]). In terms of overall approach, the Court stated that:

> [Article] 6 of the Convention guarantees the right to a fair trial, it does not lay down any rules on the admissibility of evidence as such, which is therefore primarily a matter for regulation under national law. The court therefore cannot exclude as a matter of principle and in the abstract that unlawfully obtained evidence of the present kind may be admissible. It has only to ascertain whether Mr. Schenk's trial as a whole was fair. (at para 46)

Judges Pettiti, Spielmann, De Meyer and Carrillo Salcedo dissented on the basis that the admittance of unfairly or unlawfully obtained evidence rendered a trial inherently unfair:

> [In] our opinion, compliance with the law when taking evidence is not an abstract or formalistic requirement. On the contrary, we consider that it is of the first importance for the fairness of a criminal trial. No court can, without detriment to the proper administration of justice, rely on evidence which has been obtained not only by unfair means but, above all, unlawfully. If it does so, the trial cannot be fair within the meaning of the Convention. (at p 31)

The English courts have held that the majority ruling in *Schenk* is consistent with domestic law (see *R v Khan (Sultan)* [1997] AC 558); the question is whether the proceedings as a whole were fair, and the manner in which evidence was obtained forms part of this assessment. *El Haski* v *Belgium* (2013) 56 EHRR 31 confirmed that it is not for the European Court of Human Rights to arbitrate on whether particular types of evidence should be admitted in a domestic legal system; its task is to determine whether an individual has received a fair trial, which, following *Schenk* v *Switzerland* (1988) 13 EHRR 242, can be the case in countries without a mandatory exclusionary rule.

There may be a violation of another Convention right if unlawfully obtained evidence is admitted. In *El Haski* v *Belgium* (2013) 56 EHRR 31, the example of an individual's right to respect for private life and correspondence in Article 8 was provided (at para [82]). A court will take account of any breach of a Convention right, alongside the nature of that breach, but this will inform an overarching assessment of fairness rather than leading to mandatory exclusion. There is one exception. Incriminating statements obtained in breach of Article 3, which prohibits torture, and inhuman or degrading treatment, will automatically render trial proceedings unfair, with the consequence that the evidence will be excluded (at para [85]). This recognizes that Article 3 is an absolute right and cannot be derogated from under Article 15 even in war or at a time of public emergency. Exclusion does not just extend to statements from the accused:

> The same [principle] applies to the use of material evidence obtained directly as a result of torture; the use of such evidence obtained by treatment which is contrary to Article 3 but falls short of torture is not, on the other hand, contrary to Article 6 unless it is shown that the breach of Article 3 had a bearing on the outcome of the proceedings, that is, had an impact on the conviction or sentence. (at para [85])

Rights-based justifications for excluding illegally obtained evidence can also be seen in legal systems where there are domestic constitutional rights. The Republic of Ireland operated a strict exclusionary rule (*Trimble* v *Governor of Mountjoy Prison* [1985] IR 550), which the Supreme Court deemed necessary to 'defend and vindicate the personal rights of the citizen' (*Director of Public Prosecutions* v *Kenny* [1990] 2 IR 110, at p 134).

More recently, there has been a shift in judicial thinking in *Director of Public Prosecutions* v *JC* [2015] IESC 31 (for comment see Leon and Ward, 2015). Inadvertent breaches of legal procedure no longer lead to automatic exclusion. Instead, the judiciary should balance the effect of the breach on the fairness of the trial. This makes the current Irish position difficult to classify. If rights-protection remains the paramount concern, then whether the actions of the law enforcement agent was deliberate or inadvertent should be of no relevance. Similarly, whether the mistake was made in good conscience has little bearing on the probative value of the evidence. The way in which illegally obtained evidence obtained in good faith is now dealt with appears identical to the English approach in that an overall assessment of procedural fairness determines whether the evidence should be admitted. Where bad faith can be found, though, exclusion is seen as a necessary means of protecting the victim's constitutional rights.

Canada also has a Charter of Rights and the Supreme Court has ruled that exclusion of unlawfully obtained evidence is not automatic and that courts must undertake a balancing act: '[The] more serious the impact on the accused's interests, the greater the risk that admission of the evidence may signal to the public that Charter rights, however high-sounding, are of little actual avail to the citizen, breeding public cynicism and bringing the administration of justice into disrepute' (*R* v *Grant* [2009] SCC 32, at p 376). These references to public cynicism and the reputation of the administration of justice are telling as they document an approach based on systemic integrity, which favours balancing competing policy demands, rather than a rights-based model, which tends to demand automatic exclusion. The implications of different typologies for excluding unlawfully obtained evidence will form the basis of the conclusion to this chapter.

The 'fruits of the poison tree' doctrine

Weeks v *United States* 232 US 383 (1914) must be regarded as one of the most important rulings of the United States Supreme Court. The facts are surprisingly mundane. Fremont Weeks was convicted of using the mail for transporting lottery tickets in violation of the Missouri Criminal Code. At the same time as he was being arrested at Union Station in Kansas City, officers entered his house without a warrant and took possession of papers and articles that formed the basis of the case against him. Weeks challenged his conviction on the basis that the use of unlawfully obtained evidence breached the Fourth Amendment of the United States' Constitution:

> The right of the people to be secure in their persons, houses, papers, and effects, against unreasonable searches and seizures, shall not be violated, and no Warrants shall issue, but upon probable cause, supported by Oath or affirmation, and particularly describing the place to be searched, and the persons or things to be seized.

The Supreme Court held that a warrantless search and seizure of articles from a house constituted a violation of the Fourth Amendment. The reason why the case is so significant is the consequence: evidence obtained unlawfully could not be used against an accused and a mandatory exclusionary rule in the federal courts was thereby established. In *Mapp* v *Ohio* 367 US 643 (1961), the Supreme Court went further and held that the exclusionary rule applied to state courts as well. The Court justified this approach with reference to its supposed deterrent value (*Costello* v *United States*, 365 US 265 (1961)). Citizens' Fourth Amendment rights would be meaningless if law enforcement personnel could breach the law with impunity. The stridency of these rulings has led to a consistent approach to the handling of probative but unlawfully obtained evidence by the American courts, at least until comparatively recently, when the Supreme Court has been prepared to entertain some exceptions or restrictions to the general position (see further Cammack, 2010). In part this is a recognition that deterrence cannot always justify the exclusion of unlawfully obtained evidence:

> [Police] conduct must be sufficiently deliberate that exclusion can meaningfully deter it, and sufficiently culpable that such deterrence is worth the price paid by the justice system. As laid out in our cases, the exclusionary rule serves to deter deliberate, reckless, or grossly negligent conduct, or in some circumstances recurring or systemic negligence. (*Herring* v *United States*, 555 US 135 (2009), at p 144)

The last sentence of that quotation is important as it suggests that it is not merely the malpractice of individual officers that the court will consider but, where necessary, systemic negligence. This makes sense as an exclusionary policy may be better justified on the basis of general rather than specific deterrence. The courts have also determined that whether the law enforcement officer acted in good faith is relevant to a deterrence-based exclusionary rule (*United States* v *Leon*, 468 US 897 (1984); *Arizona* v *Evans*, 54 US 1 (1995); *Herring* v *United States*, 555 US 135 (2009). Ignorance of the law or an innocent misreading of the situation arguably renders the individual blameless, which makes specific deterrence futile. However, there are a number of scenarios where the officer is to varying degrees culpable and the appeal to specific deterrence becomes more plausible from a policy perspective. Even where a mistake is innocent, however, the courts have failed to grasp that an exclusionary rule may still aid general compliance if it leads to cultural change or better training. Deterrence does not have to relate to the future conduct of the officer concerned.

Along with the limits of deterrence, the Supreme Court has also recognized the societal cost – presumably individuals escaping prosecution and possible punishment – of an automatic exclusionary rule (*Nix* v *Williams*, 467 US 431 (1984)). However, and this must be stressed, restrictions to the rule have been incremental and limited. The first exception, confirmed in *Nix* v *Williams* was that illegally obtained evidence would not be excluded if it was inevitable that the law enforcement agencies would have found the evidence in any event; this does provide ample scope for evidence to be admitted based on a subjective assessment of the likely direction of an investigation. The second exception is possibly less objectionable. Where there has been a factual break between the initial legal infraction and the discovery of the incriminating evidence, exclusion will not automatically follow (*Brown* v *Illinois*, 422 US 590 (1975); *Murray* v *United States*, 487 US 533 (1988)). If the historical basis for excluding unlawfully obtained evidence was to protect the suspect's constitutional rights, then both of these restrictions to a rigid rule of exclusion would cause concern, but it is evident that the early Supreme Court jurisprudence preferred to consider the need for a deterrent against state agencies acting unlawfully. Viewed through the prism of deterrence, it comes as no particular surprise that the boundaries of the rule have been whittled away, albeit slightly, when the practical limits of a deterrence-based approach become exposed.

Another way of framing the American jurisprudence would be to suggest that there is more of a recognition that there is a cost associated with having a strict exclusionary approach. Put simply, the court is denied the opportunity to review evidence that may be very prejudicial to an individual. Society does have a legitimate interest in securing the conviction of those who have broken the law and who may in extreme cases pose a threat to community safety. Yet, it is striking that the Supreme Court has not fully acknowledged this. What has happened instead is that the limitations of the basis for the exclusionary rule have increasingly been recognized and, in some cases where an argument founded on deterrence flounders, the rule has been rejected. It is, though, easy to overstate the shift. The United States still retains a robust exclusionary approach towards illegally obtained evidence save in limited, prescribed scenarios.

Balancing probativeness and probity

Two foundational principles, promoting the search for truth and the integrity of the criminal justice system, identified by Turner and Weigend (2019) help frame the discussion in this chapter and, indeed, in this book as a whole. First:

> A functional procedural system needs to present courts as principally fair and oriented toward a just disposition of cases in accordance with the law; this includes an orientation of fact-finding toward the 'truth', or more realistically, a renunciation of court decisions based on evident fiction. Courts are encouraged to pursue these basic goals through admitting and taking into consideration any evidence that appears to be factually relevant for the disposition of the case. (Turner and Weigend, 2019, p 257)

A lot of this book deals not only with what constitutes truth for the purposes of criminal legal-adjudication, the justice systems best placed to uncover truth, and the points in the system where the risk of error is especially great. It may, therefore, appear odd to have included a chapter where the probative value of the evidence is apparent. What this chapter highlights is that other systemic values need protecting and this can lead to an argument that probative evidence should in some instances be withdrawn. The search for truth cannot be everything:

> The reliability-based rationale has a limited area of application … It rarely comes into play with regard to physical evidence. When drugs are seized illegally or a telephone conversation

is taped without a necessary judicial warrant, the unlawful government action does not in any way reduce these items' probative value. Therefore, excluding such evidence would undermine the search for truth instead of advancing it. (Turner and Weigend, 2019, p 257)

Truth-finding favours a permissive approach to the admissibility of probative evidence obtained unlawfully. Yet, none of the legal systems surveyed in this chapter fully ignores legality in determining whether unlawfully obtained evidence should be admitted at trial. There are degrees of tolerance: England and Wales are more permissive than most other countries while the United States still excludes most illegally obtained evidence. Commonalities exist: evidence obtained following significant and deliberate breaches of procedure would likely be excluded in all of the jurisdictions considered. What differs is the legal basis for excluding potentially probative evidence. It is suggested that three broad typologies can be discerned: states that exclude on the basis of systemic unfairness; states that exclude in order to protect against domestic or international human rights violations; and states that exclude in order to deter malpractice by law enforcers. Like all typologies, these are generalizations, but they help frame the competing pressures and the way in which they are prioritized. The typologies also possess value in explaining shifts in a given jurisdiction. While some countries retain a well-established approach, the general direction of travel is to increase the circumstances when probative unlawfully obtained evidence can be admitted. None of the legal systems considered in this chapter has moved towards a more rigid exclusionary approach. Instead, there is a greater appreciation that the exclusion of relevant evidence hampers truth-finding and, particularly if the breach is minor and/or made in good faith, that the exclusion of probative evidence may be a disproportionate response. The three typologies will be considered in turn, starting with states that exclude where there is systemic unfairness.

Systemic unfairness

Some legal systems allow for the exclusion of illegally obtained evidence on the basis that admittance would undermine perceptions of the fairness of the trial process (see further Bloom and Fentin, 2010; Taslitz, 2013). Turner and Weigend explain the rationale thus:

[Courts] would taint their own reputation and dignity if they (routinely) base their decisions on evidence that has been obtained through gross violations of the law. Courts should therefore exclude tainted evidence in order to demonstrate to the public that they do not condone illegal acts of government agents and that they refuse to base their decisions on the results of such acts. (Turner and Weigend, 2019, p 258)

England and Wales epitomize this approach as section 78 of the Police and Criminal Evidence Act 1984 specifically requires judges to base decisions on whether to admit unlawfully obtained evidence on the grounds of fairness. Subsequent case law has illustrated that this exercise is a balancing act. A case like *R v Twigg* [2019] EWCA Crim 1553 shows how all available evidence is considered, not just that which was unlawfully obtained. The Court of Appeal justified the decision to dismiss the appeal on the basis of the lawfully obtained evidence, which suggested that the admissibility of the improperly obtained sample did not render the proceedings unfair. English common law might also be said to fit within this typology. Despite the courts stating that the means by which evidence was obtained was irrelevant to its admissibility, there was recognition that a trial judge had a residual duty to ensure the fairness of a trial. The Canadian Supreme Court has also articulated the need for balance in determining whether proceedings are fair (*R v Grant* [2009] SCC 32).

Given the restrictions that have been placed on the exclusionary rule by the United States Supreme Court, has systemic unfairness become the dominant concern in American law? We would argue that this point has not been reached. Automatic exclusion still occurs following many types of breach and the basis for this is a belief that exclusion encourages legal compliance. Exclusion, therefore, has a deterrent effect, at least in theory. In those limited areas where the Supreme Court has held that automatic exclusion no longer applies, the courts will look for systemic injustice (*Nix v Williams*, 467 US 431 (1984)) but this is the exception to the general rule, and to its rationale.

Systemic justice entails balance, hence an absolutist position cannot be taken. A decision must be made about the level of guidance that courts are given as to how to undertake this task. One possibility is to give the courts latitude by providing a general discretion to exclude unlawfully obtained evidence; section 78 of the Police and Criminal Evidence Act 1984 in England and Wales exemplifies this approach. Courts can then be guided by previous appellate decisions. An alternative model is found in the New Zealand Evidence Act 2006. Section 30(2)(b) stipulates that, once it has been established that the evidence has been obtained improperly, the judge must '[determine] whether or not the exclusion of the evidence is proportionate to the impropriety by means of a balancing process that gives appropriate weight to the impropriety and takes proper account of the need for an effective and credible system of justice'. This already goes beyond section 78 of the Police and Criminal Evidence Act 1984 in terms of specificity. However, section 30(3) then lists eight considerations that the court may consider:

- 'the importance of any right breached by the impropriety and the seriousness of the intrusion on it';
- 'the nature of the impropriety, in particular, whether it was deliberate, reckless, or done in bad faith';
- 'the nature and quality of the improperly obtained evidence';
- 'the seriousness of the offence with which the defendant is charged';
- 'whether there were any other investigatory techniques not involving any breach of the rights that were known to be available but were not used';
- 'whether there are alternative remedies to exclusion of the evidence that can adequately provide redress to the defendant';
- 'whether the impropriety was necessary to avoid apprehended physical danger to the police or others';
- 'whether there was any urgency in obtaining the improperly obtained evidence'.

Providing criteria may give the impression of clarity, but this is illusory. Each factor need not inform the judge's decision, nor are they listed in any hierarchy. This is important because the factors may pull in opposite directions in any given case, some favouring admission, others exclusion. What the section illustrates is that determining whether unlawfully obtained evidence should be admitted on the basis of systemic integrity, though common as an approach, depends largely on judicial perception.

Human rights protection

States, and by implication state criminal justice agencies, should not benefit from breaching an individual's rights. Excluding the use of unlawfully obtained evidence would, on this basis, seem an appropriate remedy for someone whose human rights had been violated. This would favour an automatic exclusionary rule: once a factual determination had been made that someone's rights had been violated, there could be no subsequent debate about whether the evidence should nonetheless be admitted. However, the way in which rights conventions are framed does not mandate automatic exclusion. Article 6 of the European Convention on Human Rights, for example, protects the right to a fair trial, yet the European Court of Human Rights case law is clear that this does not require state parties to exclude illegally obtained evidence (*Schenk* v *Switzerland* (1988) 13 EHRR 242; *El Haski* v *Belgium* (2013) 56 EHRR 31). The House of Lords in *R* v *Khan (Sultan)* [1997] AC 558, therefore, found no conflict between the approach taken by the European Court of Human Rights and that taken by the English courts. Whether an individual has received a 'fair trial' will be considered holistically, an approach that does not differ radically from decisions taken elsewhere about the systemic fairness of a trial.

The reasoning in the leading case of *Schenk* v *Switzerland* (1988) 13 EHRR 242 answers a simple point of law, but posits an interesting counterfactual. It will be recalled that Schenk had attempted to secure the services of someone who would kill his wife and that the prosecution's case included unlawful tape recordings of Schenk talking with the individual he planned to hire. Central to the European Court of Human Rights' reasoning were two factors: the unlawfully procured recordings were only part of the evidence incriminating Schenk; and he was given ample opportunity at trial to challenge the probity of the evidence and whether it should be admitted. What if the case against Schenk had rested solely on the illegal recordings? Suddenly, the arguments become starker. The probative value of the recordings remains, though the overall case against Schenk is presumably weakened. Does the requirement of a 'fair trial' now demand that the evidence is excluded? Thommen and Samadi (2016) have also found the Court's approach objectionable in that the seriousness of the offence increases the likelihood that improperly obtained evidence will be admitted and these are the very cases where an individual's rights are most in need of protection.

Deterrence

Basing exclusion on deterring official malpractice could be viewed as a variant of excluding evidence to ensure systemic fairness. Criminal processes that benefit from illegality forfeit legitimacy. There is also little incentive for strict compliance on the part of law enforcement agencies if evidence will be admitted regardless of whether it was obtained legally. Conceptually, deterrence is far more complex than is commonly assumed. Its effectiveness at reducing undesirable conduct rests on a number of assumptions, which are far from convincing. Two key assumptions are that: (a) individuals minded to break the law know the consequences of doing so; and (b) individuals act with sufficient knowledge and rationality that the potential penalty will impact on their behaviour.

The usual context for discussing deterrence is when determining sentencing policy. One of the reasons why setting a penalty at a certain level appears to make little difference to crime rates is because those minded to offend are unlikely to know the likely consequence if they are convicted. In the context of deterring malpractice by the police, an automatic exclusionary rule may have the virtue that there would be no ambiguity as to the outcome of an illegal search. However, this presupposes that an officer has a sufficient vested interest in an individual being convicted. More problematic is the case where the infraction is accidental. If a police officer has made a mistake in good faith and in the process has unearthed probative evidence, it is difficult to see the social value in excluding the evidence.

The relevance of whether the breach was made in good faith has been addressed directly in Australian law. Section 138(1) of the Evidence Law 1995 provides that evidence obtained improperly or in contravention of an Australian law is not to be admitted 'unless the desirability of admitting the evidence outweighs the undesirability of admitting evidence that has been obtained in the way in which the evidence was obtained'. There is, therefore, a presumption against inadmissibility but unlawfully obtained evidence can be admitted if the prosecution proves that the desirability of admitting the evidence outweighs the negative consequences. Section 138(3) lists a number of factors that the court must take into account when making this determination and this includes 'whether the impropriety or contravention was deliberate or reckless'. Where the evidence has resulted from serious and deliberate illegality it is ordinarily excluded (for example, *Ridgeway* v *R* (1995) 184 CLR 19). The Australian courts have also expanded on what is meant by recklessness in the context of gathering evidence unlawfully:

> Conduct would be reckless if the officer had foresight that it might be illegal but proceeded with indifference as to whether that was so. What is described as an alternative of a 'don't care' attitude expressed in the passage from Helmholm must be understood as meaning that the

offender, recognising that the conduct might be illegal, did not care whether it was. (*DPP* v *Marijancevic* (2011) 33 VR 440, at [85])

A general deterrent argument for excluding unlawfully obtained evidence is slightly more convincing. The purpose of exclusion is not about 'punishing' an individual officer so we should not get side-tracked by assessments of personal culpability. The focus should be on improving police practice; if evidence is excluded, and the reasons why are disseminated, procedural rules are upheld and are less likely to be breached again. Early American case law presented such arguments in compelling terms (*Silverthorne Lumber Co* v *United States*, 251 US 385 (1920); *Weeks* v *United States*, 232 US 383 (1914)).

The partial retreat from an automatic exclusionary rule in the United States (*United States* v *Leon*, 468 US 897 (1984); *Herring* v *United States*, 555 US 135 (2009)) recognizes two limitations implicit in a deterrent approach. First, that there are circumstances where the illegality is inadvertent and hence deterrence cannot secure individual compliance with the law. The second observation is that an exclusionary rule comes at a cost – the exclusion of probative evidence jeopardizes the search for truth (see Cammack, 2010). Unlike other systems, the American approach does not entail balancing competing interests. It is indisputable, however, that the value of an exclusionary rule as a means of deterring unlawful conduct by criminal justice personnel is being increasingly questioned.

Legitimate limitations on the admissibility of probative evidence

What this chapter illustrates is that a sole focus on the reliability of evidence and truth-finding would compromise the integrity of the criminal justice process. Probative evidence can be obtained unfairly, improperly or unlawfully. A policy of admitting all probative evidence regardless of how it was secured would allow law enforcement agencies to act with virtual impunity. The debate is about the extent to which other legitimate concerns should restrict the admissibility of potentially valuable evidence. Deterring illegal law enforcement, protecting citizens' rights and maintaining public confidence in the integrity of the administration of justice are vital to any democracy. The question is better framed as whether the exclusion of evidence obtained improperly is the most appropriate means to address these concerns.

Increasingly, courts have questioned this while legislation has often placed a duty on courts to balance competing demands so as to ensure a 'fair trial'. Two trends can be observed. The first is a recognition that excluding improperly obtained evidence may have minimal deterrent effect. It is not hard to discern why. Many procedural breaches are inadvertent and future behaviour will not be affected if evidence obtained as a result cannot form part of the prosecution case. This is why legal systems that still operate comparatively strict rules of exclusion consider the officer's integrity when the breach occurred. Those systems favouring systemic propriety as a justification for potential exclusion are also mindful that the officer's state of mind is relevant.

The second trend is that there has been an honest appreciation that the exclusion of probative evidence can come at a considerable cost. This is not the same thing as saying that probative evidence should always be admitted regardless of the means by which it was obtained – no legal system, at least among those under review in this chapter, adopts so lax an approach. An approach based on systemic propriety recognizes the societal cost and, by balancing the factors at play, attempts to ensure that justice occurs on a case-by-case basis. This is not to underestimate the difficulty associated with such an assessment, nor the potential for judicial inconsistency. That most legal systems are gravitating towards a variant of this model is telling. When faced with competing – and potentially irreconcilable – policy concerns, trusting the judiciary to arrive at a just outcome has much to commend it.

6

Decisions and Narratives: Factfinding and Case Construction

In the public imagination, the criminal trial is the culmination of the criminal justice process, the overriding purpose of which is to acquit the innocent and convict the guilty. As Michael Naughton writes:

> If you were to ask the 'person in the street' what he or she wants from the criminal justice system, the reply is more than likely going to be that it should convict the guilty and acquit the innocent; and, if it should happen that an innocent person is convicted in 'error', then most people would probably think that the appeals system should operate to overturn the conviction in a speedy fashion to reduce the harm that was caused to the victim and his or her family and friends and restore the legitimacy of the criminal justice system. The idea that the criminal justice system should be about convicting the guilty and acquitting the innocent is reflected in political statements about how the system should function and it is transmitted in portrayals of wrongful convictions and wrongful acquittals in the media. (Naughton, 2009, p 17)

The process starts with the allegation or discovery of a potential criminal act and proceeds through investigation and the gathering of evidence. Along the road to the criminal trial is a series of decisions to be made, gates through which the defendant must pass: Has a crime occurred? Is there justification for an arrest? Is there a basis to press charges? Is the decision to prosecute justified?

Gottfredson and Gottfredson (1988) argued that there are two types of decisions – those made by individuals and 'agency or institutional decisions' – although many individual decisions are informed by agency/institutional policy. So, for example, the decision of an individual prosecutor whether to proceed with a prosecution will be governed by agency and institutional requirements.

The Code for Crown Prosecutors provides the following:

> 2.2 It is not the function of the CPS [Crown Prosecution Service] to decide whether a person is guilty of a criminal offence, but to make assessments about whether it is appropriate to present charges for the criminal court to consider. The CPS assessment of any case is not in any sense a finding of, or implication of, any guilt or criminal conduct. A finding of guilt can only be made by a court. (CPS, 2018)

In the majority of cases, prosecutions should only be started or continued where they have satisfied both stages of the Full Code Test. The first stage is the Evidential Test:

> 4.6 Prosecutors must be satisfied that there is sufficient evidence to provide a realistic prospect of conviction against each suspect on each charge. They must consider what the defence case may be, and how it is likely to affect the prospects of conviction. A case which does not pass the evidential stage must not proceed, no matter how serious or sensitive it may be. (CPS, 2018)

If prosecutors believe that the first stage is satisfied, then they must consider whether or not the prosecution is in the public interest. In assessing the interests of the public, the Code directs prosecutors to take into account six specific matters:

- the seriousness of the offence – the more serious the offence, the more likely a prosecution will be required;
- the culpability of the suspect – the higher the levels of culpability, the more likely a prosecution will be required;
- the circumstances of and the harm caused to the victim;

- the suspect's age and maturity at the time of the offence;
- the impact on the community of the offence;
- the proportionality of the prosecution – in considering whether prosecution is a proportionate response, regard should be had to the cost to the CPS and wider criminal justice system of the prosecution and also to 'principles of effective case management' – '[f]or example, in a case involving multiple suspects, prosecution might be reserved for the main participants in order to avoid excessively long and complex proceedings' (CPS, 2018, para 4.14f).

Increasingly, 'effective case management' and other factors may divert the criminal justice process from a focused pursuit of the truth. In a case involving multiple suspects, establishing the truth of what happened would require all those to be identified. The reality is that whether or not a suspect becomes a defendant in a criminal trial will depend on the assessment of a prosecutor as to whether the suspect is a main or subsidiary participant.

The Criminal Procedure Rules 2015, which apply to all criminal trials in England and Wales, provide that the overriding purpose of the Code (and by implication of the criminal process) is that criminal cases be dealt with justly (rule 1.1(1)). Dealing with a case justly includes:

(a) acquitting the innocent and convicting the guilty;
(b) dealing with the prosecution and the defence fairly;
(c) recognising the rights of a defendant, particularly those under Article 6 of the European Convention on Human Rights;
(d) respecting the interests of witnesses, victims and jurors and keeping them informed of the progress of the case;
(e) dealing with the case efficiently and expeditiously;
(f) ensuring that appropriate information is available to the court when bail and sentence are considered; and
(g) dealing with the case in ways that take into account—
    i. the gravity of the offence alleged,
    ii. the complexity of what is in issue,
    iii. the severity of the consequences for the defendant and others affected, and
    iv. the needs of other cases. (Criminal Procedure Rules, 2018, rule 1.1(2))

Acquitting the innocent and convicting the guilty – the sole object of the criminal process according to Sir Samuel Romilly in 1810 (Romilly,

1810, note D) – is now one of nine factors to be taken into account alongside 'dealing with the case efficiently and expeditiously'.

Gottfredson and Gottfredson (1988) suggest any decision has three components:

1. A goal (or set of goals) that the decision maker wishes to achieve. A decision is made with an objective in mind: in the case of the police or prosecutors that objective has traditionally been thought to be to secure the conviction of the guilty (and, by implication, the acquittal of the innocent). Increasingly, effective and efficient case management are becoming important goals with the potential for seriously adverse effects on the pursuit of truth.
2. For a decision to be possible there have to be alternatives: decision making is about making a choice from possible options. Decision making therefore involves the exercise of considerable discretion, subject to any 'agency or institutional decisions'.
3. The decision maker requires information to guide the choice of possible options:

    In order to qualify as information in this sense, the data available about alternatives must be related to the goals of the decision – that is the data must be relevant. The definition of relevance in this context is that the data must reduce uncertainty about the consequences of the decision ... The information value of a datum is determined by the relation of the datum to the consequences of the alternative choices; if there is no relation, then there is no information ... decisions about crime, offenders and alleged offenders often are made with much data but little information. (Gottfredson and Gottfredson, 1998, p 3)

It is widely acknowledged that only a small proportion of crimes result in a criminal trial. The occurrence of a crime may be the beginning of the criminal process but in many cases the process will end there too:

> The occurrence of a crime signals the potential involvement of the criminal justice process. It is the triggering mechanism for discretionary actions on the part of victims and possibly of criminal justice functionaries. These discretionary actions are the very basis of the criminal justice system ... The occurrence of a crime is by no means a sufficient condition for the involvement of the criminal justice system. A series of decisions must take place before the criminal justice system becomes involved. First, the behaviour in

question must be noticed, and the decision to define it as a crime must be made. This discovery and definition may be made by a citizen (as a victim or a witness) or by the police. Second, someone must decide that the behaviour in question is properly within the realm of the criminal justice system. Third, the decision to enter the event into the criminal justice system must be made. (Gottfredson and Gottfredson, 1998, p 15)

We have seen in Chapter 2 that the majority of criminal incidents come to the attention of the police through public reports and in that sense it is members of the public who are the key gatekeepers of the criminal process: 'It is therefore difficult to overestimate the influence that [these] victimized decision makers have over the nature of the criminal justice process. The decision of the victim is obviously bound inextricably with the major questions and issues that confront the whole of society about the criminal justice system' (Gottfredson and Gottfredson, 1998, p 16).

Decision making, storytelling and narrative

As we have seen, the criminal process involves a large number of decisions: from the initial decision as to whether or not a crime has occurred, through the decision as to whether to report the crime, right through to the decision as to whether the defendant is guilty or not guilty. Given the centrality of decision making to the criminal process, it is perhaps surprising that there is little attention by legal academics to the decision-making process.

Lee Roy Beach et al define decisions as the process of estimating potential regret and figuring out how to avoid it if it is too great:

> The basic decision is about the regret-potential of the future you expect to occur if you stay on your present course. If what you expect to happen has a sufficiently low or negative regret-potential (ie is desirable) you can keep on with what you were planning to do anyway and just let the future unfold as expected. But, if the expected future has high regret-potential (ie is undesirable), you must decide what to do to ensure that when the actual future arrives, it is less regrettable (more desirable) than it otherwise would have been. (Beach and Bissell, 2016, p 24)

Evaluations of 'regret-potential' are made on the basis of standards: beliefs, values and preferences. For Beach et al, beliefs are declarative memories of how things work; values are declarative memories of how things should or should not be; and preferences based on both episodic and declarative memories are much more transitory and less resistant to change than values.

The prevailing theory explaining decision making in the mid-20th century was rational choice theory. It emerged in the 1940s in economic theory and an influential work was von Neumann and Morgenstern's *Theory of Games and Economic Theory* published in 1944 (von Neumann and Morgenstern, 1944). The origins of rational choice theory are often traced back to Blaise Pascal's justification for a belief in God. The choice is between believing or not believing and the correct choice will not be revealed until after death. If you choose not to believe and you are right, then there are no consequences; if you choose not to believe and are wrong, the consequences could be an eternity in hell. If you choose to believe and are wrong, there are no consequences; if you choose to believe and are right, then the consequences are an eternity in heaven. The rational choice for Pascal is therefore to believe in God.

According to rational choice theory, decisions should be made on the basis of the expected utility of the outcome. The utility is the extent to which the outcome is preferred or preferable to the alternatives. Thus, in Pascal's example, an eternity in heaven is to be preferred to an eternity in hell. A more mundane, everyday example is provided by the *Stanford Encyclopaedia of Philosophy*: You are planning a long walk and need to decide whether to take an umbrella. You would rather not carry the umbrella with you on a sunny day, but you would prefer to face the rain with rather than without the umbrella. There are three possible outcomes here: you remain dry having carried an unnecessary umbrella; you remain dry having carried the umbrella; you end up getting wet. There are two possible states outside your control: it either rains or it stays dry. There are also two acts: taking the umbrella or leaving the umbrella at home. The decision-making process then depends on a rational calculation of the relative probabilities of the states and utility of the outcomes. The decision as to whether to take the umbrella or not involves assessing the likelihood of rain and the relative utility of getting wet or remaining dry (https//plato.stanford.edu/entities/rationality-normative-utility).

Similarly, in the criminal process, an important factor in reporting theft is whether the item stolen is insured or not. The process of reporting an offence can be time consuming and frustrating. If levels of outcome utility are perceived to be low then the offence will not be reported; alternatively, if the item is insured then a claim on the insurance policy might require the theft to be reported and the outcome utility will be considerably increased.

In a landmark article in the *Stanford Law Review*, John Kaplan (1968) sought to apply the theory to the factfinding process in criminal justice. He identified the following three fundamental concepts: probability, expected value and expected utility. In many situations, the rational person will make the choice that has the greatest probability producing the highest value. In some situations, however, simple value will not determine the decision and instead expected utility will be key:

> Whereas probability is concerned with the chance of getting a reward, utility is concerned with the value to one of that reward. The utility of the same item may vary among individuals and even within the value structure of the same individual, depending upon such factors as his financial status and the demands on his resources. The expected utility of a decision – that is, the probability that the course of action will lead to the reward multiplied by the utility of the reward – will determine whether a rational man will make that decision as opposed to one with a lower expected utility. (Kaplan, 1968, p 1068)

Kaplan then outlines the basic premise:

> A businessman making a decision according to [the] precepts [of rational choice theory] first lists all of the options open to him, and then computes as best he can the probabilities attached to the different possible consequences of each option. In evaluating these probabilities he uses his experience, which in many cases is merely an educated intuition, and what scientific and quantitative studies can be brought to bear on the problem. Next, he decides on the utility associated with each possible outcome and, combining this figure with the calculated probabilities, he computes the expected utility of each option or combination of options. On the basis of this computation he then chooses the course that maximizes his expected utility. (Kaplan, 1968, p 1069)

While accepting that in the criminal context the computation of utilities might be more difficult than in a business context, Kaplan argues that the theory could usefully be applied to legal decision making: 'The criminal trial is, at least in concept, one of the simpler decision processes in the law' (Kaplan, 1968, p 1070). The decision involves calculating the probability of the defendant's guilt and the utility/disutility of acquittal/conviction. In applying the theory, Kaplan makes some disturbing points in relation to utility:

> It is obviously far less serious to society, for instance, to acquit an embezzler, who, in any event, may find it very difficult to be placed again in a position of trust, than it would be to acquit a child molester, since the latter crime is one that tends to be repeated ...
>
> Similarly we might rationally weigh Di, the disutility of convicting an innocent man, differently in different cases. The better the reputation of the defendant, the greater the tragedy of his fall from grace, and hence perhaps the greater disutility of convicting him should he be innocent. If so, we perhaps have an explanation of the relatively powerful effect of character testimony on behalf of a criminal defendant. In addition to the usual justification – that the evidence of the good character of the defendant makes it less likely that he in fact committed the crime – we have a second reason: that by raising the disutility of convicting the defendant should he be innocent, we raise P, the quantum of proof or probability of guilt necessary to convict. (Kaplan, 1968, p 1072)

This approach, if true, has worrying consequences for the pursuit of truth: making decisions on the basis of perceptions of utility demotes the centrality of accurate factfinding.

Kaplan's article led to an increasing interest in the possibilities of incorporating scientific techniques into the criminal justice system and making it 'more scientific'. In March 1991, the Cardozo School of Law held a conference on Decision and Inference in Litigation. The conference proceedings were subsequently published in a special edition of the *Cardozo Law Review*. In his preface to the collection of conference papers, Professor Peter Tillers makes reference to the development of a 'new evidence scholarship' over the preceding 25 years, which looked to the role of mathematics in evaluating evidence. Indeed, one of the conference streams was entitled 'Trial by

Logic and Mathematics'. Professor Tillers seems to confirm the view that the criminal justice process is about a search for truth and if we can find the appropriate tools we can be much closer to ascertaining the truth: 'A primary motivation for the interest of new evidence scholars in disciplines such as probability theory and statistics is their belief that formal analytical tools are useful for the analysis of factual uncertainty in litigation' (Tilliers, 1991, p 255). The 1980s had seen the first use of DNA evidence in criminal litigation. Professor Alec Jefferies at the University of Leicester had carried out pioneering work in the field of DNA profiling and, in 1988, Colin Pitchfork became the first man in the UK to be convicted on the basis of DNA evidence. In fact, Pitchfork had pleaded guilty after the DNA evidence had been presented to him. The development of DNA profiling was perhaps the biggest jump in forensic techniques since the first use of fingerprint evidence. It seemed to offer huge possibilities to get at the truth and the 1991 Carodozo conference can partly be understood in that context. Truth in criminal justice would be achieved with the rigorous appliance of science.

In fact, the idea that the criminal trial could be compared to a scientific investigation is not new. In the early 20th century, the leading Anglo-American authority on evidence was John Henry Wigmore. *Wigmore on Evidence (Treatise on the Anglo-American System of Evidence in Trials at Common Law)* became a leading work and now consists of 13 volumes revised by a variety of successors and cites some 40,000 cases from every jurisdiction in Canada, the United States and several Commonwealth countries. Wigmore was also the author of *The Science of Judicial Proof as Given by Logic, Psychology, and General Experience and Illustrated in Judicial Trials* (1937). The first two editions had referred to the 'principles of judicial proof'. In the book, Wigmore set out his chart system of analysing evidence. The chart employed a system of symbols and coloured pencils. Wigmore's work pre-dated computers and involved law teachers and students in something new at the time to law schools: examination of the facts. *The Science of Judicial Proof* set down the complex reasoning processes – the principles of judicial proof – which if correctly applied could lead to a true verdict. Wigmore was particularly concerned with the distinction between proof and admissibility and argued that too much attention was placed on rules of admissibility at the expense of proof, which had been 'virtually ignored ... and left to the chances of later acquisition, casual, empiric, in the course of practice' (Wigmore, 1937, p 3).

Wigmore's ideas fell out of favour and it was only with interest in rational choice theory and the 'science' of decision making that lawyers and legal academics renewed interest in them. Although rational choice theory was the dominant theory explaining decision making in the 1960s and 1970s, it started to come under attack during the 1970s. In a landmark paper published in *Econometrica* in 1979, psychologists Daniel Kahneman and Amos Tversky argued that '[rational choice theory], as it is commonly interpreted and applied, is not an adequate descriptive model and we propose an alternative account of choice under risk' (Kahneman and Tversky, 1979, p 263).

The alternative theory – prospect theory – was to earn Kahneman the Nobel Prize for Economics in 2002 (Tversky had died in 1996). Kahneman and Tversky were keen to describe the actual behaviour of real people. In studying real decision making, they found that people did not decide utility in absolute, objective terms but rather in relation to their individual situation. People did not always act rationally, and their decisions were informed by emotion and by their sense of self. Kahneman and Tversky found that, faced with risky choices leading to gains, individuals tended to be risk-averse. By contrast, in choices leading to losses, individuals tended to be risk seeking. They also found that people tend to attribute excessive weight to events with low probabilities and insufficient weight to events with high probabilities. Dan Gardner (2009), in *Risk: The Science and Politics of Fear*, illustrated this point with the public reaction to the events of 9/11. Although the probability of being the victim of a terrorist attack while on board an aircraft remained very low, many people cancelled flights across the United States and chose to drive. Gardner quotes the relative odds as a 1-in-135,000 chance of being killed in a hijacking, against the 1-in-6,000 odds of being killed in a car crash. Following 9/11 the number of road fatalities rose rapidly as people made decisions, not according to the rational choice model, but consistent with prospect theory (Gardner, 2009, pp 1–5).

The importance of narrative

Decisions made to report crimes, to stop and search, to arrest, to charge are not always made on the basis of a rational calculation of probability and utility. They are frequently made in relation to the individual situation and narrative. Given the centrality of storytelling to human existence, this is perhaps not that surprising.

> The twentieth-century observer looks into the night sky and sees stars and planets; some earlier observers saw instead chinks in a sphere through which the light beyond could

be observed. What each observer takes himself or herself to perceive is identified and has to be identified by theory-laden concepts. Perceivers without concepts, as Kant almost said, are blind. Empiricist philosophers have contended that common to the modern and the medieval observer is that which each really sees or saw, prior to all theory and interpretation, namely many small light patches against a dark surface; and it is at the very least clear that what both saw can be so described. But if all our experience were to be characterized exclusively in terms of this bare sensory type of description—a type of description which it is certainly useful for a variety of special purposes to resort to from time to time—we would be confronted with not only an uninterpreted, but an uninterpretable world, with not merely a world not yet comprehended by theory but with a world that never could be comprehended by theory. A world of textures, shapes, smells, sensations, sounds and nothing more invites no questions and gives no grounds for furnishing any answers. (MacIntyre, 2007, p 183)

As MacIntyre points out, perception alone is insufficient to make sense of the world. It is only through stories (narrative) that the world becomes interpreted and interpretable:

A central thesis then begins to emerge: man is in his actions and practice, as well as in his fictions, essentially a story-telling animal. He is not essentially, but becomes through his history, a teller of stories that aspire to truth. But the key question for men is not about their own authorship; I can only answer the question 'What am I to do?' if I can answer the prior question 'Of what story or stories do I find myself a part?' We enter human society, that is, with one or more imputed characters—roles into which we have been drafted—and we have to learn what they are in order to be able to understand how others respond to us and how our responses to them are apt to be construed. It is through hearing stories about wicked stepmothers, lost children, good but misguided kings, wolves that suckle twin boys, youngest sons who receive no inheritance but must make their own way in the world and eldest sons who waste their inheritance on riotous living and go into exile to live with the swine, that children learn or mis-learn both what a child and what a parent is, what the cast of characters may be in the drama into which they have been born and what the ways of the world are. Deprive children of stories and you leave them unscripted, anxious stutterers in their actions as in their words. Hence there is no way to give us an understanding of any society, including our own, except through the stock of stories which constitute its initial dramatic resources. (MacIntyre, 2007, p 183)

Recent developments in neuroscience have allowed us to gain greater insight into both perception and the neural processes involved in interpreting and acting on perceptions. Michael Gazzaniga, one of the leading authorities on cognitive neuroscience, discussed how mind and brain 'accomplish the amazing feat of constructing our past and, in so doing, create the illusion of self' (Gazzaniga, 1998, p 1):

[Reconstruction of events] starts with perception and goes all the way up to human reasoning. The mind is the last to know things. After the brain computes an event, the illusory 'we' (that is, the mind) becomes aware of it. The brain, particularly the left hemisphere, is built to interpret data the brain has already processed. Yes, there is a special device in the left brain, which I call the *interpreter*, that carries out one more activity upon completion of zillions of automatic brain processes. The interpreter, the last device in the information chain in our brain, reconstructs the brain events and in doing so makes telling errors of perception, memory, and judgment. The clue to how we are built is buried not just in our marvellously robust capacity for these functions, but also in the errors that are frequently made during reconstruction. Biography is fiction. Autobiography is hopelessly inventive. (Gazzaniga, 1998, p 2, emphasis in original)

MacIntyre, in order to show the importance of narrative, quotes from a sequence written by Dr Johnson of his travels in France:

'There we waited on the ladies—Morville's.—Spain. Country towns all beggars. At Dijon he could not find the way to Orleans.—Cross roads of France very bad.—Five soldiers.—Women.—Soldiers escaped.—The Colonel would not lose five men for the sake of one woman.—The magistrate cannot seize a soldier but by the Colonel's permission, etc., etc.' What this suggests is what I take to be true, namely that the characterization of actions allegedly prior to any narrative form being imposed upon them will always turn out to be the presentation of what are plainly the disjointed parts of some possible narrative. (MacIntyre, 2007, p 182)

A catalogue of events will only start to make sense once it has had a narrative form imposed on it. For Paul Ricoeur, 'our existence cannot be separated from the stories we tell of ourselves' (quoted in Meretoja, 2014) and decision making involves both argumentation and interpretation. In interpretation, the decision maker collects the facts together to form a story and interprets the law in the same way. At the same time, individual stories are synthesized into a plot or unified story. In the court setting, as we shall see in Chapter 7, competing narratives are subject to argumentation to arrive at the dominant, guiding narrative that frames the future events: decision to convict, sentencing and so on. For Ricoeur, the relationship between narrative and life is a dialectical one. Similarly too for Bruner:

> The concept of narrative has been called 'one of the more prominent currents in late 20th-century intellectual life' (Neisser & Fivush, 1994, p. vii), and a number of philosophers of mind have argued that the portions of human consciousness beyond the purely somatic—self-awareness, self-understanding, and self-knowledge—are products of personal narratives (e.g., Dennett, 1991). It is 'because of the nature of our minds,' as Dan P. McAdams (1993) claims, that 'we are impelled as adults to make sense of our lives in terms of narrative' (p. 134). This powerful role for narrative is realized by the linking of personal memories to present conditions and future hopes, by organizing, translating, and providing continuity and coherence to experience. Self-awareness and self-knowledge are constructed, to a significant degree, through narrative as we compose and assemble stories for ourselves and our world. In a complex interplay between the experience that makes for the personal story and the personal story that structures the experience, the narrator discovers the meaning and significance of the experience. It is through narrating that

we learn about our selves, our community, and the social world (Bruner, 1986, 1990). (Fireman et al, 2003, p 3)

For others in the narrative tradition, such as Mink (1970) and White (1980), 'stories are not lived but told' (Mink, 1970, p 557):

> In an attempt to elucidate the different approaches to this question, theorists have been divided into those who conceive of narrative primarily as a cognitive instrument for imposing meaningful order onto human reality or experience (for example, Hayden White, Louis Mink, Daniel Dennett) and those who consider it to be primarily an ontological category that characterizes the human way of being in the world, that is, something constitutive of human existence (for example, Paul Ricoeur, Charles Taylor, Alasdair MacIntyre). These can be called respectively the epistemological and ontological position on the significance of narrative for human existence. Galen Strawson, in turn, has made an influential distinction between descriptive and normative positions on the narrativity of experience (what he calls the 'psychological Narrativity thesis' and the 'ethical Narrativity thesis'). Even though these conceptual differentiations are helpful to a certain extent, such binary terms may also prevent us from paying adequate attention to the complex interconnections between the ontological, epistemological, and ethical dimension of the relation between narrative and human existence.
>
> A crucial background for the epistemological approach to narrative is the debate launched by philosophers of history such as Arthur Danto, Louis Mink, and Hayden White, who argued that historical accounts retrospectively project a narrative order on events. For example, Mink famously argues that 'stories are not lived but told,' since 'life' in itself 'has no beginnings, middles, or ends'. He agrees with White '(1) that the world is not given to us in the form of well-made stories; (2) that we make such stories; (3) that we give them referentiality by imagining that in them the world speaks itself'. White, in turn, asserts that a historical narrative 'reveals to us a world that is putatively "finished," done with, over, and yet not dissolved, not falling apart'. Thus, according to White, the 'value attached to narrativity in the representation of real events arises out of a desire to

have real events display the coherence, integrity, fullness, and closure of an image of life that is and can only be imaginary.' What these arguments are suggesting is that narratives project a false order on the disorder of human existence. (Mink, 1970, p 557)

The individual situation referred to in Kahneman and Tversky's prospect theory of decision making is dependent on narratives, stories we tell ourselves and others, the means by which we come to know ourselves. In Chapter 7 we will explore further the role of narrative in the criminal trial.

Constructing the case

The daughter of one of the editors, upon entering the fifth grade, was given the assignment of learning about a child in the class whom she did not know well. Specifically, she was instructed to develop an interview that would answer the question 'Who are you?' Of course, her collaborator was to do the same. Thus, one evening during the first week of class, in attempting to respond to her classmate she asked, 'Dad, where was my favorite vacation?' After his telling her where they went and discussing what they did on her favorite vacation, she then asked, 'What is my most frightening memory?' Unable to answer the second question, he came to the awkward realization of how quickly and thoughtlessly he was willing to answer the first. She wanted to provide stories to answer questions about who she is, and initially it seemed perfectly reasonable to both of them that he help construct them. The stories we tell to ourselves and others, for ourselves and others, are a central means by which we come to know ourselves and others, thereby enriching our conscious awareness. Narrative pervades our lives—conscious experience is not merely linked to the number and variety of personal stories we construct with each other within a cultural frame but is also consumed by them. (Fireman et al, 2003, p 3)

There are parallels here with the investigation of crimes and the joint work of the investigating officer and witness in constructing what happened. Some years ago, one of the authors had his car stolen. The car was advertised for sale and the theft occurred while the author (A) and a prospective purchaser (P) were taking the car for a test drive. To begin with, P sat in the passenger seat and A drove. P was then offered the opportunity to drive the car and both got out of the car to swap places. Before A had got back into the passenger seat, P had driven off in the car, leaving A at the side of the road. By chance, a police patrol vehicle passed by quite soon afterwards and A reported the theft. Of course, strictly speaking, the event could not truly be classified as a theft at that stage. At best it was an alleged theft. A was unaware whether the prospective purchaser possessed the necessary intention to commit the offence (section 1 of the Theft Act 1968). The police to whom A reported the event did not know whether or not A was a willing party to some insurance fraud. The prospective purchaser could have driven away as a joke. Indeed, A's immediate thought was that he would walk round the corner and find him parked up, laughing. The prospective purchaser could have been, at that moment, transferring the full purchase price to A's bank account. Nevertheless, A's past experience and knowledge told him that the event had all the characteristics that he identified as theft. The police officers in the vehicle were on other duties and took little in the way of details other than to report the car stolen. Later that day, A was required to attend a local police station to make a statement. The making of the statement consisted of A being asked a series of questions from which a police officer created a statement. The statement was then read and signed by A. It told a story of the incident, but the story was constructed through the discussion between A and the police officer.

As Fireman et al write:

> The narratives that we tell ourselves and others aid in developing our conscious awareness, since such provide a central means for us to know ourselves and others. Conscious experience is both related to and consumed by the personal stories we make up and share with each other in a cultural frame. (Fireman et al, 2003, p 3)

Construction of a criminal case is often analogous to the writing of a biography. In the 1983 novel *Edwin Mullhouse*, Stephen Millhauser writes that the fatal flaw of all biography, according to its enemies:

> [Is] its helpless conformity to the laws of fiction. Each date, each incident, each casual remark contributes to

an elaborate plot that slowly and cunningly builds to a foreknown climax: the hero's celebrated deed ... [the entire genre can only be deemed] hopelessly fictional, since unlike real life, which presents us with question marks, censored passages, blank spaces, rows of asterisks, omitted paragraphs, and numberless sequences of three dots trailing into whiteness, biography provides an illusion of completeness, a vast pattern of details organized by an omniscient biographer. (Millhauser, 1983, pp 100–1)

Similarly, Joanna Field, in *A Life of One's Own* (1934), wrote: 'I realized that the facts were not separate things which were there for anyone to pick up, but an ever-changing pattern against a boundless background of the unknown, an immense kaleidoscope changing constantly according to the different ways you looked at it' (Field, 1934, pp 105–6).

Although, as we have seen in Chapter 5, there may be rules prohibiting the use of hearsay as evidence in the criminal trial, in fact we make considerable use of hearsay in the construction of our personal narratives. They are constructed from stories we tell ourselves and are told by others. As Jerome Bruner has pointed out, our stories employ contemporary prevailing literary conventions, which are themselves inseparable from the 'folk-psychological canon' (Bruner, 1991). As we saw in Chapter 2, signal crimes and moral panics contribute to this 'folk-psychological canon' and will contribute to the content and plot of the stories we construct.

As Gazzaniga has written:

Sure, life is a fiction, but it's our fiction and it feels good and we are in charge of it. That is the sentiment we all feel as we listen to tales of the automatic brain. We don't feel like zombies; we feel like in-charge, conscious entities. [But] the interpreter constantly establishes a running narrative of our actions, emotions, thoughts, and dreams. It is the glue that unifies our story and creates our sense of being a whole, rational agent. It brings to our bag of individual instincts the illusion that we are something other than what we are. (Gazzaniga, 1998, p 172)

This clearly casts doubt on the feasibility of any search for truth in the criminal process. As Arnold Ludwig notes:

One of the major problems with any insight-oriented psychotherapy based on the uncovering of important, early-life experiences is that it is difficult if not impossible to establish the historical truth through the customary exploration of your memories, fantasies, and dreams, no matter how thorough the probing or how long the treatment. This is so for a lot of reasons. For one, your memories and perceptions are designed to support your biases. You selectively remember or repress certain information, and many of your experiences are indescribable or difficult to translate into words. Your memories tend to be shaped by the theoretical outlook of your therapist. And you tend not to include disconfirming experiences in your accounts ... For these reasons, what you come to regard as historical truth really represents plausibility. This plausibility involves how well your account embraces all the pertinent elements of your experiences and how cohesive it seems. (Ludwig, 1997, p 155)

Clearly, plausibility is not as high a standard as beyond reasonable doubt. Plausibility is perhaps more akin to the balance of probabilities, the standard of proof in civil trials. Plausibility is not the same as certainty. A criminal process that pursued plausibility rather than the truth would arguably carry much less authority and respect.

In 1982, Donald P. Spence criticized psychoanalysis for its misguided pretensions to seek historical truth when what it is really about is the pursuit of the narrative truth. There are similarities here with the trauma-based approach of the truth commission, discussed in Chapter 2:

[Throughout] psychotherapy, the patient deals with the conflict between what is true but hard to describe—that is, the pure memory—and what is describable but partly untrue—that is, the screen memory. The very attempt to translate the original memory destroys it because the words, as they are chosen, likely misrepresent the image, and because the translation, no matter how good, replaces the original ... [But] even when the reconstruction of the past is entirely imaginary, it acquires the mantle of truth if it lets patients find coherence and meaning in their personal stories and make sense out of their chaotic experiences. And it becomes officially true and sometimes more real than actual historical truth when an authoritative figure, such as their analyst, gives the narrative the stamp of approval. (Ludwig, 1997, pp 156–7)

Crime can often be a 'chaotic experience'; it will involve varying degrees of trauma. To make sense of it we construct stories. As soon as events move into retentive memory they are ordered, told and retold and a plot is constructed: '[Plot is] the intelligible whole that governs a succession of events in any story ... A story is made out of events to the extent that plot makes the events into a story. It is the plot of the narrative that unifies causal and teleological elements of an action into a whole' (Ricoeur, 1984, p 171).

The centrality of storytelling

Just as journalists are taught to address the five Ws in their stories – Where? Who? What? When? Why? – so Kenneth Burke identified the pentad all human drama unfolded in five key elements:

- scene
- cast and character
- plot
- timeframe
- human plight (Burke, 1969)

Case construction is not a careful, forensic piecing together of material that produces the truth; it is a plot-driven, narrative process:

> Law stories, like all stories, are the creations of an unseen intelligence that selects, shapes, and transforms raw material into *events* and then arranges these events into the ordered *sequence* of a story. This sequence of events, or plot, provides meaning to the human affairs depicted in the story. These events do not come ready-made like prenumbered pieces or the links to be inserted into a preconfigured chain. The nature of the plot itself determines what kind of actions can serve as events in the story and enter the plot itself. (Meyer, 2014, p 11, emphasis in original)

Research into decision making in healthcare interventions has demonstrated that the influence of narrative has a biasing effect and can lead to poorer decisions from a healthcare point of view (Winterbottom et al, 2008). The stories can appear to get in the way of the objective, scientific truth. In the field of healthcare, it may seem easier to establish a scientific truth and disengage it from narrative. But such 'scientific truth' is not immutable: it can be subject to change. The truth about the nature of light changed with the discovery by Einstein of photons. Scientific truth can be disputed as illustrated in recent debates about the efficacy of measles vaccinations and possible links to autism. Arguably in the criminal process the decisions are more nuanced; in most cases there are not clues that can be subjected to scientific analysis. Law stories are plot-driven, with clear narrative trajectories and dynamic internal movement. The audiences for law stories are intolerant and inpatient and therefore law stories are like popular films in needing strongly pro-fluent plots. As we have come to see with psychoanalysis, the criminal process may be less a search for a historical truth and more about a search for a narrative truth. If that is the case, it is possible that the criminal trial is not the most satisfactory search method to adopt.

7

Truth and the Criminal Trial: Competing Stories

Considering the centrality of the contested criminal trial in the popular imagination, there is a surprising lack of academic research into how contested trials operate. By design, alternative narratives are constructed and presented to the court to enable it to assess the factual and legal culpability of the accused. The rules of engagement are strict. Evidence that juries may find of relevance may sometimes be withheld – for example, evidence of previous bad character relating to an accused, or evidence of a complainant's sexual history in a rape case. This suggests that juries may attach disproportionate weight to evidence, jeopardizing the fairness of the trial. Issues also surround the use of expert witnesses. The presentation of complex evidence can lead to misunderstanding on the part of lay people and can also mask the fact that there can be scientific disagreement over the interpretation of evidence.

It is perhaps a common public perception that criminal trials will turn on questions of law. Legal practitioners spend approximately four years studying the law prior to qualification. In practice, however, few criminal cases are primarily about questions of law. In the overwhelming majority of criminal trials it is the facts that are disputed and in issue. The court will have to decide whether the necessary facts have been proved to a sufficient standard to meet the legal elements of the offence charged. As Susan Blake points out:

> For the litigation lawyer a case will often be concerned with the sorts of questions of fact a journalist asks—who, what, where, when, and how? Effective litigation requires close attention to establishing and analysing the facts relevant to a

123

case, and an ability to understand and address the problems that dealing with facts can present. (Blake, 2015, para 8.01)

Adversarial justice

As its name suggests, adversarial justice rests on the idea that the truth will emerge from two competing narratives of the criminal event. The state presents its case before a neutral finder of fact who has to determine, beyond reasonable doubt, whether the case against the defendant is made out. The defendant has the opportunity of contesting the prosecution case, of disputing the evidence, of questioning the witnesses and of raising potential defences. They may also choose to confess to the crime pre-trial (see Chapter 3) and forego the trial by pleading guilty in exchange for a lesser sentence (see Chapter 8). However, the defendant is under no obligation to do anything – they have the right to put the case against them to proof.

Evidence and the decision to prosecute

At least theoretically, there has to be an initial foundation to the prosecution case. As we have seen in Chapter 6, in England and Wales, for example, a two-stage test operates: a prosecution can only be brought if there is a realistic chance of conviction; and prosecution is judged to be in the public interest. The first criterion is evidential. Prosecutors have to review the evidence collated by (usually) the police and determine the strength of the case. The exercise is speculative. Cases where the initial evidential review suggests a likelihood of conviction can change during the course of a trial. However, this review represents an initial filter: weak cases should not be prosecuted. Ideally this would remove the possibility that innocent individuals face trial, but it cannot. There may, for example, be confession evidence which, at this stage, is indicative of guilt but which may be contested at trial (see Chapter 3). A distinction can be drawn between the evidence and the individual: at this stage, some cases will be brought against innocent individuals (because, for example, prosecution evidence has not been tested at trial), while other cases will be discontinued against guilty people on policy grounds. Two other observations appear relevant. First, in the context of limited resources, the Crown Prosecution Service (CPS) may interpret 'realistic chance of conviction' narrowly: the evidence may have to be compelling rather than suggestive. If this is the case, proceedings may be discontinued against a tranche of factually guilty individuals. Second, the public interest criterion is not wholly irrelevant in a discussion of truth. There may be some individuals who have offended but whom proceedings are not brought against despite strong evidence.

Selective prosecution is justifiable on a number of grounds. Some offences are so trivial that the expense of a trial and the consequences of conviction are disproportionate (this argument is developed in Dingwall and Harding, 1998). In other cases, personal characteristics of the alleged perpetrator suggest limited culpability, which casts doubt about the suitability of criminal proceedings. But these decisions are taken on pragmatic grounds (largely cost) or on penological grounds (punishment is for some reason inappropriate) rather than on concerns about miscarriages of justice. If the sole concern was truth-finding, then the only determinant of prosecution should be the strength of the prosecution case measured by the available evidence. Viewed together, this second stage could be seen as a deliberate policy of withdrawing cases against some factually guilty individuals: if the case against them was not strong, the case should have been withdrawn earlier as there was no realistic prospect of conviction.

The burden and standard of proof

Adversarial justice rests on a presumption of innocence. (This is equally fundamental to many inquisitorial justice systems.) As will be shown later, human rights obligations also require that the UK (as well as many other jurisdictions) ensures that domestic law presumes innocence. In England and Wales, in order to secure a conviction, it is for the prosecution to prove the guilt of the defendant save in limited and prescribed exceptions. In a foundational case of English criminal procedure, this procedure was referred to as the 'golden thread' of English law (*Woolmington* v *DPP* [1935] AC 462), and the situations where a burden would lie with the defence were narrow and tightly defined. Most of the occasions when the defence has a burden to discharge arise after the prosecution has established a *prima facie* case against the accused and he wishes to raise an affirmative defence. Here the defendant would have to discharge what is referred to as an 'evidential' burden – sufficient evidence would have to be adduced to suggest that it is a relevant concern. If the evidential burden is satisfied, the prosecution acquires the legal burden of disproving the defence beyond reasonable doubt.

Not only must the prosecution prove the case against the defendant, but they must do so to the criminal standard of proof – beyond reasonable doubt. In a memorable phrase from *R* v *Lifchus* [1997] 3 SCR 320, the court observed that:

> [The] standard of proof beyond a reasonable doubt is
> ... inextricably linked to that basic premise which is
> fundamental to all criminal trials: the presumption of
> innocence. The two concepts are forever as closely linked
> as Romeo with Juliet or Oberon with Titania ... If the
> presumption of innocence is the golden thread of criminal
> justice then proof beyond a reasonable doubt is the silver
> and these two threads are forever intertwined in the fabric
> of criminal law. (at [27])

When the defence has a burden to discharge, it only needs to satisfy this on the balance of probabilities. Placing the burden of proof on the prosecution and ensuring that the standard of proof remains high are designed to protect the innocent from conviction. Even where there may be substantial prejudicial evidence against the accused, conviction should not follow unless the factfinder is sure of guilt beyond reasonable doubt. The burden and standard of proof are essential due process protections and any attempt to shift the burden to the defence rightly attracts judicial approbation.

The underlying principle that the burden of proof rests on the prosecution recognizes three realities (Roberts, 1995). The first is that, were the burden of proof to rest with the defence, the factfinder would be compelled to convict where they remained unconvinced or uncertain about what the evidence established. As a matter of principle, the state should only convict and punish an individual when a strong case against them can be made out. Second, placing the burden on the prosecution ensures that the defendant has the opportunity to hear and (should they so wish) to rebut the allegations made against them. Finally, though recent years have witnessed sweeping reductions in policing budgets and funding for the CPS, the state can still employ resources denied to most defendants – portraying adversarial justice as a contest between two equal parties masks the fact that one party is better equipped for the fight and has much less to lose than the other.

Woolmington allows for two exceptions: where the accused pleads insanity or where there is a statutory exception to the rule. Both require more comment given the significance of placing a burden of proof on a defendant in criminal proceedings. The law concerning insanity is found in the *M'Naghten Rules*, which pre-date the decision in *Woolmington*. The rules – which show scant regard to modern psychiatric understanding – stipulate that:

[Jurors] ought to be told in all cases that every man is to be presumed to be sane, and to possess a sufficient degree of reason to be responsible for his crimes, until the contrary be proved to their satisfaction; and that to establish a defence on the ground of insanity, it must be clearly proved that, at the time of the committing of the act, the party accused was labouring under such a defect of reason, from disease of the mind, as not to know the nature and quality of the act he was doing; or, if he did know it, that he did not know he was doing what was wrong. (*M'Naghten's Case* (1843) 10 CI & F 200, at p 210)

This does contravene a presumption of innocence, and introduces inconsistency when a defendant seeks to rely on a defence to a criminal charge. Where an individual seeks to rely on an affirmative defence, such as duress, they have to satisfy an evidential burden. Should they do so, it is for the prosecution to prove beyond reasonable doubt that the circumstances of the defence do not apply. This may be expedient: the alternative would be that the prosecution would have to dispel all plausible defences in all cases. What is problematic is why the position should be any different when the potential defence is insanity? An argument that only the defendant can testify as to their thought process at the time the offence occurred is flawed in so far as the prosecution routinely has the burden of proving that the *mens rea* requirements of an offence (for example, that the defendant's actions were intentional) are satisfied. On one level this is a point of academic interest. Insanity is seldom raised as a defence because the disposals available to the court risk a significant deprivation of liberty. However, placing the burden of proof on the defence will also affect the likelihood of the defence being pleaded, and being pleaded successfully.

In fact, as Lord Steyn pointed out in *R* v *Lambert* [2002] 2 AC 535, Parliament has 'frequently and in an arbitrary and indiscriminate manner made inroads on the basic presumption of innocence' (p 569). Ashworth and Blake's (1996) empirical research found that statutory exceptions to the presumption of innocence are not exceptional but are commonplace. Statutes can place a burden on the accused expressly or, more problematically, by implication. The strongest argument for placing a burden on the defence is that, on occasion, it is in a far better position to produce evidence that will help the factfinder arrive at the truth. Sometimes what is asked is not especially onerous; for example, a defendant might be asked to produce a permit to establish that they were permitted to engage in a particular activity. It can also be the case that proving the lawfulness of an activity can be more straightforward than proving that the conduct was illegal. The example of a permit is a good one – the defendant should easily be able to produce one, while it could be time consuming to establish that the defendant did not possess the relevant authority. Ashworth and Blake's (1996) study demonstrates that a principle like that in *Woolmington* may no longer reflect reality due to an increasing political readiness to place burdens of proof on the defence.

In *McIntosh* v *Lord Advocate* [2001] 3 WLR 107, Lord Bingham of Cornhill referred to the judgment of Sachs J of the South African Constitutional Court in *State* v *Coetzee* [1997] 2 LRC 593:

> There is a paradox at the heart of all criminal procedure, in that the more serious the crime and the greater the public interest in securing convictions of the guilty, the more important do constitutional protections of the accused become. The starting point of any balancing inquiry where constitutional rights are concerned must be that the public interest in ensuring that innocent people are not convicted and subjected to ignominy and heavy sentences, massively outweighs the public interest in ensuring that a particular criminal is brought to book ... Hence the presumption of innocence, which serves not only to protect a particular individual on trial, but to maintain public confidence in the enduring integrity and security of the legal system. Reference to the prevalence and severity of a certain crime therefore does not add anything new or special to the balancing exercise. The perniciousness of the offence is one of the givens, against which the presumption of innocence is pitted from the beginning, not a new element to be put into the scales as part of a justificatory balancing exercise. If this were not so, the ubiquity and ugliness argument could be used in relation to murder, rape, car-jacking, housebreaking, drug-smuggling, corruption ... the list is unfortunately almost endless, and nothing would be left of the presumption of innocence, save, perhaps, for its relic status as a doughty defender of rights in the most trivial of cases. (Sachs J, at pp 677–8)

The views of Sachs J are worth contrasting with John Kaplan's application of rational choice theory to legal decision making, discussed in Chapter 6. For Kaplan, and other adherents of utility-based decisions, the seriousness of the offence would be among the factors to be weighed in for the balancing exercise.

In relation to reverse-onus provisions, a series of cases has been taken to the European Court of Human Rights and to appellate courts in the UK. The argument advanced in each case is that the reverse burden conflicts with the right to the presumption of innocence found in Article 6(2) of the European Convention on Human Rights. The European Court of Human Rights, though, has held that the presumption of innocence is not an absolute right and that statutory exceptions, whether express or implied, are permissible provided that they are confined within reasonable limits and balance community interests with the rights of the individual (*Salabiaku* v *France* (1988) 13 EHRR 379; *Telfner* v *Austria* (2001) 34 EHRR 7; *Janosevic* v *Sweden* (2002) 38 EHRR 22). In *Salabiaku* v *France*, the European Court of Human Rights accepted that the European Convention did not prohibit presumptions of fact or law but 'requires states to confine them within reasonable limits which take into account the importance of what is at stake and maintain the rights of the defence' (p 388, para 28).

In *R* v *Lambert* [2002] AC 535, the majority of the Supreme Court found that they did not need to consider the human right point in the context of the particular case. Lord Steyn, however, dissented from the majority view on that question and went on to consider the proportionality of the justification for reversing the burden of proof in regard to the particular offence:

> The basis for this justification is that sophisticated drug smugglers, dealers and couriers typically secrete drugs in some container, thereby enabling the person in possession of the container to say that he was unaware of the contents. Such defences are commonplace, and they pose real difficulties for the police and prosecuting authorities. (p 571)

The English courts have also heard a number of cases where a reverse-onus statutory provision was challenged on the basis of a conflict with the defendant's Article 6(2) right. These are important cases as many concern serious offences but, as the approach taken is highly fact-specific, it can be difficult to discern general patterns. However, some important principles have emerged. *R* v *Lambert* concerned the Misuse of Drugs Act 1971. Lambert was detained by the police at Runcorn railway station in possession of a duffle bag that contained two kilograms of cocaine, with an estimated value of £140,000. Lambert told police he had been paid to pick up the bag but was told it contained scrap gold and had no knowledge or reason to suspect it contained cocaine. He was stopped by the police very soon after collecting the bag and was subsequently charged with possession of a class A drug with intent to supply contrary to section 5(3) of the Misuse of Drugs Act 1971. At his trial at Warrington Crown Court, Lambert accepted that he had been in possession of the drugs but denied knowledge of the drugs. Judge Hale in the summing up to the jury said:

> A person who is in possession of a controlled drug shall be acquitted if he proves that he neither believed nor suspected nor had reason to suspect that the substance in question was a controlled drug. He doesn't have to know the type of drug, but he must prove that he neither believed nor suspected nor had reason to suspect that the substance or product was a controlled drug. Now whenever the criminal law requires a defendant to prove a defence of this type, then he does not have to prove it to the same high standard that the prosecution have to prove their burden. The prosecution has to make you sure of anything that they have to prove. A defendant has a lower standard of proof. Is it more probable than not, on the balance of probability? (p 611)

The jury were not convinced by the defendant's story and brought in a verdict of guilty. Interestingly, Lord Hope speculated on what the jury would have decided had the burden of proving knowledge of the contents of the bag been with the prosecution:

> I think that it is unclear what they would have made of the case if they had been told that proof of knowledge that the bag contained controlled drugs was an essential element of the offence of possession which the prosecution had to prove to the required standard so that they were sure of what was being alleged. (p 578)

Lord Steyn also considered the factual issues in his conclusion:

> My Lords, this is a case of an accused found in possession of two kilograms of cocaine worth over £140,000. It must be comparatively rare for a drug dealer to entrust such a valuable parcel of drugs to an innocent. In any event the

appellant's detailed story stretches judicial credibility beyond
breaking point. (p 575)

In the light of what has been said about narrative and storytelling
in Chapter 6, it is interesting to see a Justice of the Supreme Court
speculate on the limits of trust of 'drug dealers'. Evidence about the
characters of the men who gave Lambert the duffle bag was not heard
at first instance or at the appeal hearings. The truth of whether they
were drug dealers or not was not tested. Nor do we have any evidence
on which to make an assessment of the rarity of drug dealers entrusting
'a valuable parcel of drugs to an innocent'. Lambert's story did not
seem plausible to Lord Steyn; it stretched credibility, but as was argued
in Chapter 6, that is not quite the same thing as demonstrating the
proposition is untrue.

Withdrawing evidence from the factfinder: the example of complainants' previous sexual history

Factfinders are generally trusted to review all available relevant evidence
in order to determine guilt to the criminal standard. But some forms
of evidence are excluded on the basis that the prejudicial effect is
likely to outweigh any probative value. The most contentious example
relates to evidence about complainants' previous sexual history in
sexual offence trials.

Empirical studies conducted with mock juries have shown
consistently that many adverse inferences can be drawn from prior
sexual behaviour with men other than the accused. It was a known
tactic for defence lawyers in the past to question complainants about
their sexual history in an attempt to prejudice the jury into believing
that the complainant's testimony was at odds with her prior sexual
behaviour. Evidence still had to be 'relevant' to be admitted but case
law from this era shows how ready courts were to admit previous sexual
history evidence on the most spurious basis; for example, in *R v Viola*
(1982) 75 Cr App R 125 the defence was allowed to question a young
complainant about previous sexual activity on the supposed basis that
she would never have consented to losing her virginity with a man of
the defendant's age. It is impossible to escape the conclusion that this
line of questioning was in truth a crude attempt to cast doubt on the
complainant's integrity by introducing evidence that had absolutely
no probative value to the present case. This actually is a question of
evidential relevance in so far as any search for the truth has to be
rigorous in excluding evidence that adds very little and which has the

potential to lead to a false conclusion. Yet determinations of relevancy seldom lend themselves to easy resolution and so the current statutory regime is complex.

Section 41(1) of the Youth Justice and Criminal Evidence Act 1999 severely restricts the circumstances where evidence of a complainant's previous sexual history can be admitted at trial. Courts interpret sexual history widely to include, for example, engaging in sexually charged messaging on Facebook (*R* v *D* [2011] EWCA Crim 2305) and taking part in an online quiz about sexual behaviour (*R* v *Ben-Rajab and Baccar* [2012] 1 Cr App R 4). There are four 'gateways' that allow an application to adduce evidence of prior sexual history:

- the evidence or question relates to an issue that is not an issue of consent (section 41(3)(a)); or
- the evidence or question relates to consent and the sexual behaviour is alleged to have taken place at or about the same time as the event in issue (section 41(3)(b)); or
- the evidence or question relates to consent and the sexual behaviour to which the evidence or question relates is so similar to behaviour which, according to the evidence, took place as part of the event or other behaviour by the complainant at about that time that the similarity cannot reasonably be explained as a coincidence (section 41(3)(c)); or
- the evidence or question relates to and rebuts evidence adduced by the prosecution about the complainant's sexual behaviour (section 41(5)); and
- that a refusal of leave might have the effect of rendering unsafe a conclusion of the jury or (as the case may be) the court on any relevant issue in the case.

The final statutory requirement is vital – the evidence or question can only be admitted if it satisfies the requirements in sections 41(3)(a)–(c) or section 41(5) if a failure to admit the evidence or question would render unsafe a conclusion of a jury or the court. Generally, admitting evidence of a complainant's previous sexual history is seen as a way of compromising the truth – and the empirical evidence supports this – but the Act recognizes that achieving justice in an individual case exceptionally does require use to be made of such evidence. In the leading case of *R* v *A (no 2)* [2002] 1 AC 45, Lord Hope referred to evidence that is used for specific reasons, which point to guilt or innocence as opposed to impermissible generalizations about consent.

What, of course, is critical is how the courts interpret the Act. There certainly is the potential for the exceptions to be applied liberally, which would undermine parliamentary intent and place prejudicial evidence before the jury. Two cases concerning the third potential 'gateway' provide a useful contrast.

In *R v White* [2004] EWCA Crim 946, the prosecution alleged that White had met the complainant and returned to her flat where the rape took place. White maintained that the sex was consensual and that he woke to find her stealing his wallet. A fight broke out, after which he left. An application was made by the defence to question the complainant about the fact she had been engaged in sex work for 19 years. The trial judge refused the application. The Court of Appeal upheld the conviction on the basis that being a sex worker had no bearing on whether there was consent. It was not alleged by the defence that White had been a client and so her previous convictions for offences related to prostitution were not sufficiently similar to the circumstances of the charge for the purposes of section 41(3)(c).

The facts in *R v Evans* [2017] 1 Cr App R 13 were different in that the complainant could recall nothing of the incident, which occurred in a hotel bedroom. Evans stated that sexual intercourse had taken place but that it was consensual or that he had reasonable belief that the complainant was consenting. His account included details of particular sexual activity and words spoken by the complainant at the time. He was convicted at trial. The Criminal Cases Review Commission referred the conviction to the Court of Appeal where leave was sought to adduce fresh evidence. Two men alleged that they had sex with the complainant, one before the alleged rape and the other afterwards. Both claimed the activity and the words spoken by the complainant were similar to Evans's account at trial. The Court of Appeal admitted the fresh evidence and allowed the appeal, though with hesitation.

Withdrawing evidence from the factfinder: the defendant's prior character

Empirical research with mock juries has shown that knowledge of past misconduct on the part of the defendant can influence findings of guilt. Mock juries who were told that the defendant had a recent prior conviction for a similar crime were more likely to convict than juries who were unaware of the defendant's past or who were told that the defendant had offended before but that the offence was of a different type. Two factors may explain this. The first is cognitive bias; jurors may attach disproportionate weight to prior misconduct, and this may lead them too readily to the conclusion that past criminality serves as a useful guide to whether the defendant is responsible for the offence before them. Credibility is the second factor. If it is known that the defendant has a criminal past, the jury may be less likely to believe their account. How the law deals with character evidence is central to a fair trial. If evidence that is known to be highly prejudicial and yet of limited value is routinely disclosed, the potential for miscarriages of justice to occur is very real. Anyone with similar previous convictions would, in practice, have to convince the jury that, although they had committed previous similar offences, they had not committed the specific offence under consideration. Jurors, however, may well believe that evidence of past criminality is valuable and would enhance their ability to arrive at the correct conclusion. There are also scenarios where the past misconduct is of such similarity that its probative value simply cannot be ignored, but in such cases the prejudicial effect is manifest and the past conduct may carry as much or more weight than the evidence linking the accused to the crime for which they are being tried.

Before turning to bad character, however, attention needs to be given to how a defendant may seek to adduce favourable evidence of their character into play, presumably in the belief that the jury may draw favourable inferences from it. Denial of the offence is not in itself suggestive of good character (*R v Ellis* [1910] 2 KB 746) – the claim made has to be a positive assertion. Two examples from the case law would be where a defendant testified about their regular attendance at church services and their involvement in religious societies (*R v Ferguson* (1909) 2 Cr App R 250), and a line of questioning designed to lead the jury to conclude that the defendant was a person of integrity who would give up property that they found (*R v Samuel* (1956) 40 Cr App R 8). Good character evidence may be adduced to lend credibility to the defendant's account, though it is impossible to know how much weight is in fact given to it. There is, however, considerable risk attached to raising evidence of good character. By so doing, the defendant 'brings character in' with the consequence that the prosecution may introduce evidence of bad character to counter the potentially misleading impression given. In determining the truth of an incident, therefore, the jury would either know nothing of the defendant's character or would be faced with evidence that presents a supposedly rounded picture of the defendant's character. Whether or not the jury have this evidence is determined by the defendant, meaning that the determination of admissibility – and of whether character evidence should or should not inform the jury's decision – is largely left to the person whose guilt or innocence they are deciding.

It is necessary to briefly consider what amounts to bad character evidence before turning to the situations in which it can be admitted. According to the Criminal Justice Act 2003, it constitutes 'evidence of, or of a disposition towards, misconduct on [the defendant's] part' other than evidence that relates to the offence charged (section 98). Misconduct is also defined in the Act as 'the commission of an offence or other reprehensible behaviour' (section 112(1)). There is no requirement for the earlier offence to be similar, nor any requirement for it to be recent. As was said earlier, mock jury research suggests that juries distinguish between like offences and different offences in making decisions about guilt. Indeed, there is some evidence to suggest that mock jurors may find evidence that shows a dissimilar pattern of prior offending suggestive of innocence, presumably on the basis that the current offence is inconsistent with past behaviour.

According to the Court of Appeal in *R v Renda* [2005] EWCA Crim 2826, reprehensibility denotes 'some degree of culpability or blameworthiness' (at [24]). Obvious examples would include the possession of a DVD in which the defendant was seen engaging in violent and racist behaviour (*R v Norris* [2013] EWCA Crim 712) and evidence that the defendant had previously attacked someone viciously with a chair leg even though they had subsequently been found unfit to plead (*R v Renda* [2005] EWCA Crim 2826). It is equally illuminating to see what is not judged to be reprehensible conduct, and, by implication, conduct that is not seen as being culpable or blameworthy. Evidence of a consensual relationship between the defendant when he was aged 34 and a 16-year-old girl was held not to amount to evidence of bad character in a case involving alleged sexual offences committed against a 13-year-old girl (*R v Manister* [2005] EWCA Crim 2866). Nor was the taking of an overdose following an argument (*R v Hall-Chung* [2007] EWCA Crim 3429).

Section 101(1) of the Criminal Justice Act 2003 lists 'seven gateways' through which evidence of the defendant's bad character may be admitted:

- All parties to the proceedings agree to the evidence being admissible.
- The evidence is adduced by the defendant themselves or is given in answer to a question asked by them in cross-examination and intended to elicit it.
- It is important explanatory evidence.

- It is relevant to an important matter in issue between the defendant and the prosecution.
- It has substantial probative value in relation to an important matter in issue between the defendant and a co-defendant.
- It is evidence to correct a false impression given by the defendant.
- The defendant has made an attack on another person's character.

The journey to beyond reasonable doubt

As we have seen, the archetypal adversarial criminal trial involves the weaving of golden and silver threads. The golden thread of the presumption of innocence together with the silver thread of proof beyond a reasonable doubt produce the fabric of the criminal law. We have seen that there are exceptions where the law may require the defendant to prove some aspect of the defence on the balance of probabilities and there are situations where evidence, which otherwise might assist the decision maker, is withheld, but in most cases the archetype holds good. The question then arises as to the basis on which the factfinders in the criminal trial make their decisions. As Amsterdam and Bruner point out:

> [T]he administration of the law and even much of its conceptualization rests upon 'getting the facts.' Every recognized legal situation (whether problem or solution) is taken to involve a distinctive state of facts (actual or potential). In each situation, some arbiter or agency or adviser is presumed to be able to decide what the facts are, at least for the purposes at hand. Relevant facts, 'found' or hypothetically imagined, are presumed to frame the issue in debate, delimit the choices of action that can be pursued, determine the visitation or the vindication to be authoritatively pronounced. (Amsterdam and Bruner, 2000, pp 110–11)

Kaptein et al (2009) identify the three main approaches to legal proof: statistics, storytelling and logical argument. In the past 50 years there has been a number of writers who have argued for a more statistical and scientific approach to evidence in criminal trials. More recently with the developing possibilities of artificial intelligence (AI), the idea of deciding cases on the basis of algorithms and statistical methods has gained further support. As noted in the previous chapter, in 1991 the Cardozo School of Law hosted a conference on Decision and Inference in Litigation. The conference proceedings were published in the 1991 volume of the *Cardozo Law Review*. The conference took place at a time of a number of important scientific developments with relevance for factfinding in the trial process. Perhaps the most discussed was the emergence of DNA evidence already referred to in the last chapter. With increasing use of expert evidence in trials and the need for factfinders to understand complicated statistics and the nature of probability, there was considerable academic debate as to the basis of decision making in litigation.

Paul Bergman and Al Moore considered the validity of taking a statistical approach in litigation decision making:

> Maria and David, two intrepid skydivers, are about to leap from the belly of an aircraft. David suddenly snaps his fingers, removes his parachute, and prepares to jump.
>
> 'Hey!' yells Maria. 'What are you doing? You can't jump without a parachute – you'll be killed!'
>
> 'Nothing to worry about,' David replies. 'Didn't you read the paper this morning? A new study showed that people's life expectancies are longer than ever.'
>
> Inferential errors are not always as potentially lethal as David's. However, the thought that the Davids of this world sometimes wind up as jurors rather than skydivers has led many theorists to look for methods of minimizing what they regard as triers' tendencies to make inferential errors during the fact-finding process. Some of these theorists have suggested that we might be better off replacing the Davids with clones of the Reverend Thomas Bayes, who just over two centuries ago developed the mathematical formula known as Bayes' Theorem. (Bergman and Moore, 1991, p 589)

Bergman and Moore cite the 1968 article by John Kaplan discussed in the last chapter and refer to others who have argued in favour of adopting a Bayesian methodology in analysing and assessing evidence. They accept that most proponents accept that Bayesian theory or rational choice theory is not the way in which real judges and juries decide cases, but it is the way in which such cases should be decided. It is a similar argument to that put forward for increased use of AI in the criminal process today. Bergman and Moore reject such an approach on the basis partly that decisions in criminal trials are often much more nuanced, dealing with soft, rather than hard, facts. They also point out that:

> Instead of determining what they think happened in a particular case, triers following Bayesian precepts would produce a frequentist decision. That is, they would determine what is most likely to happen in 'cases such as these.' As Bayesian methodology does not produce individualistic judgments, it fails as a theoretical fact-finding model. (Bergman and Moore, 1991, pp 591–2)

In responding to Bergman and Moore, James Brook, Professor of Law at New York Law School, defended a statistical approach to evidence: 'Professors Bergman and Moore insist that jurors make determinations based not on probability assessments, but on their beliefs as to "what really happened" and what really happened "in this particular case"' (Brook, 1991, p 623). Brook drew attention to the case of *Kaminsky* v *Hertz Corporation* 94 Mich App 356, 288 N W 2d 426 (1979), decided by the Michigan Court of Appeals. The case was brought by Joyce Kaminsky who, together with five others, was riding in a Volkswagen south on Highway M-52 in Saginaw County, Michigan. The windshield of her car was struck by a large sheet of ice, which flew off the top of a passing truck. The truck, all agree, was yellow. It bore the distinctive Hertz company logo. The car's windshield was shattered. Kaminsky was the most seriously injured of the passengers, losing her right eye and suffering serious facial lacerations. Along with the other passengers, she brought an action against the Hertz Corporation. It turned out, and it was stipulated at trial, that a truck identified only by its yellow colour and the Hertz logo would not necessarily be one owned by Hertz, or one for which it would otherwise be responsible. Hertz owned approximately 90 per cent of such vehicles. The other 10 per cent were owned by licensees or franchisees or were vehicles sold without removal of the Hertz logo and colours:

> Presented only with these facts, the trial court granted summary judgment to the defendant corporation, concluding in the words of the appellate court that 'a jury could not find ownership in Hertz Corporation and that any verdict for plaintiffs would be based on guess and conjecture.' All in all a pretty poor result for the probabilist camp, we would have to say. And, more to the point, a

very poor result from Kaminsky's point of view. But all is not and was not lost. (Brook, 1991, p 624)

On appeal, the Michigan Court of Appeals reversed. 'In a civil case,' the court opined, 'the quantum of proof required as [sic] a "preponderance of the evidence".' It cannot be said that the preponderance of the evidence showed non-ownership of the truck by Hertz, when the facts stipulated showed 90 percent of the vehicles bearing the Hertz logo are owned by Hertz. (Brook, 1991, p 624)

Whether the court of appeals was 'right' is, for my present point, not really the issue. I must say, however, that in my experience, most people to whom the story of this case has been told have no problem with the ultimate result. (Brook, 1991, p 625)

Brook's approach has similarities to that of Lord Steyn in *R v Lambert* [2002] 2 AC 535. It was unlikely that Lambert was unaware of the content of the duffle bag; it was unlikely that the 'drug dealers' would hand over £140,000 worth of cocaine to 'an innocent'. The probability was high that Lambert knew what the bag contained. Similarly, there was a high probability (90 per cent) that the passing truck in the *Kaminsky* case was owned by Hertz. But probability is not the same as truth. Deciding criminal cases on the basis of statistical analysis and probability theory may be more efficient but it may undermine the legitimacy that the claimed search for the truth provides.

Dispelling doubt through storytelling

Also speaking at the Cardozo conference in 1991 were psychologists Nancy Pennington and Reid Hastie. They had spent the previous 10 years carrying out research into how jurors arrived at their decisions: 'Our conclusion is that the juror is a sense-making information processor who strives to create a meaningful summary of the evidence available that explains what happened in the events depicted through witnesses, exhibits, and arguments at trial' (Pennington and Hastie, 1991, p 519). Pennington and Hastie had found a lack of research into the decision-making process:

Probably the most unified descriptions of the juror's thought processes are mathematical models based on Bayesian probability theory, variants of traditional probability theory, and other algebraic models. However, none of these approaches has dominated legal scholarship or practice and none has been supported as a descriptive model by empirical research on realistically complex juror decision making tasks. (Pennington and Hastie, 1991, p 519)

Their empirical research led them to discover that 'a central cognitive process in juror decision making is story construction' (Pennington and Hastie, 1991, p 520). Their 'storytelling model' comprised three component processing stages:

- evidence evaluation through story construction;
- representation of the decision alternatives by learning verdict category attributes;
- reaching a decision through the classification of the story into the best-fitting verdict category.

In addition, the model made the further claim that the story the juror constructs determines the decision.

In a passage that is redolent of Lord Steyn's views about drug dealers, Pennington and Hastie describe the jury's deliberations in a knife crime case and the interpretation of what it means to carry a knife:

Some jurors (usually from 'better' residential neighborhoods) would not at first accept that a person could carry a knife without intending to do specific harm with it. Other jurors pointed out during deliberation that either they or members of their families regularly carried knives because of the neighborhoods they lived or worked in, even though they had no specific intentions of using the knives. (Pennington and Hastie, 1991, p 556)

Johan van Zyl Steyn, a 69-year-old white male, educated at the Universities of Stellenbosch and Oxford, who had spent much of his working life at the commercial bar, found it unbelievable that a drug dealer would hand over a substantial quantity of cocaine to 'an innocent'. The only credible explanation, consistent with the stories Lord Steyn possessed, was that drug dealers are untrusting fellows and that Lambert knew full well what was in the bag. Any other explanation would not make sense to Lord Steyn. Similarly, those from 'better residential neighbourhoods' do not ordinarily carry knives. They do not have stories that include the legitimate carrying of knives. Their knowledge of the topic comes primarily from news stories and fictional representations. They therefore find it difficult to believe, or find it unbelievable, that someone would carry a knife without intending to do harm with it. The jurors who did not come from the 'better residential neighbourhoods' told themselves different stories; stories that contained instances of people carrying knives for self-defence without any intention of causing harm.

Pennington and Hastie found some evidence that when jurors shared knowledge and experience it could affect the decisions reached but found that there was some evidence to suggest that 'once a juror has committed to a decision, it becomes more difficult for that juror to change stories' (Pennington and Hastie, 1991, p 556). As we have already seen, many cases are decided without any jury deliberation. Where decisions are made by single judges or benches of three magistrates there is limited opportunity for the sharing of knowledge and experience.

Pennington and Hastie conclude their paper by remarking: 'Perhaps the most satisfying characteristic of the Story Model approach for us, as cognitive experimental psychologists, is the extent to which it connects important naturally occurring decision-making phenomena to accounts from the mainstream of modern information processing theories of the mind' (Pennington and Hastie, 1991, p 557).

The debate between the two main opposing analyses of proof in the criminal trial is neatly summarized by John Leubsdorf:

> One, probability analysis, has created a large body of scholarly literature, to which this symposium makes a number of further contributions. Its proponents march under the banners of mathematics, and perhaps under those of science – though if so it is usually a normative rather than a descriptive science. The second means of analysing trials describes litigators as proposing stories for the trier of fact to accept or reject. This approach is a more recent development, though its ancestry can be traced back to classical works on rhetoric. Its advocates tend to favor a more humanistic and literary approach, though they do include among them some people of numbers. (Leubsdorf, 1991, p 455)

Both approaches, the one more normative in nature, the other grounded in human behaviour, conflict with the idea that the criminal trial is about the pursuit of the truth, the whole truth and nothing but the truth. It is either about identifying the most probable and plausible explanation for an event or series of events or about constructing a story that makes the event(s) comprehensible and consistent with a prevailing view of the world.

Stories defence lawyers and defendants tell

The focus of this chapter has primarily been the decision making of the factfinders in the criminal trial. It is worth also considering the role of defence lawyers and defendants. In one of the largest empirical studies of its kind for several decades, Daniel Newman carried out ethnographical research to investigate the relationship between defence lawyers and their clients. In doing so he shed considerable light on the attitudes of defence teams and the role they play in the construction of trial stories. The research was published in *Legal Aid Lawyers and the Quest for Justice* (Newman, 2013). Newman found that while, in interview, lawyers claimed a positive relationship with their clients, participant observation revealed a very different picture. The lawyers were observed treating their clients with wanton disrespect, talking over them and pushing them to plead guilty.

For Newman, attitudes underpin the entire lawyer–client relationship:

> At root, the relationship is a social interaction, an interpersonal encounter premised upon a fundamental 'exchange of knowledge'. Understanding the manner in which lawyers relate to their clients offers a means of comprehending the lawyer's practice as a whole, assessing the foundations so as to pass judgement on the stability of the overall structure. (Newman, 2013, p 40)

Newman's observations revealed that defence lawyers 'seemed to share the opinion that the fundamental character trait of their clients was that they were mentally lacking' (Newman, 2013, p 45). They had a poor view of their client's character. Newman quotes from three solicitors (Newman, 2013, p 47):

> This is just what they're like. They won't accept reality. They think they can live their lives like that [committing crime]. It's a total lack of responsibility. They don't deserve help. (Bob, solicitor, Radford Hope, IC)

These are regular clients. They come from one of our crime families. Crime's a way of life for that kind. (Ed, senior partner, Swining MacSage, IC)

She'll be back. As soon as she needs something, she'll just steal it. It's a way of life. She's bound to activate that suspended sentence. They're all the same. (Leland, solicitor, Radford Hope, IC)

Perhaps most importantly, they did not share their client's story: they believed them to be guilty (Newman, 2013, p 49):

Lawyers from all firms routinely discussed and approached clients as if they were guilty, whether or not they had talked to them or read their file. Sometimes this was based on what the prosecutor told them, others on past experience of that client; it could even be premised on the area in which they lived. Regardless of the reasons, I witnessed each lawyer treat a client as if they were guilty before they had heard their story, as reflected in these examples whereby lawyers had received instructions to proceed to trial:

Believe her? Look at the colour of this file. Never believe a client from there. Did I just say that? Whoops! (Teresa, solicitor, Radcliffe and Musk, IC – at this firm, files were colour-coded for different areas of the city. This one came from a notoriously run-down, working-class, estate)

If there's one person you shouldn't lie to it's your solicitor. But they all do. They all lie! Just lie after lie, like I don't know they did it. (Leland, solicitor, Radford Hope, IC)

He doesn't know lies from truths any more. People like that get to a point where they start believing their own lies and no longer know the truth. (Bob, solicitor, Radford Hope, IC)

Newman's research clearly undermines the idealized view of the adversarial trial where two sides, equally armed, present their argument to enable the factfinder to arrive at the truth. Mike McConville and Luke Marsh draw parallels between the modern criminal justice system and factory farming:

This state practice [of the annexation of criminal justice systems by state-induced guilty pleas], developed in England and Wales and elsewhere, has come to subvert traditional understandings, values, principles and justifications on which those systems, both common law and civilian, were avowedly based. Participants in the process today have become entrapped in an elaborate charade in which they act out prescribed roles, whilst lawyers who invoke traditional process protections and safeguards are exposed to judicial criticism and censure. Romilly's orthodox contention that 'the object of penal laws is the protection and security of the innocent' sounds almost anachronistic. The volte-face in penal rationalisations adopted by judges and prosecutors and increasingly enforced upon defence lawyers is eroding the integrity, both of individual practitioners and of the criminal justice system itself. (McConville and Marsh, 2016, p 100)

Just as defence lawyers may share a narrative that undermines the pursuit of the truth, defendants too can adopt a narrative that may have adverse effects on their prospects of acquittal. There is quite a long tradition in criminology of exploring the stories defendants tell to justify or neutralize their actions. Most famously, perhaps, Sykes and Matza (1957) explored the 'techniques of neutralisation' employed by offenders. More recently, Fiona Brookman (2015) cast light on the stories told by violent offenders. She quotes earlier work:

For example, Presser (2004) interviewed twenty-seven violent male offenders and found that they all claimed an identity as morally decent in the present. How they arrived at such decency varied. Some told a return narrative (from offender back to the good person they were before); others told a stability narrative (of an essentially consistently good person); and, yet others told elastic narratives (stories of change that were contradictory or vague). (Brookman, 2015, p 208)

Brookman then discusses three case studies of violent offenders. The interpretations and conclusions drawn are, however, based on an analysis of a much wider group of violent offenders. Brookman observes that:

[Offenders] generally provide complex narratives of their lives and past acts of violence. They can shift, from one breath to the next, from a gangster narrative to one of vulnerability, or from a narrative of agency and responsibilization to one of structural disadvantage. Oftentimes these narratives seem in conflict, and sometimes they are ... Most of the violent offenders, initially at least, minimized the levels of harm and violence enacted ... When pressed, some talked in detail about how doing harm felt to them in the moment. Put another way, while violent offenders neutralize, excuse, and justify, they may also relive the excitement and pleasures ... While some offenders are more embedded in and committed to a criminal lifestyle and may speak more to gangster discourse, they nevertheless are not hermetically sealed off from wider society and immune from broader discourses. Hence, even the most authentically violent offenders will often present themselves and their violence in ways that are complex and seemingly contradictory. (Brookman, 2015, pp 225–6)

The dissonance between the competing narratives of lawyer, defendant and factfinder can only make the pursuit of truth more elusive. As Amsterdam and Bruner point out:

Law begins, as it were, after narrative. It is shaped in some measure not only by the narrative claims of contending parties in litigation, not only by 'findings of fact' and 'rules of law' announced by judges who have heard testimony and legal argument, but by the stock of familiar categories and story types within which all people in a culture live their lives. It is shaped, too, by adversarial rhetorics. For we almost always tell our stories to convince, not simply to inform. The rhetorics of legal contention and adjudication are a sort of choreography of disputation whose permissible maneuvers are limited both by the law's established precepts of logic and procedure and by the conventions of viable narrative. (Amsterdam and Bruner, 2000, p 283)

The disappearing trial

This chapter has focused on the criminal trial and the extent to which it is the culmination of the criminal process's pursuit of truth. In fact, as has already been discussed in earlier chapters, it is only a minority of potentially criminal incidents that conclude with a contested trial.

McConville and Marsh point to the parallels between plea bargaining and the industrialization of the global meat industry:

> Like factory farming, state-induced guilty pleas are portrayed as an inevitable or required response to uncontrolled demand rather than as a preferred model chosen for its inherent qualities ... The depressing reality of most farming structures is supplanted by nostalgic, comforting images of farms through 'countrified labelling and advertising of animal products'. The ideological functions of imagery recalls Lord Hewart's familiar but solemn mantra that it is in the public interest not only for justice to be done, but to be seen to be done. The UK Ministry of Justice, eager to demonstrate that the state-induced guilty pleas process is 'working' with cost-efficiency programmes designed to deliver a 'simpler, swifter and more transparent service', in fact shrouds from public gaze the reality of its architecture and questionable purpose. (McConville and Marsh, 2016, pp 99–100)

In criminal justice, the 'nostalgic, comforting images of farms' are replaced by images of be-wigged and be-gowned lawyers eloquently arguing before a red-robed judge and 12 members of the jury. Neither image accurately reflects the system. In its report *The Disappearing Trial* (Fair Trials, 2019), the Fair Trials project points to a 300 per cent worldwide increase in trial waiver systems (in the United States, 97 per cent of convictions follow a guilty plea):

> But the trial is starting to disappear. In many parts of the world, trials are being replaced by legal regimes that encourage suspects to admit guilt and waive their right to a full trial. Of the 90 countries studied by Fair Trials and Freshfields, 66 now have these kinds of formal 'trial waiver' systems in place. In 1990, the number was just 19. Once introduced, trial waivers can quickly dominate. In Georgia, for example, 12.7% of cases were resolved through its plea-bargaining system in 2005, increasing massively to 87.8% of cases by 2012. (Fair Trials, 2019, p 1)

Trial waiver schemes are justified on the basis of efficiency and allocation of resources. It is clear that it would not be possible to subject every reported crime to a full criminal investigation and trial:

New York City courts processed 365,000 arraignments in 2013; well under 5 percent of those cases went all the way to a trial resolution. If even a small fraction of those defendants asserted their right to a trial, criminal courts would be overwhelmed. By encouraging poor defendants to plead guilty, bail keeps the system afloat. (Pinto, 2015)

In the next chapter, we consider trial waiver schemes and the pressure to plead guilty in the context of the sentencing process and the implications they have for the pursuit of truth.

8

Truth, Sentencing and Punishment

The contested trial, and the search for truth that takes places in that forum, may be central to popular perceptions of justice. For reasons documented elsewhere in this book, though, an adversarial trial has many deficiencies as a means for discerning the truth surrounding a criminal event. It has also been seen that the trial process is concerned with more than truth-finding and that this function may, on occasion, be subordinated to potentially competing values, for example by excluding potentially incriminating evidence that has been obtained unlawfully (see Chapter 5). The popular belief that a contested trial is the normal means of determining whether an offence occurred and, if so, who bears responsibility, is incorrect. Contested trials are rare. In England and Wales, the majority of offenders admit guilt pre-trial. In most cases, the only thing to be determined in court is the appropriate sentence. This might suggest that factfinding is of limited relevance in the daily life of the criminal courts. Questions of fact, however, remain vital even when a plea of guilty is tendered. An initial task for the court is to determine what precisely the offender is admitting to. This is a factual question (what does the individual accept responsibility for?) as much as it is a legal one (the offence admitted to may not reflect the real gravity of the actual conduct and/or may misrepresent their culpability at the time).

Also of potential relevance are the circumstances surrounding a guilty plea. A court might, for example, seek supporting evidence in order to stop a potential miscarriage of justice. Or a sentencer might differentiate between someone who had no realistic choice but to admit their guilt given the strength of the prosecution case, from someone who admits guilt when there is little incriminating evidence. Finally, the judge must determine the relevance of particular facts in order to impose an appropriate sentence. This assessment might appear to be wholly subjective but determinations have already been made by a Sentencing Council about what 'facts' are relevant to sentencing and how these 'facts' should influence the punishment.

This chapter will consider these three issues: the facts surrounding a guilty plea; how facts inform decisions about offence severity; and the impact sentencing guidelines have on determining an accurate account of the circumstances surrounding an offence. The focus will be on the law in England and Wales, although limited reference will be made to other jurisdictions as there is a marked disparity of approach to some of the issues under discussion. In particular, some legal systems prescribe the factors that should influence judges when arriving at a sentence, which reduces or removes the scope for judges to determine what occurred and what weight to give to competing facts. Elsewhere, judges operate with more freedom. This may be preferable if a just sentence depends on an accurate and balanced picture of the crime. But, as we shall see, competing concerns have to be recognized, if not necessarily accommodated. The perceived need for a consistency of sentencing approach is perhaps the most pressing. First, though, it is necessary to consider issues regarding plea, given the overwhelming proportion of defendants who admit guilt. What the offender is admitting to is the first concern.

Admitting to what?

In the United States, where there is a far more developed and accepted system of charge and plea bargaining, the term 'negotiated justice' is used to describe the process whereby the defence and the prosecution will agree a charge to which the offender will admit guilt (see further Morrison and Bushway, 2007; Johnson et al, 2016; Redlich et al, 2017). Officially, 'charge bargaining' does not exist in England and Wales although more serious charges are dropped on occasion where a willingness to admit guilt to a lesser charge is made known. The way in which violent offences in particular are structured provides plenty of room for manoeuvre. There is in effect a hierarchy of offences determined by the severity of injury and the offender's intent at the time. The most serious non-fatal harm is classified as 'grievous bodily harm' (Offences against the Person Act 1861, sections 18 and 20), which the courts have defined as 'serious harm' (*DPP* v *Smith* [1960] 3 WLR 546). CPS charging standards listed injuries that would ordinarily fall within this category (for example a broken limb) but the standards had no legal force and have since been revised. Sitting below 'grievous bodily harm' in terms of injury to the victim is 'actual bodily harm', which again is not defined in the Offences against the Person Act 1861, section 47, but which has been interpreted by the courts to mean injury that is more than 'transient and trifling' (*R v Donovan* [1934] 2 KB 498). (The offence descriptor is clumsy as it suggests that there is a form of non-existent bodily harm.) The Crown Prosecution Service (CPS) provided examples of injuries that would usually be charged as 'actual bodily harm', an example of which would be extensive bruising. An individual who has allegedly caused 'grievous bodily harm' may make it known that they would be willing to admit to assault occasioning 'actual bodily harm' and the CPS may accept this plea rather than continue with the more serious charge.

The motivation for the offender is obvious – they are likely to receive a lesser penalty – but an over-stretched and under-resourced prosecution service may also find offers of this nature attractive. Punishment, though, should reflect the seriousness of the offence that was committed and not the offence that was admitted to, unless one takes a very legalistic position. It will be shown later in the chapter that a sentence in England and Wales should depend on the seriousness of the offence, which is calculated with reference to the harm caused and the offender's culpability (Sentencing Act 2020, section 63). Admitting to a lesser offence means that the seriousness of the offence will not be reflected in the sentence. Taking the example before, admitting causing 'actual bodily harm' to the victim when the injuries were more severe means that the sentence will be unduly lenient.

A variant of this is for the defendant to accept that they caused the harm but to dispute the intent. There are two offences that broadly cover 'grievous bodily harm' (Offences against the Person Act 1861, sections 18 and 20), the primary (but not the only) distinction being the offender's intention at the time the harm was inflicted. The more serious of the two offences (section 18) – which carries a potential life sentence – demands intent on the part of the offender. The lesser offence (section 20) – which carries a maximum penalty of five years' imprisonment – does not. In neither case is the maximum penalty likely to be imposed, but the difference in sentence is likely to be marked (Sentencing Council, 2011a, 2011b). Admitting to the lesser offence may prove expedient, particularly if there is little doubt that the injury caused was severe. Personal culpability is also relevant to the determination of how serious an offence is (Sentencing Act 2020, section 63(a)) and so a charge bargain of this nature can also result in the offender receiving an unduly lenient sentence.

These examples relate to negotiations over charge but it is also possible that an offender will negotiate over factual involvement. Gang-related offending, to take an example, is viewed as especially serious when it comes to sentencing and will ordinarily result in the sentence being increased (Sentencing Council, 2019). Exceptionally, it could make the difference between a custodial sentence and a community punishment. Gang leaders can expect to be dealt with particularly harshly and it may be that an individual would admit guilt on the condition that it is accepted that their involvement in the gang was peripheral. Once again, this distortion has the effect of minimizing the offender's culpability and ensuring that the sentence does not reflect the actual gravity of the offence.

The most honest way of viewing 'charge bargaining' or 'fact bargaining' is to accept that they expedite the criminal justice process (see Chapter 10). Because it minimizes the seriousness of the offence and leads to disproportionate punishment, it appears unjust and, perhaps, slightly tawdry. Ultimately, it rewards a lie. What it exposes is that people are not necessarily being sentenced and punished for what they have done. Even if someone who pleaded guilty to assault occasioning actual bodily harm received the 'correct' sentence for assault occasioning actual bodily harm, they did not receive the 'correct' penalty if they actually inflicted grievous bodily harm. Distorting the offence in this way means that many offenders are being sentenced incorrectly even if the sentencing guidelines are followed meticulously.

The circumstances surrounding the plea

Admitting guilt pre-trial attracts an automatic sentence discount in England and Wales. The difference in sentence can be profound: pleading guilty can make the difference between a custodial sentence and a community disposal (Sentencing Council, 2017a, E1). Depending on the stage in the proceedings where the offender makes known his intention to plead guilty, there is a maximum sentence discount of a third (Sentencing Council, 2017a, D1). The official rationale for rewarding guilty pleas is largely administrative. According to the relevant sentencing guideline, a guilty plea 'reduces the impact of the crime upon victims', 'saves victims and witnesses from having to testify' and 'saves public time and money on investigations and trials' (Sentencing Council, 2017a, B). These are valid concerns but they are generic and have no bearing on the offence for which the offender is being sentenced. This might explain why remorse is not seen as relevant to a plea discount but is a distinct ground for mitigation (Sentencing

Council, 2019). Providing a powerful incentive to admit guilt could pressurize defendants into confessing when the evidence against them is weak or they have an arguable defence (Dervan and Edkins, 2013; Blume and Helm, 2014; Helm, 2019). The guideline stresses that a defendant must not be encouraged to admit guilt – the defendant is at liberty to put the prosecution case to the test (Sentencing Council, 2017a, B). Nonetheless, recognizing that the defendant has the right to put the prosecution case to the test but with the caveat that, if it is exercized unsuccessfully, the consequence will be detrimental, must challenge the notion that a defendant should be at liberty to hear the case against them and provide evidence in their defence if they so wish (Gilchrist, 2011; Lippke, 2014).

Two factors are relevant when a court decides how to sentence an offender who has pled guilty (Sentencing Act 2020, section 73(2)):

- the stage in the proceedings at which the offender indicated their intention to plead guilty;
- the circumstances in which the indication was given.

The first factor follows from the justifications for rewarding a guilty plea outlined earlier: the sooner someone admits guilt, the greater the public benefit and, potentially, victims' suffering is also dependent on when they are made aware that they will not be called upon to testify. What, though, does the second factor relate to?

A traditional justification for rewarding a guilty plea was that it evidenced remorse. In that context, the surrounding circumstances make a great deal of difference. If the evidence against the offender is overwhelming, the inference that a guilty plea demonstrates remorse lacks credibility. In contrast, where incriminating evidence is scant, a confession followed by a guilty plea may lead to an inescapable conclusion that the offender genuinely regrets their behaviour. Section 73(2) of the Sentencing Act 2020 suggests that a guilty plea needs to be contextualized. However, the sentencing guideline (Sentencing Council, 2017a) contradicts this: 'The benefits apply regardless of the strength of the evidence against an offender. The strength of the evidence should *not* be taken into account when determining the level of reduction' (emphasis in original).

Two seemingly contradictory dangers then arise. The first is that it increases the potential for a miscarriage of justice if someone admits guilt in the absence of a robust prosecution case. The onus remains on the defence to submit that there is no case to answer, but, given the increased sentence that would follow conviction, pleading guilty may appear preferable (Dervan and Edkins, 2013). Conversely, if someone admits guilt early in the process in the face of compelling evidence, that may result in a disproportionately lenient sentence being imposed (Galoob, 2017).

Automatically rewarding guilty pleas has had the effect of categorizing 'remorse' and 'assisting with the investigation' as distinct grounds of mitigation. This could be defended as the reasons why a guilty plea and remorse should result in a lesser sentence differ according to the Sentencing Council. Rewarding a guilty plea is justified on policy grounds relating primarily to expense (though the beneficial impact on victims and witnesses is also cited). Remorse and assisting the authorities, however, speak to the offender's post-offence culpability. The next section will show why this is of importance in determining an appropriate sentence in England and Wales.

Truth and the sentencing decision

The importance of quantifying offence severity

Calculating the seriousness of an offence is paramount in all sentencing decisions as fairness dictates that there is commensurability between the gravity of an offence and the penalty. Penal proportionality matters both in theory and in practice, particularly in those criminal justice systems that prioritize retribution as a sentencing objective. Unlike other sentencing objectives, such as deterrence or rehabilitation, retribution seeks no consequential benefit from punishment (Oldenquist, 1988). The penalty is no more than a deserved response to the offender's criminality (von Hirsch and Ashworth, 2005). A deserved penal response is one that is proportionate to the seriousness of the offence. This seemingly straightforward requirement necessitates two interlinked calculations. How serious is the offence? And how does one reflect that severity in a proportionate penalty? Both questions are complex if the exercise is to be meaningful. Both questions are also vital – a sentence that fails to reflect the seriousness of the offence, regardless of whether it is too lenient or too harsh, is disproportionate and offends the essential retributive principle of matching offence severity to penal outcome. How a crime is portrayed has to be accurate if the measurement of the seriousness of the offence is to have value.

Sentencing decisions in England and Wales are meant to accommodate various objectives: punishing the offender; protecting the public; reducing crime, including via deterrence; rehabilitating the offender; and recompensing the victim (Sentencing Act 2020, section

57(2)). These aims may conflict: a sentence designed to rehabilitate an offender, for example, may look very different from one whose purpose is to protect the public from potential harm. Dingwall (2008), though, has argued that the Criminal Justice Act 2003, which listed these factors for the first time, implicitly prioritized retribution in two ways: first, due to the structure of the Act and, in particular, the tests that determine whether or not particular punishments can be imposed; and second, through the structure of sentencing guidelines, which the courts are compelled to follow (Sentencing Act 2020, section 59(1)). Questions of truth arise in both of these contexts. This section will focus on measuring offence severity. The relevance of sentencing guidelines will be considered in a separate section later in the chapter.

Although the Sentencing Act 2020 provides various justifications for sentencing, and demands that each should inform all sentencing decisions, it is apparent that the severity of the offence is central to the statutory framework. Section 63 of the Act specifies the factors that are relevant when calculating offence severity:

> Where a court is considering the seriousness of any offence, it must consider–
> (a) the offender's culpability in committing the offence, and
> (b) any harm which the offence–
>   (i)   caused,
>   (ii) was intended to cause, or
>   (iii) might foreseeably have caused.

Both the offender's culpability in committing the offence and the harm that was caused, might have been caused or that the offender intended to cause have to be determined – this constitutes a truth-finding exercise. Earlier chapters have highlighted a number of evidential risks. Offenders, victims and witnesses can be mistaken or confused even though there may be no wilful deception. Partial accounts can also mislead. Ultimately, assessments of an offender's culpability are often highly subjective, in part because of a lack of independent and verifiable evidence.

The Sentencing Act 2020 states that the first thing that must be considered is the offender's culpability in committing the offence. Some facts, such as the age of the offender, are easy to ascertain. Others may be highly contested. Consider two assault scenarios. In the first, the offender claims that he had been provoked by the victim and, in the second, the offender maintains that he had used disproportionate force to defend himself from the victim. Provocation (now technically loss of control; Coroners and Justice Act 2009, section 54) can only act as a partial defence to murder in English law but especially severe provocation can be considered as a mitigating factor in cases of non-fatal violence (Sentencing Council, 2011b, 2011c). (As murder carries a mandatory life sentence, the only way in which the sentence can be mitigated is to afford a partial defence.) Proportionate self-defence can act as a defence to fatal and non-fatal violence (Criminal Justice and Immigration Act 2008, section 76). Disproportionate self-defence can be treated as mitigation (Sentencing Council, 2011b, 2011c). One might suppose that a sentencer would have more sympathy for the victim of a physical attack who retaliated excessively than to someone who responded violently to a non-violent provocation. It may well be the case, however, that the same incident could be presented in two ways. Deciding whether someone was responding to a provocative comment or to an initial strike could be near impossible, especially if there were no independent witnesses or if the witness testimony is uncertain. Regardless, a judgment about culpability has to be taken and this will inform the punishment.

Past criminality is seen to have a bearing on culpability. Where the person being sentenced has a prior conviction for a similar offence, this should have the effect of increasing the sentence. If the offender's prior record demonstrates an ongoing pattern of dishonest behaviour, for example, this should affect any decision about their culpability (Sentencing Act 2020, section 65(2)). From a theoretical stance, this is deeply problematic as the offender has already been punished for these offences and relying on these convictions to augment the sentence for the current offence means that there is an element of double punishment (see Roberts, 2008; Bagaric, 2014; Hester et al, 2018). But, on a more prosaic level, the court will have to review the facts of these earlier offences, so far as they are known, to determine both how relevant they are to the current case and, once this assessment has been made, the effect on the sentence.

If the primary objective of sentencing is not retribution, taking account of prior criminality makes far more sense. For example, logic suggests that punishment must escalate incrementally if the purpose is to deter a prolific offender who refuses to desist (Jacobs, 2010). Prior record would also appear to be highly important if a judgment is being made about whether society needs protection from a potentially high-risk offender (Hamilton, 2015). However, risk-based sentencing in England and Wales remains exceptional and the majority of sentences are calculated on the basis of proportionality. Prior record should then play a minimal role in determining culpability but the Sentencing Act

2020 demonstrates a governmental belief that recidivism should be punished, which means that sentencers must make judgments about the facts of previous offences as well as the one for which the offender is being punished.

Calibrating the seriousness of the offence is vital as, under the Sentencing Act 2020, each potential punishment depends on an assessment of offence severity. There are exceptions, but a discretionary prison sentence can only be imposed if '(a) the offence, or (b) the combination of the offence and one or more offences associated with it, was so serious that neither a fine alone nor a community sentence can be justified for the offence' (Sentencing Act 2020, section 230(2)). If this threshold is satisfied, the term that is imposed must be the shortest that 'in the opinion of the court is commensurate with the seriousness of (a) the offence or, (b) the combination of the offence and one or more offences associated with it' (section 231(2)). Similarly, a court cannot pass a community sentence 'unless it is of the opinion that (a) the offence, or (b) the combination of the offence and one or more offences associated with it, was serious enough to warrant such an order' (section 204(2)). A court must also ensure that the amount of a fine (the most common punishment) 'reflects the seriousness of the offence' (section 125(1)). If the seriousness of the offence is misrepresented, the 'wrong' sentence may be imposed. Unduly lenient or unduly severe penalties arise then from a flawed factual assessment of the crime as much as from the conceptual difficulties of determining how calculations of offence severity or punitive proportionality are made. Sentencing guidelines, which will be considered in the next section, can give the impression of accepted wisdom through clarity of expression. Issues of contention, though, are seldom far away.

'Facts' and the impact of sentencing guidelines

England and Wales have an increasingly developed system of sentencing guidelines issued by an independent Sentencing Council. The Council is autonomous and comprised of individuals from various professional backgrounds in the criminal justice system, most of whom have acted in a judicial capacity. Courts 'must ... follow any sentencing guidelines which are relevant to the offender's case' (Sentencing Act 2020, section 59(1)(a)) and 'must, in exercising any other function relating to the sentencing of offenders, follow any sentencing guidelines which are relevant to the exercise of the function' (section 59(1)(b)) unless the court is satisfied that it would be contrary to the interests of justice to do so. How sentencing guidelines are framed is, therefore, central to any understanding of the sentencing process in this jurisdiction.

Sentencers maintain (correctly) that every case is unique. This is, in effect, a plea to recognize factual distinctions and to provide scope for judicial discretion so as to accommodate difference. The legislation does not compel sentencers to follow a relevant guideline; there is a residual power to depart from a guideline where following it 'would be contrary to the interests of justice' (section 59(1)). It is impossible to know how often judges depart from a guideline on this basis, but the Sentencing Act 2020 provides legitimate scope to do so. What we do not know is what facts make this course of action acceptable to the judiciary.

Guidelines take distinct forms. The majority are offence-specific. Others prescribe principles about sentencing particular categories of offender (for example, children and young people: Sentencing Council, 2017b) or generic sentencing issues such as determining the effect of a guilty plea (Sentencing Council, 2017a). This section will assess the impact of sentencing guidelines on issues of fact and truth. In order to do so, attention will be given first to the generic guideline on determining offence seriousness as this provides a detailed list of factors that are deemed relevant to assessing the gravity of an offence. After that, by way of example, the offence-specific guideline for benefit fraud (an offence requiring dishonesty) will be considered.

The Sentencing Council (2019) recently issued an overarching guideline on the principles of sentencing. The reach of the guideline is deliberately wide: it is designed to be read alongside offence-specific guidelines and used for offences lacking specific guidance. It starts by identifying four statutory factors that must increase the sentence: the offender has relevant previous convictions; the offence was committed while the offender was on bail; the victim was an emergency worker; and the offence was motivated by hostility based on religion, race, disability, sexual orientation or transgender identity. In effect, Parliament has declared that these facts are relevant to all sentencing decisions and, where present, can only have the effect of increasing the sentence. Does a fact, though, always carry the same meaning? To take an example, it may well be highly relevant that an assault victim was a paramedic tending to a patient, but does it follow that this finding is universal? In some cases, the victim's professional status may be highly pertinent and should rightly inform an assessment of offence severity but, in other cases, the relevance of the victim's occupation may be less apparent. The point is not that a victim's occupation is inherently irrelevant, it is that the relevance varies and the statutory provision does not reflect this. If sentencing is about reflecting offence severity in a proportionate sentence (see earlier), then restricting what can be considered and restricting the effect that a particular fact can have on the overall calculation is regrettable. What lies behind this list of statutory aggravating factors is a policy determination that offending in certain contexts is always more culpable and a belief that this should be stated explicitly in statute.

The Sentencing Council provides an additional 23 aggravating and 17 mitigating factors. Examples of the aggravating factors include:

- The offence was committed under the influence of alcohol or drugs.
- The offence was committed as part of a group.
- There was evidence of planning.
- The offence was committed in a domestic setting.
- The offence is prevalent.

Two of the aggravating factors are particularly relevant to a discussion about how truth should inform sentencing. Offenders who blame others incorrectly for the crime are seen to be especially culpable. The potential harm caused by lying here is self-evident and so treating this as an aggravating factor is appropriate even though the dishonesty occurs after the offence has been committed. There is an interesting argument to be had about whether this dishonesty relates to the offender's culpability or to the potential harm caused by the claim; there would have been an additional victim if the wrong person had been convicted following the offender's lie. Deflecting the blame deceptively can be viewed as the polar opposite of admitting guilt. Rather than admitting responsibility, or simply denying responsibility (which could be viewed as a morally neutral response), there is a deliberate attempt to wrongly attribute and a disregard for the fate of the person now subject to police attention.

In effect, this creates a hierarchy of dishonesty: if an offender lies about their whereabouts at the time of the offence, for example, this will not impact on their sentence, whereas if they dishonestly claim that someone else committed the offence, they will receive a harsher punishment. The Sentencing Council also states that actions taken by the offender after the event, such as attempting to cover up the crime or conceal evidence, must be treated as aggravation. Again this appears to relate to honesty but, unlike lying about the culprit, this should perhaps be viewed as natural post-offence conduct and it is difficult to see why taking measures to avoid detection should attract an enhanced penalty.

Integrity is central to many of the mitigating factors listed (Sentencing Council, 2019). A lack of previous convictions has long been seen as one of the most powerful forms of mitigation and can reduce a sentence significantly. 'Good character' is a more nebulous personal characteristic but it is clear from case law that it can relate to meritorious behaviour prior to the offence as well as to exceptional conduct between the offence and the sentence (see also Chapter 10). As with the first-time offender, the claim is that culpability should be viewed in the round, and that the criminal conduct was unprecedented or, at least, atypical. Good character will not benefit the serially dishonest but character does not simply relate to honesty. Someone with a history of violence would also struggle to convince the court that he was of previous good character. Further mitigating factors that indicate honesty include self-reporting the crime to the police and cooperating fully with the investigation (Sentencing Council, 2019).

In order to scrutinize more fully how the courts deal with dishonesty when passing sentence, it is instructive to review the sentencing guideline for benefit fraud (Sentencing Council, 2014). There is no specific offence of benefit fraud in England and Wales but those who engage in this activity can be convicted of several offences (Fraud Act 2006, section 1; Social Security Administration Act 1992, section 111A; Social Security Administration Act 1992, section 112; Tax Credits Act 2002, section 35; Theft Act 1968, section 17). As was mentioned earlier, there are statutory aggravating factors that a court must take into account regardless of the offence, including whether the offender has relevant previous convictions. In order to assess the weight that should be given to prior offending, the guidelines state that the nature of the prior offence(s) and the time that has elapsed since the last offence are relevant. This gives courts latitude. Courts will not just consider offences that are identical to the present conviction. Some prior convictions clearly have no relevance whatsoever. Perhaps what the courts look for is a pattern of similar (as opposed to identical) offending. Dishonesty is a characteristic that links many property offences of varying degrees of severity. It is a requirement of handling stolen goods (Theft Act 1968, section 22(1)), theft (Theft Act 1968, section 1), robbery (Theft Act 1968, section 8) and most burglaries (Theft Act 1968, section 9) as well as the fraud offences listed earlier. It would presumably be appropriate for a judge to consider prior convictions for any property offence involving dishonesty; this will often be damning as many minor property offenders have extensive criminal records (although fraud has one of the lowest reconviction rates: Ministry of Justice, 2019, Table A4).

A separate and distinct list of aggravating factors for benefit fraud is provided in the guideline. Some of the factors relate to the offender's integrity. Features that aggravate the offence could be characterized as those which make a dishonest offender an especially dishonest offender. These aggravating factors include: the claim was fraudulent from the outset; the length of time over which the offending was committed; the number of false declarations made; whether there were attempts to conceal evidence; and whether the offender placed the blame knowingly on an innocent person.

The benefit fraud guideline is unusual in that few of the aggravating factors relate to the harm of the offence (although courts must take account of whether the proceeds of the fraud were used to fund a lavish lifestyle and whether there was damage to a third party). It is important to remember that dishonesty is integral to fraud – all those sentenced for benefit fraud offences were found by the courts to have been dishonest or admitted that their behaviour was dishonest. What the guideline is in effect trying to do is calibrate the individual's dishonesty in order to arrive at a proportionate penal response. Can one talk sensibly of a continuum of dishonesty? (Just as all lies are lies, all liars are liars.) An alternative way of framing this would be to acknowledge that the offender's behaviour in committing the offence was (deliberately) dishonest. Dishonesty (among other offence requirements) determines criminal liability. But the sentencing concern is broader and relates to culpability. If someone's dishonesty is repeated or is designed not only to obtain money but also, vicariously, to risk an innocent party, the offender's culpability is magnified. Someone who commits benefit fraud is dishonest but some benefit fraudsters are more culpable than others, and in a desert-based sentencing system deserve a more severe sanction.

What is the effect of sentencing guidelines on the search for truth at the sentencing stage? Facts surrounding the offence and the offender are filtered twice. First, statute states that some facts must augment the sentence if they are present. Second, guidelines provide at both a generic and an offence-specific level detailed lists of facts that sentencers must take account of when determining a sentence (Sentencing Council, 2019). The guidelines do not exclude other facts that the court may consider to be relevant as aggravation or mitigation, but many facts are now deemed *prima facie* relevant. It is true that the weight to be attached to these facts is not generally specified but it is suggested that the process of identification and demarcation affects the way in which these facts are interpreted. Familiarity can suggest that questions of relevance and impact are resolved when they are not. Similarly, the clarity with which guidelines are presented can hide the reality that the classifications can be suspect or debatable. To take one example, the generic guideline on offence seriousness (Sentencing Council, 2019) states that an offence is always more serious if the offender was under the influence of drugs or alcohol at the time. The consequence is that a violent drunk will always receive a harsher sentence than someone who inflicts similar violence sober, even though, in some cases, intoxication may help frame the offence. The argument is not that sober violence is worse than drunken violence, merely that the guidelines do not allow for the fact that sometimes sober violence may be more culpable. Nuance is forfeited in the pursuit of clarity.

There is an interesting subtext. It is sometimes argued that the benefit of clear sentencing guidelines is that it leads to a consistency of approach – like sentences are imposed for like offences. The way in which this is supposedly achieved is to identify which facts are relevant – like offences are those with like facts. But the artificial and selective nature of this exercise minimizes the importance of other facts that should properly inform the sentence: through a process of selection and prioritization, the truth is distorted and the criminal event is presented in a skewed way. Sentencers can depart from the sentencing guidelines if it is felt that compliance would be 'contrary to the interests of justice' (Sentencing Act 2020, section 59(1)). One cannot know how often judges rely on this provision (but they would be acutely aware that a decision to do so could be challenged on appeal). Perhaps of more interest, is the way in which the guidelines allow courts to consider additional aggravating and mitigating factors. This means that overall assessments of offence severity may be more individualistic and sophisticated than the guidelines would suggest.

Another unknown is how the existence of detailed and prescriptive sentencing guidelines has changed the way in which defence lawyers frame pleas in mitigation. Pleas in mitigation have always been formulaic. Guidelines now provide a template on how best to present a case by highlighting facts that are recognized explicitly as mitigation and listing aggravating factors that it would be wise not to draw attention to. Pleas in mitigation have always had the potential to mislead, as the story presented is partial and possibly exaggerated. What has changed is that there is now an 'accepted' view on how certain facts should be treated and so it is easier to construct a compelling (if inaccurate) narrative – the intoxicated assailant mentioned earlier would be well advised not to bring his inebriation to the court's attention.

Victims' perceptions and the sentencing process

A final issue that must be considered is the extent to which current sentencing processes enable victims' narratives to be heard. As we shall see in Chapter 9, it has been argued that the current model of adversarial justice fails victims (as well as offenders). One of the key objections is that the forum is ill-designed to allow the truth to emerge once guilt has been admitted or established. Victims, therefore, can feel that their experience of the offence and of its aftermath is not given the attention warranted. If, for the reasons outlined earlier, a deserved sentence should take account of the harm caused (Sentencing Act 2020, section 63(b)), this is an unwelcome limitation. Subjective experience is relevant to harm (and likely harm) and should inform any assessment of the gravity of an offence.

Victims can document the effect of a crime by providing a Victim Personal Statement (known in most jurisdictions as a Victim Impact Statement), which the victim can read out in court, have someone else read out on their behalf, or provide as a written statement (College of Policing et al, 2018, para 22). The official guidance notes:

> When assessing the nature and seriousness of the offender's actions, courts will take into account the physical, emotional and financial harm caused to a victim or his or her family. Whilst the court is aware of the likely impact of most offences, the VPS [Victim Personal Statement] can help them understand better how they apply to the particular case before them. In other words, it can help them understand how the crime has affected the victim. (College of Policing et al, 2018, para 40)

Having recognized why the victim's narrative is important, the guidance lists what they may include in their statement:

- any physical, financial, emotional or psychological injury they have suffered and/or any treatment they have received as a result of the crime;
- if they feel vulnerable or intimidated;
- if they no longer feel safe;
- the impact on their family;
- how the quality of their life has changed on a day-to-day basis;
- if they need additional support, for example, if they are likely to appear as a witness at the trial;

- the ongoing impact of the crime on their lives (College of Policing et al, 2018, para 32).

Expectations have to be managed as such a statement is likely to be one factor among many that determine the sentence. Sentencing remarks can sometimes make brief and selective mention of Victim Impact Statements, which risks victims feeling marginalized. Research suggests that the statements have not made victims more satisfied with the criminal justice process (Davis and Smith, 1994).

Misrepresenting the sentence: the length of determinate custodial terms

Most prison sentences in England and Wales are determinate (Office for National Statistics, 2019, Table Q5.4). The prisoner's release date is known at the time that the sentence is passed. Offenders seldom serve the full term in custody; having served a proportion of the sentence in prison, they are released and serve the remainder of the term on licence. This practice appears disingenuous and has led to calls for 'truth in sentencing' whereby those sentenced to determinate sentences serve the whole term in prison. Automatic release (on licence) was a pragmatic response to the pressure facing the prison system at a time when the number of people in custody was rising. Releasing prisoners part-way through their sentence circumvented the need to either restrict the number of people being sentenced to custody or to address escalating sentence lengths, both of which would have faced political opposition. Masking the fact that those serving determinate prison sentences do not serve their full term in custody is more a question of transparency than honesty – no one is claiming that they do. But a sense that the public is being misled lingers.

Public confidence is jeopardized through duplicity so the anger felt when an offender is released having served only part of their term is understandable. There would also appear to be political mileage in assuaging this perceived injustice. The Prime Minister has recently expressed the view that prisoners should serve their full term in custody (Hope, 2019), despite the fact that the prison system would be unable to cope. Other jurisdictions have passed legislation designed to provide greater transparency. Canada introduced a Truth in Sentencing Act in 2009, while the stated objective of the Sentencing Act 1989 in New South Wales was 'to promote truth in sentencing by requiring convicted offenders to serve in prison (without any reduction) the minimum or fixed term of imprisonment set by the court' (section 3(a)).

Recognizing the victim's voice in parole decisions: a new paradigm of inclusivity?

The parole board is responsible for determining whether approximately 26,000 prisoners a year should be released from custody (Parole Board, 2019, p 16). The statutory test requires the board to decide whether the individual's risk can be 'safely managed in the community' (Criminal Justice Act 2003, section 239(1)(b)). Parole boards have the legal status of courts; however, hearings are not held in public, evidence (which is often of a sensitive nature) is not made public, and release decisions are not routinely reported. Parole boards are not tasked with deciding whether the time served is an adequate punishment for the crime committed. Instead, they undertake a risk assessment. As release is a part of the sentencing process, it is necessary to consider how the board deals with alternative accounts of the risk posed. The task is different from that of the sentencing court in that the facts relating to perceived risk (which may include disputed evidence of past behaviour and of the crime itself) are evaluated. Determinations of harm caused by the offence (where the victim's narrative is valuable) and culpability when the offence was committed (where the offender's account, among those of others, may have relevance) took place before the sentence was passed. Assessing culpability and assessing risk are distinctive undertakings, and the conclusions can vary. A highly culpable offender may pose a low risk of future harm, and *vice versa*. Truth matters to both decisions, but for different reasons.

What evidence does the parole board have at its disposal when making a risk assessment? Some decisions are taken purely on the basis of evidence contained in the case dossier. If there is a hearing, the prisoner may provide oral testimony to the panel. This will be supported by evidence from individuals who have observed and worked with the offender in custody and, perhaps, expert psychiatric assessments. Victims have no opportunity to feed into the process. The purpose of victim participation is perhaps less obvious at parole than at sentence as the focus has shifted from an assessment of harm and culpability (which, for the reasons discussed earlier, require subjective experience to be included) to an assessment of risk (which requires expert opinion). To a victim, though, a parole decision may cause alarm – after all, the offender is not being sent to prison, but being released back into the community. Historically, some victims have not been informed that the offender is being considered for parole or that release has been granted. The covert way in which parole operated in England and Wales also meant that the process did not receive the level of academic scrutiny that it merited.

The infamous case of *R (on the application of DSD and NBV & Ors) v The Parole Board of England and Wales & Ors and John Radford* [2018] EWHC 694 (Admin) reviewed how parole boards should use evidence to inform release decisions. Radford, formerly known as John Worboys, was an exceptionally prolific sex offender dubbed the 'black cab rapist' due to the distinctive pattern of his offending. All of his victims, of whom there were in excess of 100, were lone female passengers in his taxi. Radford would produce a wad of cash, which he claimed he had won, and invite his victims to celebrate with him. The drink he provided was laced with sedatives. Radford was sentenced to Imprisonment for Public Protection. This is a form of indeterminate sentence. (Although Imprisonment for Public Protection was abolished in 2012, almost two thousand prisoners are still serving it, the vast majority having failed to convince the parole board that their risk can be managed safely in the community.) Nine years after having been sentenced, Radford became eligible for parole. His case was considered by a panel who reviewed a large dossier and heard testimony from Radford. The board concluded that his risk could be safely managed in the community provided extensive licence conditions were attached.

The ensuing judicial review made legal history: it was the first time in England and Wales that a victim successfully challenged a parole board decision to release. Many aspects of the ruling are legally significant but will be glossed over here so that the issues relating to (dis)honesty on the part of the offender and the relevance of victims' opinions can be developed. The first ground for appeal was that the decision taken by the parole board was 'unreasonable'. While the decision was 'surprising' and 'concerning', the High Court concluded that it could not be regarded as 'unreasonable' as the board had considered a thick dossier of expert evidence, which included expert psychiatric opinion that Radford's risk could be managed in the community (at [130]). Moreover, the panel had questioned Radford and, although the court recognized that he was someone who was inherently manipulative, they were satisfied that the board would have been aware of this (at [131]). Radford may have tried to mislead the board, in other words, but the High Court held that it was for the parole board to assess the probity of his evidence.

Radford had been convicted of multiple serious offences, but the Metropolitan Police believed that his offending had been far more prolific. The dossier before the parole board made several references to more than 80 unproven allegations and a central aspect of the ruling was whether these allegations should have informed the risk assessment. Radford had only admitted to the offences that he had been convicted of belatedly and he made no mention of any additional offences. None of the further allegations had been put to proof in a criminal court; however, the number and similarity of the allegations may well have supported a finding that Radford would continue to present a significant risk if at liberty. The High Court ruled that the allegations should have been considered by the parole board when assessing Radford's present risk (at [159]). Perhaps a distinction can be drawn between the probative value of this evidence in establishing Radford's risk as opposed to his culpability, but this is somewhat artificial: for both assessments to be meaningful, the available evidence has to be as accurate as possible. Inaccurate evidence may jeopardize public safety in a risk assessment; similarly, inaccurate evidence is prone to lead to a disproportionately lenient or severe punishment if the court is measuring personal culpability.

The final aspect of the ruling related to 'open justice'. The High Court held that the procedure at the time lacked transparency and required urgent revision (at [177]). New rules have allowed both victims and members of the public to access release decisions and victims now have the right to give evidence to parole boards. What value does this bring? An obvious claim is that it might address perceptions of marginalization in the release process. Obtaining the victim's perspectives may inform the board, but risk is not static and the victim's input may be less valuable than supposed when an offender's current risk is being assessed. There is also the potential for disappointment if victims engage with the process, feel that their views have been taken on board and the offender is still released.

As a court, it is for the Board to decide the weight that should attach to the victim's testimony. The testimony that the offender provides to the board may be untrue but a victim may also over-estimate the risk that the offender poses. One of the unappreciated effects of the *Radford* case is that additional evidence, which may contextualize the initial offence and which has the potential to inform a risk assessment, will be considered. This is to be welcomed if the additional evidence will not only enhance the evidence base for panels but also increase the chance that an accurate assessment is made.

The danger is that an inclusive approach may complicate the evidence and compromise the panel's ability to make an appropriate determination. Unproven allegations may be untrue (although the volume and similarity of those in the *Radford* case support the view that his convictions only partly reflected his offending) and could misinform a risk assessment. And, it should not be forgotten that while a distinction can be drawn between a decision to imprison and a later decision to release, the impact on the offender – the length of time served in custody – is identical. The High Court was clear in the *Radford* case that the unproven allegations should have informed the release decision and quashed the decision on the basis that the board had ignored them. The judges decided that the unproven allegations may have exposed the true pattern of Radford's offending, which would have led to a more informed risk assessment. The risk that the allegations were incidental to an assessment of Radford's risk, or indeed whether they had any factual basis, was not mentioned despite the fact that parole decisions affect an individual's liberty.

Why truth is integral to sentencing

There is a temptation to think of the trial as the forum where competing narratives are presented, tested, believed or disbelieved. However, for the reasons documented earlier, the trial is exceptional as most defendants plead guilty. This may be due to a recognition on the part of many defendants (often after legal advice) that they have no plausible account – the facts tell their own story. Lawyers can influence decisions on plea. The situation in which the suspect/defendant finds themself can be presented in multiple ways. A lawyer has to evaluate the facts incriminating the client, potential means of rebuttal or justification, and the likely penalty, before offering professional but subjective advice. The client may or may not be swayed, even if the advice is clear.

This chapter has made the case that competing factual accounts are integral to the sentencing process. An acceptance of guilt may suggest agreement, but of what? Precision and accuracy matter as the penalty imposed may differ. Offence severity usually determines the penalty in England and Wales and this is quantified with regard to the magnitude of the harm (real, intended or likely) and the offender's culpability. Truth can be negotiated, just as it can be accepted or denied. For example, gang participation is seen to make an offence worse but the role that each individual played in the gang is apposite. Even where evidence suggests that an offender instigated the offence, they might be prepared to admit to an offence on the basis that their involvement was peripheral.

A second argument that has been advanced in this chapter is that the way in which facts are handled has altered due to the development of more structured sentencing guidelines. Offence-specific guidelines have the potential to reduce disparity in outcomes for like offences (although this is not a given). The Sentencing Council can review particular facts objectively and decide whether or not they should influence a sentence and, if so, whether the presence of the fact should aggravate or mitigate. Consistency demands that like offences are treated in a like manner and this requires that cases with like facts are treated in a like manner. This process is artificial and leads to partiality. Other relevant facts pertaining to the offence are marginalized (the guidelines do not strictly exclude them) while the existence of a listed factor makes it intrinsically relevant. Truth can easily be jeopardized when simplicity and clarity trump complexity and ambiguity.

9

Restoration, Reconciliation and Reconceptualizing Justice

Earlier chapters have cast doubt on the ability of adversarial justice systems, including that in operation in England and Wales, to arrive at the truth despite procedural rules and safeguards designed explicitly to facilitate factfinding by discriminating between probative evidence and evidence likely to lead to inappropriate (though not necessarily false) conclusions. There is frustration that the current rules can hamper the search for truth, as well as a realization that the supposed due process protections may be overstated or illusory. To some writers, though, the failure is more profound: despite vast expenditure on the apparatus of a justice system, few criminals are held to account and, even when a culprit is convicted, the trial process causes victim dissatisfaction and current forms of punishment seem more adept at entrenching criminal behaviour than aiding desistance (Mitchell et al, 2017; Ministry of Justice, 2019). As the factually guilty usually avoid detection (and hence possible prosecution, conviction and punishment), the truth only emerges sporadically and arbitrarily. Moreover, even if one could design a system which ensured that only the factually guilty were convicted, the penal response is unsatisfactory. Critics point to the mass of empirical evidence which demonstrates that those punished are seldom deterred by the experience (Nagin, 2013a, 2013b; Chalfin and McCrary, 2017).

This is an account of systemic failure. Consequently, it should come as no surprise that these critics advocate for a radical recasting of how society conceptualizes and reacts to harm and to those who cause it. Part of this critique, at both a macro and a micro level, is how an event should be constructed. Rather than an adversarial model, which presents two (or possibly more) rival accounts to the factfinder (see Chapters 6 and 7), the alternative model discussed in this chapter seeks an agreed truth. The primary motivation for moving towards a restorative model is the individual and societal harm caused by traditional criminal justice processes (the critique transcends individual jurisdictions and adversarial and inquisitorial models of justice), allied to their evident limitations as a means of reducing crime (Pali and Pelikan, 2014; Richards, 2014).

The claim that a restorative approach is preferable has been presented and challenged at length and so the focus of this chapter is somewhat different: as alternative models of justice gain traction worldwide, what are the implications for truth-finding in the resolution of criminal disputes? Do alternative approaches adequately protect individuals from wrongful conviction? Restorative justice may reject traditional forms of punishment (particularly imprisonment), but a finding of guilt (or more accurately, and for reasons expanded upon later, an admittance of culpability) remains stigmatic and, despite the avowed aim of reintegrating the offender back into society, is likely to hold far-reaching consequences (Pinard, 2005–06). In the search for a more effective response to criminal behaviour, one has to ensure that procedures to establish the truth remain robust (Pavlich, 2017). According to Roche:

> Accountability is essential, for the simplest of reasons: it is one of the most important checks on the exercise of power. Many familiar principles and practices – such as the practice of democratic elections, the doctrine of ministerial responsibility, the principle of open justice, the practice of auditing – are based on the important supposition that decision-makers are less likely to abuse their discretion when they know that at some stage they will have to explain and justify their decisions. This need to ensure that decision-makers are accountable has become one of society's central preoccupations. One of the reasons that many people are uneasy about the rise of restorative justice is the perception that such programmes lack the sort of public accountability we expect from criminal justice institutions, even if we do not always receive it. (Roche, 2003, p 3)

This chapter will commence with a brief review of the perceived failings of traditional justice processes so as to understand the background to the calls for a different process of obtaining justice in interpersonal disputes (whether they are cast as civil, criminal or both). The differences with a restorative model will then be explored. Consideration will be given to an in-depth evaluation of a restorative justice scheme that operated in London and Northumbria, England. The evaluation allows one to see what victims and offenders hoped to achieve prior to the conference and the extent to which these aspirations were realized. It will be shown that both victims and offenders valued the opportunity to discuss the offence, including the background and context (which was particularly important to perpetrators) and the aftermath (a notable concern to the victims). This process was, in fact, more beneficial than any subsequent agreement between the parties as to how the harm could be repaid.

Having looked at a domestic use of restorative justice, the discussion will turn to the use of 'truth commissions', a restorative approach that has been employed in the aftermath of civil war. Finally, and by way of conclusion, the chapter will consider whether restorative justice could be incorporated into or act as an adjunct to traditional criminal justice processes. Were this possible it may provide a means of resolving some disputes in a more effective and participatory manner, while allaying fears that accountability and procedural safeguards can be sacrificed in restorative processes. The conclusion we draw may surprise but certain aims – including the search for truth – appear identical. What differs is process. Restorative justice advocates have provided a great service in challenging the assumption that traditional models and processes are the only or the best way to achieve justice (Zehr, 1985, p 4). Many of their criticisms are trenchant and powerful. But so are some of the concerns that have been raised about restorative justice. The number of restorative schemes in existence demonstrates, perhaps, an acknowledgement of genuine potential but their marginal overall use shows a wariness to reject the due process protections associated with existing models of justice.

Alternative means of dispute resolution

It is evident that traditional means of resolving legal disputes have been found wanting in many contexts. Alternative processes with varying degrees of formality are now commonplace. Marital breakdown and child custody disputes, to take but two examples, will often now be mediated. Commercial arbitration is frequently preferred to litigation, even in high-value cases. This is not necessarily a new phenomenon in civil (see Edwards, 1986) or criminal (Dingwall and Harding, 1998) justice, yet there is no doubt that this trend has accelerated over the past 20 years. Rather than a court being seen as the primary means of resolving a dispute, in many legal contexts it is more accurate to view courts as a forum of last resort when alternative routes have been exhausted. Criminal justice, at least in the context of adult offenders, is behind the curve.

Various factors lie behind this shift. The economic motivation is obvious: there is the potential for cost and delay to be reduced considerably. One should perhaps guard against cynicism at this point as an expensive system that fails in its primary purpose *is* a waste of state resources that could be spent more effectively to reduce crime, or on other areas of social importance. Another valid concern is the recognition that adversarial justice is highly stressful for all participants. The recognition that adversarialism can entrench, and sharpen, polarized accounts has acted as an incentive to find an empowering alternative means of dispute resolution that may increase the possibility of an amicable settlement.

In the criminal context, though, the primary driver for change has been the despair associated with the high rates of recidivism by those convicted and sentenced by the courts (Nagin et al, 2009; Mitchell et al, 2017). In England and Wales, adult offenders have a proven reoffending rate of 29.3 per cent (Ministry of Justice, 2019). Prison appears especially ineffective: 62.2 per cent of adults sentenced to a prison term of fewer than 12 months reoffend within a year of release. More could undoubtedly be done to reduce the pressure on the prison system and to improve the physical estate so as to facilitate meaningful rehabilitation. However, increasing numbers of criminologists believe that it is not a question of reforming traditional modes of trial and punishment but of abandoning them and searching for something preferable (Ruggiero, 2010, 2011). Most alternative models are variants of restorative justice and the essential features of this approach will be mapped out in the next section.

Defining restorative justice

It would, of course, be helpful to start with a precise definition of restorative justice, but there is a surprising lack of agreement even among its many advocates (Daly, 2016; Wood and Suzuki, 2016). Dignan believes that:

> [This] failure is not altogether surprising. After all the restorative justice movement draws ... on a rather disparate collection of intellectual currents. The term itself has been applied to a bewildering wide range of practices operating in a variety of different contexts. And while some view

restorative justice rather narrowly, as simply an alternative way of responding to criminal wrongdoing, others see it as a far more radical and potentially transformative social movement. Perhaps the mistake lies in the quest for an exact word or phrase that would encompass all these elements, which probably is impossible. In which case a more productive response might be to abandon the quest for a traditional 'stipulative' definition in favour of a more discursive one that sets out simply to describe the term according to its main essential properties. (Dignan, 2007, p 310)

The failure to agree a stipulative definition has resulted in a variety of terms being employed to describe similar paradigms and processes (Dignan and Cavadino, 1996, p 153): 'communitarian justice', 'making amends', 'peacemaking', 'positive justice', 'reconciliation', 'redress', 'relational justice', 'reparative justice', 'restitution' and 'restorative justice' have all been used. There are distinctions but, for reasons of simplicity, this chapter will adopt the term 'restorative justice' throughout as it is the term most commonly used by policy makers and in the academic literature. The exception will be when the discussion turns to international criminal justice, when the term 'truth commission' will be preferred, again on the grounds that this reflects academic and official terminology.

Given the impossibility of agreeing on a definition, it is more fruitful, as Dignan suggests, to draw a comparison between 'old' paradigms of justice (which in England and Wales equates to the adversarial process) and 'new' restorative paradigms. Arguably, the most influential account of the key distinctions was provided by Zehr (1985), a leading early advocate of restorative justice. Not all of Zehr's distinctions are discussed here as some have marginal bearing on the ability to expose truth, but several of Zehr's distinctions are highly relevant. The most significant distinction is a shift from an 'old' focus on establishing blame and guilt (did the individual do it?) to a 'new' focus on problem solving, liabilities, obligations and the future (what should be done to resolve the dispute?). Both a process of establishing blame (under the old paradigm) and a process of 'problem solving' (under the new paradigm) would appear to necessitate a search for truth. We shall return to this in the chapter conclusion where it will be suggested that this aim is not as binary as Zehr suggests.

The traditional emphasis placed on adversarial relationships by old paradigms would be replaced by an ethos of dialogue and negotiation between the offender and the victim. The concept of 'justice' also differs: under old criminal justice paradigms, justice relates to process whereas new approaches measure justice by outcome, a relational goal. Here it is worth commenting that empirical evidence suggests that process appears to be more important to victims under a restorative model than outcome (see further on). Punishment (regardless of its philosophical foundation) is rejected under new paradigms in favour of restitution; the focus is on repairing injury rather than causing intentional and unnecessary harm to the offender. The new paradigm, Zehr contends, recognizes that crime is an interpersonal conflict whereas old paradigms create a fiction that the dispute is between the offender and the state. The community (as opposed to the state) is also seen to be marginalized under the old paradigm whereas its significance is reinstated in restorative approaches as society has a pivotal role in facilitating restoration: restorative justice, if successful, must lead to community reintegration.

Restorative approaches reject state punishment. While old paradigms of justice simply require passive accountability on the part of the offender, restorative approaches demand more. Not only must the offender accept culpability for causing the harm, they also have direct involvement in resolving the dispute through a process of dialogue. The rejection of punishment is radical but how a criminal dispute is perceived is also transformational (see also Hulsman, 1986). According to the old paradigm, criminal harms are a legal construct. Offences are defined in law and established following legal procedure. Moral, social, economic and political context are seen, at best, as marginal concerns. A broader appreciation of the circumstances surrounding the offence – including the factors just outlined – is necessary under the new paradigm if a meaningful resolution is to be agreed (see later). The implication is that, if victims were aware of the background to the offence, restoration and reintegration are more likely. This speaks to a different conception of truth. The old paradigm narrows what is adjudged to be relevant. New paradigms differ in two regards. First, truth encompasses more. Second, relevance is not legally prescribed – the process allows the parties to determine what factors have a bearing.

Zehr's account is comprehensive, analytically useful and has endured, but it cannot capture the defining features of all restorative programmes. Wright argues that one overarching premise can be identified:

> This is the crux: the restorative case is that the infliction of pain because it is painful is likely to be counterproductive; if the aim is to increase awareness, understanding and empathy,

the measures should be designed for that purpose. If they succeed they may prove painful, but the pain will come from within the offender, and that is what is needed in order to generate repentance and the willingness to apologise and make reparation. (Wright, 2003, p 9)

Self-evidently, this relates to purpose rather than process, and this is important because drawing a distinction between process, outcomes and values allows a better understanding of restorative justice (Dignan, 2007, p 310). All three aspects have some bearing on the search for truth. Restorative processes aim to create space for stakeholders to resolve disputes. This necessitates allowing those harmed and those responsible to contribute by presenting their version of events, their fears and their views on how the dispute could be settled. This discussion may include factors that the offender believes influenced their conduct and the victim's account might include how they have been affected. The process requires active victim participation, although Dignan notes that direct personal contact with the offender can be avoided if a mediator conveys information between the parties. A victim may find the process more empowering if they can confront the offender directly (as will be seen later, this is the reason many victims choose to participate), but presenting their concerns in writing may retain value for those unwilling to meet the offender. For Daly, restorative justice is best viewed as a mechanism for achieving justice:

> Restorative justice is a contemporary justice mechanism to address crime, disputes, and bounded community conflict. The mechanism is a meeting (or several meetings) of affected individuals, facilitated by one or more impartial people. Meetings can take place at all phases of the criminal process, pre-arrest, diversion from court, pre-sentence, and post-sentence, as well as for offending or conflicts not reported to the police. Specific practices will vary, depending on context, but are guided by rules and procedures that align with what is appropriate in the context of the crime, dispute, or bounded conflict. (Daly, 2016, p 14)

Outcomes emanate from the process. Some may 'restore' victims – to take an obvious example, when an offender agrees to repair the damage caused by the offence. Other outcomes, though, might be aimed at 'restoring' an offender. An example here would be where services are made available to deal with an addiction. Truth is essentially found in process, not outcome, but the interrelationship means that a successful outcome is dependent on the truth emerging in the process. When the chapter assesses two large-scale restorative conferences in the next section, it will be seen that the most disappointing outcomes followed conferences where no factual agreement was reached between the parties.

Finally, Dignan identifies a number of values associated with restorative justice:

> They include the principle of inclusivity that seeks to engage all the relevant stake-holders in the restorative justice process; an attempt to balance the different sets of interests that are known to be affected when an offence has been committed; a commitment to the principle of 'non-coerciveness'; and a problem-solving orientation. (Dignan, 2007, p 311)

An alternative, and equally illuminating, account is provided by Rossner, who identifies three aspects of restorative processes that are distinctive: the process relies on the 'active participation' of *lay people*; the process is designed to develop a *narrative* that focuses on the *emotions* of these participants; and the process has a *ritual dynamic* (Rossner, 2018, p 232, emphasis in original). More is said about narrative:

> Here, victims (and in conferencing models, supporters and community members) are invited to articulate a narrative about how they have been harmed by the offence. Offenders are invited [to] contribute to a narrative that acknowledges any harm, accepts responsibility, and expresses remorse. In these narratives, a range of emotions can be expressed, including anger, fear, anxiety, shame, guilt, remorse, and hope. (Rossner, 2018, p 323)

The next section will provide an evaluation of whether restorative processes can fulfil these aspirations.

Restorative justice and the search for truth: empirical findings

In order to assess the extent to which restorative processes can deliver on their promise, this section will review the evidence from one large study funded by the Ministry of Justice in England and Wales

(Shapland et al, 2007). This was an analysis of three different schemes but for the purposes of this chapter, consideration will only be given to the largest of the schemes, which operated in two locations in England (London and Northumbria) and were run by the Justice Research Consortium (JRC). The JRC facilitated the conferences, which involved participation by offenders and victims, both of whom were encouraged to have supporters present. Many of the offenders had committed serious offences and were serving long prison terms.

The methodological approach was robust. Cases were randomized to a conference (152 offenders and 216 victims) or to a control group (118 offenders and 166 victims) after consent had been given by both parties. Views were obtained prior to the conference, immediately afterwards and eight or nine months later. Expectations before the conference were mixed. The participants consented to take part but, even so, only 61 per cent of offenders and 60 per cent of victims expressed a desire to meet the other party (Shapland et al, 2007, Table 2.2). This suggests reticence but only 24 per cent of offenders and 16 per cent of victims said they did not want to meet the other party. It will come as little surprise that, prior to the conference, 69 per cent of offenders and 53 per cent of victims stated that they felt very or somewhat nervous – only 17 per cent of offenders and 32 per cent of victims claimed to not be at all nervous (Shapland et al, 2007, Table 2.2). (It is interesting that the offenders were more nervous than the victims beforehand.) A key finding from the pre-conference interviews is that both parties believed that the conference was designed to benefit the other party: 71 per cent of offenders thought the event was for the benefit of victims and 73 per cent of victims believed it was for the benefit of offenders.

Victims and offenders were both asked why they had chosen to participate. Presenting their version of events was central to the decision. Eighty per cent of offenders and 77 per cent of victims said it was quite important or very important to them to be able to 'express [their] feelings and speak directly to the other person' (Shapland et al, 2007, Table 2.3). Meanwhile, 78 per cent of victims and 54 per cent of offenders said it was quite important or very important to 'have some questions about the offence answered'. It is useful to compare these motivations with the next two. Although 81 per cent of offenders said it was quite important or very important to repay the harm caused, only 44 per cent of victims claimed that this factor was quite important or very important. The final reason for participation also illustrates that the outcome was not as critical to the victims as the opportunity to express feelings and speak with the offender. Seventy per cent of offenders stated that it was quite important or very important to them to help the other person. Only 40 per cent of victims said the same. What this suggests is that, to victim participants, the process and, more specifically, the opportunity for direct engagement are more important than the outcome. Offenders also cite the value of discussion as a frequent motivation, alongside a desire to repay the harm caused.

Participants were asked to comment on the conference afterwards. Ninety-three per cent of victims and 85 per cent of offenders stated that they had been given the opportunity to express their point of view (Shapland et al, 2007, Table 3.1). The vast majority of offenders (85 per cent) and victims (81 per cent) also felt that they had been listened to carefully. There was a mutual perception that all sides had been given a fair chance to 'bring out what happened': 90 per cent of victims and 80 per cent of offenders answered this question in the affirmative. Eighty-three per cent of victims and 76 per cent of offenders said that their concerns and questions had been taken seriously. While these percentages are somewhat lower, it is important to note that only 4 per cent of offenders and 3 per cent of victims said that their concerns and questions had not been treated seriously. Finally, 89 per cent of victims and 82 per cent of offenders reported that they had been given the opportunity to explain the consequences of the offence. These findings suggest that restorative justice holds great potential as a means of providing a forum where alternative accounts can be presented and discussed, with the possibility that resolution and restoration will follow.

The fact that someone was given the opportunity to present their feelings during the conference did not always mean that they found participation easy. One victim explained:

> It was a very difficult situation – the offender was extremely upset during the conference. It was touching. But if I were to have expressed my true resentment it would have been a touch cruel. I wanted to see an offender who could take my anger – I felt like I was kicking him when he was down. I liked him. He was a good person who had done bad things. He undertook to repair the damage done. I will feel satisfied if those things are undertaken. (Shapland et al, 2007, p 21)

Despite the positive findings presented here, doubts were expressed about the sincerity of the other party in many cases: 65 per cent of offenders said that they thought that the victim was sincere but only 45 per cent of victims said that they thought the offender was sincere (although 23 per cent said that the offender was sincere 'to some extent') (Shapland et al, 2007, Table 3.1). This raises the intriguing question of why participants benefited from a discussion with someone who they often felt was being insincere.

Overall, the majority of victims and offenders were positive about the experience: 40 per cent of offenders and 45 per cent of victims were 'very satisfied' with what happened at the conference, while an additional 40 per cent of offenders and 40 per cent of victims were 'quite satisfied' (Shapland et al, 2007, Table 3.3). Only 6 per cent of offenders and 6 per cent of victims were 'not at all satisfied'. The process was seen as 'very fair' by 71 per cent of victims and 67 per cent of offenders and 78 per cent of offenders and 75 per cent of victims were satisfied with the agreement that was reached. It is important, though, to recognize that both parties found the experience emotional: 34 per cent of offenders and 30 per cent of victims found the conference 'very emotional', while 30 per cent of offenders and 36 per cent of victims found it 'fairly emotional'.

The researchers sought to identify the factors that led to dissatisfaction or poor outcomes. Here the analysis was more speculative but they found that 'unresolved and significant dispute' about 'what happened during the offence itself' – or a failure to agree on the truth – was the main reason:

> This might be that the offender would not take any responsibility for the offence (which we would see as potentially fatal for restorative justice); that the offender or co-offenders only took some responsibility (could be difficult, but not always); that the offender made light of the offence; that the offender would not apologise (not always fatal to restorative justice – some offences have a complicated history); or that the offender blamed the victim. *Note that problematic disputes are those between offender and victim. In some instances, there might be a dispute on some aspect between the participants and official criminal justice versions of the offence, but this does not necessarily cause difficulties for restorative justice.* (Shapland et al, 2007, p 47, emphasis added)

Such a failure, though, is common under the old paradigm where participants may feel that the process does not allow their version of events to be shared and discussed, and where arriving at an accepted account involves intervention by various criminal justice personnel, from police officers initially responding to an incident, through prosecutors determining whether the victim's account will survive rigorous scrutiny, and then, at trial, lawyers who are well versed in presenting facts in a favourable way and exposing weaknesses in the opposing case (see Chapters 6 and 7). In other words, those restorative conferences that fail share many of the characteristics of old paradigms of justice: truth fails to emerge because the process never moves beyond two mutually opposing accounts. But, what the evaluation shows is that this is rare. Most conferences that were studied did result in beneficial outcomes for both the victim and the offender. In terms of being able to delve further into the circumstances surrounding the offence, the process offered something that a trial cannot: the means to explore motive (if there was one), why the victim was targeted (and, again, this may simply have been random) and the consequences of the crime for both the victim and the offender. When a restorative process works, it would appear to offer far more than old justice paradigms and, even when it fails to bring satisfaction, the outcome may be no worse than that achieved currently.

'Truth commissions' and 'extraordinary crime'

Traditionally, diversionary approaches in criminal justice were seen as an equitable means of responding to minor delinquency, particularly when committed by those with reduced culpability (Marshall, 1996; Dingwall and Harding, 1998). Few would object to keeping such individuals out of court on the basis of proportionality. More recently, though, there has also been an argument that traditional criminal justice processes are not an effective response to those who commit the gravest of offences in international criminal law. The justification here differs as it most certainly is not an argument based on proportionality – were that the case, how could a burglar be prosecuted but not someone implicated in genocide? Rather, it is a recognition that the standard justifications for punishment (retribution, deterrence, rehabilitation and public protection) do not necessarily provide a sound normative basis for punishing extraordinary crime (Dingwall and Hillier, 2010). Moreover, as the current authors have argued, any sentence imposed is likely to appear inadequate given the magnitude of the harm involved (Dingwall and Hillier, 2010).

Tokenism is also a concern. At a domestic level, most criminals are not apprehended, convicted or punished for their actions. In the context of crimes against humanity, this is magnified: there would likely be thousands of perpetrators of extraordinary crimes and only a very few appear before the International Criminal Court or international tribunals. Punishing these people risks scapegoating them. Highly selective prosecution in conjunction with the apparent leniency of the sentences imposed may lead to victim dissatisfaction. (To take the case of the Rwandan genocide, the death penalty remained the penalty for murder in Rwandan law but was not available for the genocidal crimes committed during the civil war.) Geographically remote tribunals or courts also hinder the ability of victims to testify, further marginalizing their input and reducing the significance of their personal account. There may be a number of factors that explain the limited success of the International Criminal Court in achieving justice for the victims of extraordinary crime – the failure of the United States to engage being especially problematic in political terms – but, as with the challenge to old criminal justice paradigms, some have argued that there is a need to escape the legalism inherent in how the Court operates.

The notion of 'reconciliation' is central to the concept of 'restorative justice'. Genocidal behaviour often occurs in the context of civil war and reconciliation is paramount to peace-building. Reconciliation, in turn, demands that the truth is exposed. This is sometimes reflected in the title of the commissions, for example the *Truth and Reconciliation Commission of South Africa* and the *Timor-Leste Commission for Reception, Truth, and Reconciliation*. Recording often thousands of accounts means that truth commissions do not provide speedy resolution. The National Commission for the Disappearance of Persons (CONADEP) in Argentina took 50,000 pages of depositions from survivors prior to publishing its 1984 report (Crenzel, 2008, 2017).

Truth commissions do not prosecute individuals but the possibility sometimes remains for them to name individuals responsible for particular atrocities and recommend that prosecution takes place. Other commissions grant amnesties to participants on certain conditions. Truth seeking may therefore coexist with, rather than replace, prosecution at either a national or an international level. This is similar to the current use of restorative justice in domestic legal systems where schemes operate alongside the traditional criminal justice process. The flourishing of truth commissions as a means of achieving transitional justice suggests value (Gibson, 2009), but that success does not necessarily mean that they are an effective means of uncovering the truth. Rushton (2006) argues that truth commissions fail to provide an accurate and complete record of atrocities but serve a valuable social and political purpose. To this end, she distinguishes between truth as a process and truth as an end product in the form of a document or report.

Conclusion

Restorative justice now forms an integral and well-established part of many countries' official response to crime. Generally, though, its use is limited to discrete categories of offender (for example, children), conduct (for example, antisocial behaviour) or context (for example, school-related disputes). Some jurisdictions have embraced restorative approaches more readily than others. In Northern Ireland, for example, it is the most common means of responding to crime by young people and has been seen as a means of addressing the individual and societal trauma associated with decades of violence (McEvoy and Mika, 2002). The question can no longer be *whether* restorative justice has a role to play in resolving criminal disputes, but how *significant* that role should be. Unfortunately, the debate regarding restorative justice – like many in penal policy – tends to be polemic. Luna explains the dynamic:

> Punishment theories brutalize one another, staking out turf on principle and refusing to budge from their respective positions. As a result, the various theoretical camps spend most of their time on three endeavours: demonstrating the superiority of their approach to criminal sanctioning, subjecting all other theories to harsh criticism, and repairing the damage done to their own theory from equally severe attacks. The upshot is an unwinnable war of critiques within an ethos of mutual exclusivity. It is either one theory or another, but certainly not both. (Luna, 2003, p 205)

The authors, though, would contend that there are noticeable commonalities between new and old (or restorative and adversarial) models of criminal justice if one considers some of the underlying objectives, including the search for truth. Recognizing that there are multiple and diverse aims to restorative justice, and we would concede that some do differ from the aims of adversarial justice systems, Easton and Piper note:

> [The] objectives of restorative justice are [not] in practice necessarily different from those of the traditional criminal justice system. The restorative aim of reintegrating the offender into the community entails preventing the offender from reoffending, a traditional aim of the criminal justice system. Nor is a desire to be cost-effective and to 'do justice' excluded from thinking in restorative justice. However,

> the concept of justice is different and the criteria for cost-effectiveness will relate not only to the narrow objectives of the criminal justice system, but may well also relate to community 'health' as well as to victim satisfaction and offender reformation. (Easton and Piper, 2016, p 176)

Willemsens' observation that the perceived difference between traditional criminal justice and restorative justice depends to a large extent on the definition of punishment is also pertinent. He argues that many definitions of punishment attach too much emphasis on the associated pain:

> Restorative sanctions/punishments are not primarily intended to cause pain and suffering – their primary aim is to achieve restoration. They should be socially constructive in that they contribute in a reasonable manner to the repair of harm, suffering and social unrest caused by the crime. They should confirm social norms by censuring transgressions, and they should try to influence the offender in a positive way. They should be imposed in such a way as not to stigmatise the offender. (Willemsens, 2003, p 40)

This is not wholly convincing. Something can be painful *and* well intentioned. This is why punishment always demands normative justification. Moreover, a restorative resolution can also be painful. Roche (2003, p 1) provides two vivid Australian examples. Several children caught lighting bushfires were referred to restorative conferences. The New South Wales Premier, Bob Carr, claimed publicly that 'juvenile prison is in some respects too good for them'. He wanted to 'rub their noses in the ashes they've caused', make them 'work with the victims' and 'go into a burns ward and talk to people who've suffered from fire'. In the second case, a 12-year-old shoplifter 'agreed' to sit outside the store in a T-shirt carrying the message 'I am a thief'. This was resolution of sorts – though it was agreed by his mother and the shop manager – but it would be disingenuous not to describe the outcome as punishment.

Determining whether restorative justice can run in tandem with traditional means of resolving disputes or should be an alternative in all cases raises some challenging issues (Lemonne, 2003). Some are logistical: what should happen in a case where the victim or the offender do not want to engage or refuse to engage? If the process emphasizes understanding and consensus, coercion is inappropriate, unlike adversarial models where forced participation is integral unless one forfeits the right to a trial, in which case participation in the punishment is obligatory. The use of a proxy victim may be one solution but it is hard to see how the truth could emerge without the actual victim participating. This gives rise to an element of chance: depending on a victim's willingness to take part, an offender may be dealt with in one of two ways, one of which is punitive and one of which seeks to reject punishment. (Although, for the reasons just outlined, we are not wholly satisfied that restorative resolutions always lack punitive impact.) The degree to which this is seen as problematic depends largely on how important consistency of process and outcome is viewed.

A secondary issue is whether the severity of the harm is relevant. While the community might be persuaded that restorative justice is an appropriate response to minor offending, they may balk at the suggestion that seriously violent individuals are not brought before a court and imprisoned in order to protect the public. One needs, though, to recognize that this is, in effect, a retributive argument, which casts restorative justice as a minor intervention that is a proportionate response to minor delinquency. But the views of the community must be taken seriously as restorative justice seeks community reintegration.

There are several points to make here. First, there is no evidence to suggest that offence severity has any bearing on the likelihood of participants to engage meaningfully in a restorative process. The process may be more traumatic for the participants (but this should not be assumed), yet the truth may still emerge in a way that leads to a successful resolution. It will be recalled that the evaluation considered earlier involved many serious offences and yet the rates of satisfaction were high. Second, public protection and restorative justice are not mutually exclusive. Prisoners can still participate (see further Dhami et al, 2009; Gavrielides, 2014). Entering a prison may make the experience more unsettling for victims, but the possibility remains. Finally, if one of the drivers behind restorative justice is the marginalization of victims, is it not particularly important to give them a voice when the harm that they suffered was serious?

Some categories of offence may be regarded as *sui generis* and the suitability of restorative approaches in such cases has been questioned. The desirability of utilizing restorative justice in cases of domestic abuse and sexual violence is particularly contentious (see, for example, Hudson, 1998, 2002; Naylor, 2010; Koss, 2014; Joyce-Wojtas and Keenan, 2016). However, one must not be too hasty to make value judgments in the absence of evidence. Some victims may see value. In a case reported by McGlynn et al (2012), the victim drew comfort from the opportunity to present her experience to her attacker as she 'just wanted him to hear me'. One cannot draw broad conclusions – and even less determine policy – on the basis of one particular case, but what this comment highlights is the desire that victims must not be silenced in proceedings. Traditional models of justice grant a complainant the same status as any other witness at trial: they will be led through their testimony by the prosecution and then cross-examined by the defence. The account that they present may represent the truth (like all witnesses, they are testifying under oath and are under a legal obligation to tell the truth), but the story is partial and may omit factors that they perceive to be relevant and necessary. In a restorative forum, participants are free to determine relevancy. Doing so may be traumatic. Victims' accounts may be challenged or trivialized by offenders. Offenders' versions of events may cause upset; there are few constraints about what they can say was relevant. At trial, for example, evidence about the complainant's previous sexual history with third parties is generally inadmissible on the basis that the prejudicial effect outweighs any possible probative value (see Chapter 7). In a restorative conference, though, there is no jury to be prejudiced. If an offender perceives the victim's previous sexual history to be worthy of comment, should he be stopped, challenged or left to express his view?

There is a final, and often forgotten, way in which the truth that emerges in a restorative setting has the potential to benefit society. Wright (2003, p 21) argues that in a non-adversarial, non-punitive system (and both conditions matter), people would 'speak more freely'. A deeper understanding of the factors that make offending more likely would emerge and this evidence base could inform a meaningful crime reduction strategy.

10

The Truth, the Whole Truth and Nothing but the Truth: The Truth of Who Is to Blame

In a previous book (Dingwall and Hillier, 2016) we discussed the role of blame in the criminal process, arguing that blame and the identification of who is to blame is a central aspect of the criminal justice system. We sought to argue that 'over the last 35 years we have moved to a more judgmental, less sympathetic, and more punitive society. This change is reflected in the growth of criminalization. Central to the change is blame' (Dingwall and Hillier, 2016, p 23).

In Chapter 1 of this present book we made reference to the case of *Jones* v *National Coal Board* [1957] 2 QB 55, which concerned the death of a mineworker in a mining accident. We remarked on the fact that if the event had occurred today it may well have led to a prosecution for corporate manslaughter. There has been a large increase in the number of criminal offences in recent years. In 2015, the Criminal Justice and Courts Act created a new offence for an 'individual who has the care of another individual by virtue of being a care worker to ill-treat or wilfully to neglect that individual' (Criminal Justice and Courts Act 2015, section 20). The legislation was passed following the publication of a report produced by a government-initiated inquiry into patient care. The inquiry, chaired by Professor Don Berwick, had, in fact, emphasized the need to learn from the no-blame culture that had successfully reduced accidents in the aviation industry (Department of Health, 2013). In introducing the Berwick Report to the House of Commons in November 2013, the Secretary of State for Health had reflected the overall tone: '[The report] is not about penalising staff for making mistakes; it is about enabling them to learn from them' (*Hansard*, 2013). The reference to possible criminal action came towards the end of the report: 'We believe that legal sanctions in the very rare cases where individuals or organisations are unequivocally guilty of wilful or reckless neglect or mistreatment of patients would provide deterrence while not impeding a vital open, transparent learning culture' (Department of Health, 2013, p 33).

The extent to which the possibility of legal sanctions deters behaviour is a discussion outside the ambit of this book, but the retention of the possibility of sanctions raises the issue of two competing approaches when bad things happen. Studies of human error identify two main approaches: the person approach and the system approach. The person approach:

> [Views] ... unsafe acts as arising primarily from aberrant mental processes such as forgetfulness, inattention, poor motivation, carelessness, negligence and recklessness ... If something goes wrong, it seems obvious that an individual (or group of individuals) must have been responsible. Seeking as far as possible to uncouple a person's unsafe acts from any institutional responsibility is clearly in the interests of managers. It is also legally more convenient, at least in Britain. (Reason, 2000, p 768)

The system approach, by contrast, sees human error as normal, expected behaviour and focuses instead on changing the conditions under which humans operate:

> In an ideal world, each defensive layer would be intact. In reality, however, they are more like slices of Swiss cheese, having many holes – though unlike the cheese, these holes are continually opening, shutting, and shifting their location. The presence of holes in any one 'slice' does not normally cause a bad outcome. Usually, this can happen only when the holes in many layers momentarily line up to permit a trajectory of accident opportunity – bringing hazards into damaging contact with victims. The holes in the defences arise for two reasons: active failures and latent conditions. Nearly all adverse events involve a combination of these two set of factors. (Reason, 2000, p 769)

Active failures usually arise from the conduct of individuals with direct contact with the system and may involve rule violation. Crimes can be viewed as 'bad outcomes' arising from the conduct of individuals involving rule violation. Latent conditions are the inevitable 'resident pathogens' within the system.

In January 1993, the then Shadow Home Secretary, Tony Blair, was interviewed by the *New Statesman*. The interview focused on a future Labour government's policies towards crime and criminal justice. The interview is perhaps best remembered, however, for one sentence: 'We should be tough on crime and tough on the underlying causes of crime' (Blair, 1993). In government, Labour perhaps focused more on the first half of the sentence than the second. Yet in his interview, Blair was advocating a radical approach to criminal justice, which had much in common with the Swiss cheese model. The paragraphs immediately before the 'tough on crime, tough on causes of crime' soundbite are significant:

> [W]e are moving the debate beyond the choice between personal and social responsibility, the notion that there are only two sides to the 'law and order' debate – those who want to punish the criminal and those who point to the poor social conditions in which crime breeds. The obvious commonsense of the matter – which would be recognised instantly by any member of the public – is that the choice is false and indeed misleading.
>
> People have a right to go about their business without being attacked or abused or having their property stolen. They have a right, and society has a duty, to bring those who commit these crimes to justice, and to a punishment that properly reflects the seriousness of the crime. To act otherwise would be to betray the interests of those we serve.
>
> Equally, the purpose of any system of justice should not just be to punish and deter, but also to rehabilitate, for the good of society as well as the criminal. Which is why there are practical reasons, as well as those connected with civil liberties, for reforming our monstrous prison regime.
>
> Above all, any sensible society acting in its own interests as well as those of its citizens will understand and recognise that poor education and housing, inadequate or cruel family backgrounds, low employment prospects and drug abuse will affect the likelihood of young people turning to crime. If they are placed outside mainstream culture, offered no hope or continuity, shown no respect by others and unable to develop respect for themselves, there is a greater chance of their going wrong. This cannot be challenged other

than through active community intervention. To see this requires not a PhD in sociology, but a small experience of life. Yet the Tories are destroying hope for young people, slashing training programmes, closing youth clubs. They are inert in the face of rising youth unemployment. (*New Statesman*, 1993)

We shall discuss 'the right to bring those who commit crimes to justice' later in the chapter but in this section the focus is on the wider, crime prevention rhetoric. If people have a right not to be the victims of crime then the role of society should be to prevent those crimes occurring. Viewed in these terms, concentrating on investigating the individual who stole the property or carried out the attack is to adopt a narrow, blinkered view of the crime phenomenon. If we can recognize that 'poor education and housing, inadequate or cruel family backgrounds, low employment prospects and drug abuse' affect the likelihood of people turning to crime then it would seem that any effective crime prevention approach needs to ascertain the 'truth' of the background and context of crime.

Although many justifications for punishment are underpinned by a view of the criminal as a rational being, we know that many crimes are committed on the spur of the moment, spontaneously and without thought for consequences. In the early 1990s, there was a big increase in the level of vehicle crime and the news media ran stories of car theft and 'joy riding'. The machinery of the criminal justice system could investigate and identify those guilty of taking a vehicle without consent contrary to section 12 of the Theft Act 1968. The conviction and punishment of car thieves, most of whom were children, did little to reduce the levels of the offending behaviour. What did significantly reduce car crime was the introduction of greater security measures by car manufacturers.

To the extent that the criminal process involves a pursuit of truth, it is but one narrow aspect of a much wider truth. A 'person approach' may (mostly) attempt to identify correctly the person most deserving of blame, but it rarely succeeds in revealing the whole truth of the offence.

Crime, truth and children

In the year ended March 2019, there were just over 60,200 arrests of children (aged 10–17) by the police in England and Wales; of those, 27,352 were proceeded against at court and 19,316 were convicted and sentenced (Youth Justice Board, 2020). The number of proven offences committed by children has fallen rapidly over the past 10 years and the 2019 figure was 76 per cent lower than the year ended March 2009, and 16 per cent lower than the year ended March 2018. In the year ended March 2019, there were around 58,900 proven offences committed by children.

Unlike the case for the adult system, Parliament has expressly stated the aims of youth justice: section 44 of the Children and Young Persons Act 1933 provides that courts must always consider the welfare of the offender; section 37 of the Crime and Disorder Act 1998 states that the main aim of the youth justice system is the prevention of offending by children and young people. Nonetheless, these specific aims must also be read alongside the general aims and purposes of the criminal justice system. In England and Wales, children aged from 10 upwards are subject to the criminal law and the criminal process.

England and Wales have one of the lowest ages of criminal responsibility in the world: few countries allow the criminal prosecution of children as young as 10. There have been proposals to raise the age but they have met with little success. In September 2017, Lord Dholakia introduced a Bill in the House of Lords that would have raised the age from 10 to 12. During the second reading of the Bill, Lord Dholakia was keen to stress that:

> Taking 10 and 11 year-olds out of the criminal justice system does not mean doing nothing with children who offend; it would mean doing what other countries do with 10 and 11 year-old offenders; it would mean doing what we do with delinquent nine year-olds. In other words, it would mean dealing with the causes of these children's offending through intervention by children's services. In the minority of cases where court proceedings are necessary, it would mean bringing children before family court proceedings, which can impose compulsory measures of supervision and care. In the most serious cases this can mean detention for significant periods in secure accommodation, but this would be arranged as part of care proceedings, rather than as a custodial punishment imposed in criminal proceedings. (*Hansard*, 2017, column 2187)

Lord Dholakia referred to the evidence that shows that children dealt with through the criminal justice process are more likely to reoffend than those diverted from the criminal justice system and dealt with in other ways: 'Children who are officially labelled as offenders often react by trying to live up to the label and acting in increasingly delinquent ways to achieve status in front of their friends' (*Hansard*, 2017, column 476):

> Children who go through the criminal process at a young age are often young people from chaotic, dysfunctional and traumatic backgrounds involving a combination of poor parenting, physical or sexual abuse, conflict within families, substance abuse or mental health problems. The prospects for diverting the child from offending will be far better if these problems are tackled through welfare interventions, rather than by imposing punishments in a criminal court. (*Hansard*, 2017, column 2190)

The Bill eventually fell but was reintroduced to the House of Lords on 4 February 2020. It remains the case, however, that it has little or no chance of becoming law. The public view, certainly as expressed in the media, would seem opposed to any change in the law. When the topic is subject to media attention it is almost always linked to the murder, in 1993, of Jamie Bulger by two 10-year-old boys. Rather than investigate the 'truth' of what led two 10-year-old children to abduct, mutilate and kill a two-year-old, the trial of Robert Thompson and Jon Venables at Preston Crown Court in November 1993 focused on the narrow truth of who did what to whom. The main discussion centred on the issue of whether the defendants understood the difference between right and wrong. Until abolished by section 34 of the Crime and Disorder Act 1998, the presumption of *doli incapax* had required the prosecution, in cases involving defendants under the age of 14, to prove that the defendant knew the difference between right and wrong in addition to proving guilt beyond a reasonable doubt.

In sentencing Thompson and Venables, Mr Justice Morland told them that they had committed a crime of 'unparalleled evil and barbarity ... In my judgment, your conduct was both cunning and very wicked' (*R v Secretary of State for the Home Department, Ex parte V. and R v Secretary of State for the Home Department, Ex parte T.* [1997] Lexis Citation 3962). It is at least questionable whether the two 10-year-olds understood the meaning of 'unparalleled evil and barbarity', which calls into question the purpose of sentencing remarks and the requirement of the presence of the defendant. We will discuss this point later in this chapter.

After the two boys had left the court, Mr Justice Morland commented: 'How it came about that two mentally normal boys aged

10 of average intelligence committed this terrible crime is very hard to comprehend' (quoted by Lord Goff in R. v Secretary of State for the Home Department, Ex parte V. and Reg. v. Secretary of State for the Home Department, Ex parte T. *[1997]* Lexis Citation 3962). The judge's difficulty in understanding the crime is not perhaps surprising but it does speak directly to the pursuit of truth. The fact that a senior High Court judge can sit through the trial proceedings and yet not understand the context and motivation of the offence suggests that although the truth is pursued, it is not captured.

Prosecuting counsel in the Venables and Thompson case was Richard Henriques QC, who would later carry out the investigation into the Metropolitan Police's *Operation Midland*. In May 2020, Sir Richard spoke to the *Daily Mail* about the case. He described that although the trial took place at Preston Crown Court, 'the Old Bailey of the North', Mr Justice Morland was fastidious in ensuring that the most appropriate arrangements were made for the defendants, given their age:

> We sat school hours with no session exceeding 45 minutes. The boys were not locked in cells and they were accompanied throughout by social workers.
>
> Junior defence counsel for Thompson even took the commendable step of bringing their own Nintendo games in order to play with him when he was not in court, to put him at ease. (Henriques, 2020)

Thompson and Venables elected not to give evidence. It is perhaps difficult to see how they made an informed decision. It is a question that faces a defendant of any age and will often depend more on the attitude and advice of defence advisers than the reasoned choice of the defendant themselves. Again, one wonders whether the pursuit of truth might have been better served had Thompson and Venables been able to offer some explanation to Mr Justice Morland of their behaviour at the Liverpool shopping centre on 12 February 1993. In his closing speech, Sir Richard Henriques:

> [Submitted] that a child half the age of the defendants would know what they did was seriously wrong, and it was clear from their police interviews that each knew abducting and killing a child was seriously wrong.
>
> I submitted that a manslaughter verdict would grossly understate the gravity of this crime. This was a

murderous, prolonged attack on a small, defenceless child.
(Henriques, 2020)

Had Thompson and Venables been five years old rather than 10, one wonders whether Sir Richard Henriques would have been arguing for their prosecution.

There was criticism of the decision to prosecute the two 10-year-olds and of the fact that they were tried in an adult court. The law has since been changed in relation to the second point but Sir Richard Henriques remains convinced that prosecution was the right thing to do: 'Failure to prosecute these boys would not have been fair to James's parents and his family. The importance to them of convictions in a criminal court is inestimable' (Henriques, 2020). Sir Richard Henriques concluded the *Daily Mail* interview with reference to his sympathy for the mother of Jamie Bulger and the fact that '[n]o sentence can adequately recompense a bereaved and loving family' (Henriques, 2020). The trial and subsequent proceedings expended considerable financial and emotional resources. If 'no sentence can adequately recompense' a victim and if the trial leaves the trial judge lacking comprehension about the reasons for the offence, one is left wondering at the overriding purpose of the criminal justice system.

To encourage the others?

In *R* v *Ward* (1993) 96 Cr App R 1, the Court of Appeal stated that the task of judges is:

> [To] ensure that the law, practice and methods of trial should be developed so as to reduce the risk of conviction of the innocent to an absolute minimum. At the same time we are very much alive to the fact that, although the avoidance of the conviction of the innocent must unquestionably be the primary consideration, the public interest would not be served by a multiplicity of rules which merely impede effective law enforcement. (p 52)

We have seen in earlier chapters that the regulation of the criminal process can involve a balancing act between competing interests. The rhetoric emphasizes concepts of 'fairness' and 'justice' and the importance of avoiding the conviction of the innocent. Yet the criminal process is also said to be about enforcing the criminal law and maintaining social order: 'The detection and prosecution of at least some suspected criminals is vital to punish and deter criminal behaviour, to declare and uphold important social values and, ideally, to encourage people to lead more law-abiding lives' (Sanders and Young, 1994, p 3). Throughout the book we have seen that a recurrent theme in the pursuit of truth is that it is necessary to ensure that the right people are convicted *and* punished. Punishment, and the justification of punishment, are seen to be central to the criminal justice endeavour: either because criminals 'deserve' punishment or because punishment will reduce criminal behaviour through deterrence. Detecting and punishing the guilty will encourage us all to lead more law-abiding lives.

Yet there is little in the way of evidence to support these claims. We have seen in Chapter 9 that punishment does not have to be inevitable; there are societies that function harmoniously by adopting a more restorative justice approach. The most recent statistics for England and Wales record an overall proven reoffending rate of 28.7 per cent; adults released from custody have a reoffending rate of 36.7 per cent, while the rate for juveniles is 39.2 per cent. The rate is considerably higher for those who have 11 or more previous convictions (nearly 50 per cent for adult offenders and 72 per cent for juvenile offenders). The reoffending rate is also particularly high for those who serve sentences of 12 months or less: those who serve a sentence of less than 12 months reoffend at a rate of 62.7 per cent and those who serve a sentence of less than or equal to six months have a proven reoffending rate of 64.8 per cent. There is considerable variation in reoffending rates between types of offences: reoffending is much higher for the volume crimes than it is for more serious offences (Ministry of Justice, 2020).

Many are clearly not deterred as a result of detection and prosecution. Reoffending and reconviction rates remain high, many individuals drift in and out of offending behaviour, while others simply grow up and grow out of offending. Most models of criminal justice also depend on the existence of offenders making rational decisions about whether or not to offend. We have seen in earlier chapters the links that exist between rational choice theory and the criminal process.

In 1986, Clarke and Cornish published *The Reasoning Criminal: Rational Choice Perspectives on Offending* (Clarke and Cornish, 1986). The previous year they had noted that a 'considerable body of recent psychological research on information processing and decision making has passed largely unnoticed by criminologists' (Clarke and Cornish, 1985, p 158). The 1986 book developed a framework of criminal decision making based on the recent psychological research. More recently, Jean-Louis Van Gelder et al have pointed out that: 'Ironically, while crime researchers busied themselves with researching the rational choice perspective and examining its applications over the past decades, some major advances in the psychological study of information processing and decision-making research have gone largely unnoticed' (Van Gelder et al, 2014, p 1). More recent research in cognitive psychology and neuroscience has highlighted the importance of 'emotions, moods and related visceral factors' in human decision making (Van Gelder et al, 2014). These developments have yet to be reflected fully in criminal justice studies.

In the 2017 Parmoor Lecture to the Howard League for Penal Reform, the President of the Family Division, Sir James Munby QC, told the story of one offender:

> I was recently concerned (in every sense of the word) with a suicidal teenager, X. I do not propose to discuss the case: it would not be appropriate to do so. I refer to it only because it might be thought to exemplify some of the systemic difficulties we face and because it illustrates some of the problems I wish to address today. For present purposes, all I need to say about X is that she was a gravely disturbed teenager who came from a troubled home and whose mother (her father was dead) had her own difficulties. X was taken into care in accordance with the Children Act 1989 but the various plans approved by the family court did not work. The time came when she needed, for her own safety, to be placed in secure accommodation; no suitable accommodation was available in England, so the placement was in Scotland. Returned to a placement in England, X's behaviour led to her being sentenced by the Youth Court to a Detention and Training Order and placed in another institution where the intensity and frequency of her self-harming and suicidal actions increased. Eventually, a place was found for her in a clinical setting to which she was transferred by the Secretary of State in accordance with the Mental Health Act 1983. (Munby, 2017)

The criminal process's pursuit of truth involves ascertaining whether or not X had committed the offence leading to her Detention and Training Order (DTO); it did not establish the wider, and much more nuanced, 'whole truth' of what had led to the offending behaviour. We do not know how X's story has continued but we can hazard a guess that the DTO would have done little to address her offending behaviour. Nor would her treatment encourage the rest of us to leave law-abiding lives.

Sir James Munby, who had spent his time as a barrister in the commercial and civil courts, found that his subsequent experience of family justice led him to consider whether there might be better, alternative ways to ascertain the truth and encourage us to lead law-abiding lives:

> Unlike the civil courts, which essentially look only to the past, the criminal court and the family court look both to the past and to the future: to the past to help determine what should happen in the future. That is all to the good, but, too much of the time, the exercise is still limited to determining what is the appropriate disposal for the case: what is to happen to the prisoner or to the child in future. In the family court, where the welfare of the child is, by statute, the court's paramount concern, it is all too easy to focus on the child's future, without paying adequate attention to what it is that has brought about the court's involvement in the first place. And, especially with younger children, that has to do almost exclusively with the parent, not the child. For, typically, the problems are those of the parent, not the child. So, far too little time is spent identifying the underlying problem or, more typically, problems and then to setting out to find a solution for the problem(s). In a sentence: family courts, and where children are involved criminal courts also, ought to be but usually are not problem-solving courts. (Munby, 2017)

Sir James Munby was focusing on the family courts but his remarks apply equally to the adult criminal courts: with a focus on acquitting the innocent and convicting the guilty, courts spend far too little time on identifying the underlying problems and finding solutions to those problems:

> We tend to see negative emotions and 'punitiveness' as understandable and appropriate responses to criminality. People who have transgressed the criminal law and caused harm to others are believed to be deserving of punishment for their offending regardless of whether this punishment makes any difference to their likelihood of reoffending in

the future. Punishment conveys society's disapproval and condemnation of such behaviour. (Knight, 2014, p 1)

In earlier chapters we saw how trauma-informed approaches and truth commissions can reveal a wider truth and that a narrow focus on particular aspects of historical truth can adversely affect the ability to discover a deeper narrative truth. Discovering the deeper truths may well provide better outcomes for all connected with the system of criminal justice.

'Do you know your case is going badly?' asked the priest. 'That's how it seems to me too,' said K. 'I've expended a lot of effort on it, but so far with no result. Although I do still have some documents to submit.' 'How do you imagine it will end?' asked the priest. 'At first I thought it was bound to end well,' said K., 'but now I have my doubts about it. I don't know how it will end. Do you know?' 'I don't,' said the priest, 'but I fear it will end badly. You are considered guilty. Your case will probably not even go beyond a minor court. Provisionally at least, your guilt is seen as proven.' 'But I'm not guilty,' said K., 'there's been a mistake. How is it even possible for someone to be guilty. We're all human beings here, one like the other.' 'That is true,' said the priest, 'but that is how the guilty speak.' 'Do you presume I'm guilty too?' asked K. 'I make no presumptions about you,' said the priest. 'I thank you for that,' said K., 'but everyone else involved in these proceedings has something against me and presumes I'm guilty. They even influence those who aren't involved. My position gets harder all the time.' 'You don't understand the facts,' said the priest, 'the verdict does not come suddenly, proceedings continue until a verdict is reached gradually.' (Kafka, 1953, p 232)

List of Cases

Australia

DPP v *Marijancevic* (2011) 33 VR 440
Ridgeway v *R* (1995) 184 CLR 19

Canada

R v *Grant* [2009] SCC 32
R v *Lifchus* [1997] 3 SCR 320

England and Wales

Attorney General v *Bradlaugh* (1885) 14 QBD 667
DPP v *Smith* [1960] 3 WLR 546
Jones v *National Coal Board* [1957] 2 QB 55
Kuruma v *The Queen* [1955] AC 197
M'Naghten's Case (1843) 10 Cl & F 200
Omichund v *Barker* (1745) 1 Atk 21
Owners of Steamship Hontestroom v *Owners of Steamship Sagaporack* [1947] AC 37
Paty's Case (1704) 2 Salkeld 503
R v *A (no 2)* [2002] 1 AC 45
R v *Alladice* (1988) 87 Cr App R 360
R v *Aspinall* [1999] 2 Cr App R 115
R v *Beech* (2019) Unreported, Newcastle Crown Court, 26 July 2019
R v *Ben-Rajab and Baccar* [2012] 1 Cr App R 4
R v *Bryant* v [2016] EWCA Crim 1245
R v *Chalkley* [1998] QB 848
R v *D* [2011] EWCA Crim 2305
R v *D(R)* [2014] 1 LRC 629
R v *Delaney* (1988) 88 Cr App R 338

R v Donovan [1934] 2 KB 498

R (on the application of DSD and NBV & Ors) v The Parole Board of England and Wales & Ors and John Radford [2018] EWHC 694 (Admin)

R v Duncan (1881) 7 QBD 198

R v Dunn (1990) 91 Cr App R 237

R v Ellis [1910] 2 KB 746

R v Evans [2017] 1 Cr App R 13

R v Ferguson (1909) 2 Cr App R 250

R v Fulling [1987] QB 426

R v Gill [2003] EWCA Crim 2256

R v Goldenberg (1988) 88 Cr App R 285

R v Hall-Chung [2007] EWCA Crim 3429

R v Hasan [2005] UKHL 22

R v Horncastle [2009] UKSC 14, [2009] EWCA Crim 964

R v J [2003] EWCA Crim 3309

R v Jelen (1989) 91 Cr App R 456

R v Keenan [1990] 2 QB 54

R v Khan (Sultan) [1997] AC 558

R v Kirk [2000] 1 WLR 567

R v Lambert [2002] 2 AC 535

R v Manister [2005] EWCA Crim 2866

R v Mason [1988] 1 WLR 139

R v Miller [2010] EWCA Crim 1578

R v Norris [2013] EWCA Crim 712

R v Paris (1992) 97 Cr App R 99

R v Renda [2005] EWCA Crim 2826

R v Riat [2012] EWCA Crim 1509

R v Samuel (1956) 40 Cr App R 8

R v Samuel [1988] QB 615

R v Sang [1980] AC 402

R v Secretary of State for the Home Department, Ex parte V. and R v Secretary of State for the Home Department, Ex parte T. [1997] Lexis Citation 3962

R v Taylor (2006) EWCA Crim 260

R v Twigg [2019] EWCA Crim 1553

R v Viola (1982) 75 Cr App R 125

R v Wahab [2002] EWCA Crim 1570

R v Walsh (1989) 91 Cr App R 161

R v Ward (1993) 96 Cr App R 1

SS (Sri Lanka), R (On the Application Of) v The Secretary of State for the Home Department [2018] EWCA Civ 1391

The Rioters' Case (1683) 1 Vern 175

Thomson v R [1988] 2 WLR 927

Woolmington v *DPP* [1935] AC 462

European Court of Human Rights

Al-Khawaja and Tahery v *UK* (2011) 54 EHRR 23
El Haski v *Belgium* (2013) 56 EHRR 31
El-Masri v *Former Yugoslav Republic of Macedonia* (2012) 57 EHRR 25
Ireland v *UK* (1978) 2 EHRR 25
Jalloh v *Germany* (2006) 44 EHRR 32
Janosevic v *Sweden* (2002) 38 EHRR 22
Kafkaris v *Cyprus* (2008) 49 EHRR 35
MSS v *Belgium and Greece* (2011) 53 EHRR 2
Salabiaku v *France* (1988) 13 EHRR 379
Schenk v *Switzerland* (1988) 13 EHRR 242
Telfner v *Austria* (2001) 34 EHRR 7

Republic of Ireland

Director of Public Prosecutions v *JC* [2015] IESC 31
Director of Public Prosecutions v *Kenny* [1990] 2 IR 110
Trimble v *Governor of Mountjoy Prison* [1985] IR 550

Scotland

Clarke v *Edinburgh and District Tramways Co* 1919 SC (HL) 35
McIntosh v *Lord Advocate* [2001] 3 WLR 107

South Africa

State v *Coetzee* [1997] 2 LRC 593

United States

Arizona v *Evans*, 54 US 1 (1995)
Brown v *Illinois*, 422 US 590 (1975)
Burlington v *Missouri*, 451 US 430 (1981)
Costello v *United States*, 365 US 265 (1961)
Herring v *United States*, 555 US 135 (2009)
Kaminsky v *Hertz Corporation*, 94 Mich App 356, 288 NW 2d 426
  (1979)
Mapp v *Ohio*, 367 US 643 (1961)
Murray v *United States*, 487 US 533 (1988)

Nix v *Williams*, 467 US 431 (1984)
Silverthorne Lumber Co v *United States*, 251 US 385 (1920)
Tehan v *United States ex rel. Shott*, 382 US 406 (1966)
United States v *Leon*, 468 US 897 (1984)
Weeks v *United States*, 232 US 383 (1914)

References

ACPO (Association of Chief Police Officers) (2009) *Practice Advice on the Management of Priority and Volume Crime (The Volume Crime Management Model)* (2nd edn), London: ACPO.

Aitkenhead, D. (2014) 'There is No Doubt in My Mind that At Least One Politician Abused Kids', *The Guardian*, 28 November, available at: https://www.theguardian.com/politics/2014/nov/28/tom-watson-interview-no-doubt-one-politician-abused-kids, accessed: 29 March 2021.

Alhoff, F. (2012) *Terrorism, Ticking Time-Bombs and Torture: A Philosophical Analysis*, Chicago: University of Chicago Press.

Allison, M. and Brimacombe, E. (2010) 'Alibi Believability: The Effect of Prior Convictions and Judicial Instructions', *Journal of Applied Social Psychology*, 40(5): 1054–58.

Amsterdam, A. G. and Bruner, J. (2000) *Minding the Law*, Cambridge: Harvard University Press.

Aquinas, T. (2018) *The Complete Works*, Omaha: Catholic Publishing.

Aristotle, *The Metaphysics* (1998) (trans Hugh Lawson-Tancred), London: Penguin Books.

Ashworth, A. and Blake, M. (1996) 'The Presumption of Innocence in English Criminal Law', *Criminal Law Review* (May): 306–17.

Austin, J. L. (1950) 'Truth', *Proceedings of the Aristotelian Society Supplementary Volume XXIV*, London: Aristotelian Society, available at: https://www.aristoteliansociety.org.uk/pdf/2013%20AS%20Virtual%20Issue.pdf, accessed: 29 March 2021.

Austin, J. L. (1962) *How to Do Things with Words*, Cambridge: Harvard University Press.

Bagaric, M. (2014) 'The Punishment Should Fit the Crime – Not the Prior Convictions of the Person that Committed the Crime: An Argument for Less Impact Being Accorded to Previous Convictions in Sentencing', *San Diego Law Review*, 51(2): 343–417.

BBC (2012) 'Jimmy Savile Abuse Allegations: Timeline', 2 November, available at: https://www.bbc.co.uk/news/uk-19921658, accessed: 9 February 2021.

BBC News (2014a) 'Lord Mayor Fiona Woolf to Lead Child Abuse Inquiry', 5 September, available at: https://www.bbc.co.uk/news/uk-politics-29076504, accessed: 9 February 2021.

BBC News (2014b) 'Abuse Inquiry: Fiona Woolf Steps Down as Chairwoman', 31 October, available at: https://www.bbc.co.uk/news/uk-politics-29855265, accessed: 9 February 2021.

Beach, L. R. and Bissell, B. L. (2016) *A New Theory of Mind: The Theory of Narrative Thought*, Cambridge: Cambridge Scholars Publishing.

Beccaria, C. (1769) *Essay on Crimes and Punishments*, London: Newbery.

Beck, L. W. (ed and trans) (1949) Kant, I., 'On a Supposed Right to Lie from Altruistic Motives' in *Critique of Practical Reason and Other Writings in Moral Philosophy*, Chicago: University of Chicago Press.

Bentham, J. (1817) *Works of Jeremy Bentham*, London: Simpkin, Marshall & Co.

Bergman, P. and Moore, A. (1991) 'Mistrial by Likelihood Ration: Bayesian Analysis Meets the F-Word', *Cardozo Law Review*, 13: 589–619.

Bicak, A. V. (2001) 'Police and Criminal Evidence Act 1984, s.76(2): Re-Emergence of the Involuntariness Test', *The Journal of Criminal Law*, 65(1): 85–92.

Binet, A. (1900) *La Suggestabilite*, Paris: Schleicher Freres.

Blair, T. (1993) 'Why Crime is a Socialist Issue', *New Statesman*, 23 January, available at: https://www.newstatesman.com/2017/04/1997-election-archive-tony-blair-why-crime-socialist-issue, accessed: 10 March 2021.

Blake, S. (2015) *A Practical Approach to Effective Litigation* (8th edn), Oxford: Oxford University Press.

Bloom, R. and Fentin, D. (2010) 'A More Majestic Conception: The Importance of Judicial Integrity in Preserving the Exclusionary Rule', *University of Pennsylvania Journal of Constitutional Law*, 13(1): 47–80.

Blume, J. H. and Helm, R. K. (2014) 'The Unexonerated: Factually Innocent Defendants who Plead Guilty', *Cornell Law Review*, 100(1): 157–91.

Bok, S. (1999) *Lying: Moral Choice in Public and Private Life* (2nd ed), New York: Vintage Books.

Bond, C. F. and DePaulo, B. M. (2006) 'Accuracy of Deception Judgments', *Personality and Social Psychology Review*, 10(3): 214–34.

Bowling, B., Reiner, R. and Sheptycki, J. W. E. (2019) *The Politics of the Police* (5th edn), Oxford: Oxford University Press.

Brook, J. (1991) 'The Blue Bus Stop: On Professors' Stories and the Stories Plaintiffs Tell', *Cardozo Law Review*, 13: 621–7.

Brookman, F. (2015) 'The Shifting Narratives of Violent Offenders' in Presser, L. and Sandberg, S. (eds) *Narrative Criminology: Understanding Stories of Crime*, New York: New York University Press.

Bruner, J. (1991) 'The Narrative Construction of Reality', *Critical Inquiry*, 18(1): 1–21.

Bufacchi, V. and Arrigo, J. M. (2006) 'Torture, Terrorism and the State: A Refutation of the Ticking Bomb Argument', *Journal of Applied Philosophy*, 23(3): 355–73.

Burke, K. (1969) *A Grammar of Motives*, Berkeley: University of California Press.

Burnett, R. (2016) *Wrongful Allegations of Sexual and Child Abuse*, Oxford: Oxford University Press.

Cammack, M. E. (2010) 'The Rise and Fall of the Constitutional Exclusionary Rule in the United States', *The American Journal of Comparative Law*, 58(1): 631–58.

Campbell, E., Ashworth, A. and Redmayne, M. (2019) 'The Criminal Process' (5th edn), Oxford: Oxford University Press.

Chalfin, A. and McCrary, J. (2017) 'Criminal Deterrence: A Review of the Literature', *Journal of Economics Literature*, 55(1): 5–48.

Childline (2019) Childline Annual Review 2018/19, available at: https://learning.nspcc.org.uk/media/1898/childline-annual-review-2018-19.pdf, accessed: 9 February 2021.

Choo, A. L-T. (2018) *Evidence*, Oxford: Oxford University Press.

Clarke, R. V. and Cornish, D. B. (1985) 'Modeling Offenders' Decisions: A Framework for Research and Policy' in Tonry, M. and Morris, N. (eds) *Crime and Justice: An Annual Review of Research, Vol. 6*, Chicago: University of Chicago Press.

Cohen, S. (2011) *Folk Devils and Moral Panics* (3rd edn), Abingdon: Routledge.

College of Policing (2012) 'College of Policing Analysis: Estimating Demands on the Police Service', available at: https://www.college.police.uk/News/College-news/Documents/Demand%20Report%2023_1_15_noBleed.pdf, accessed: 12 February 2021.

College of Policing (2018) 'Review into Believing Victims at the Time of Reporting', London: College of Policing, available at: https://www.college.police.uk/News/College-news/Pages/review-into-believing-victims-at-the-time-of-reporting.aspx, accessed: 29 March 2021.

College of Policing (2020) 'Investigation: Introduction', London: College of Policing, available at: https://www.app.college.police.uk/app-content/investigations/introduction, accessed: 29 March 2021.

College of Policing, Crown Prosecution Service, HM Courts and Tribunals Service, HM Prison & Probation Service, Ministry of Justice, Judicial Office, NPCC and the Parole Board (2018) *Joint Agency Guide to the Victim Personal Statement: A Guide for All Criminal Justice Practitioners*, London: Ministry of Justice.

Conti, R. P. (1999) 'The Psychology of False Confessions', *The Journal of Credibility Assessment and Witness Psychology*, 2(1): 14–36.

Cornford, M. (1976) *A Theory of Knowledge Volume 3* (4th edn), London: Lawrence and Wishart.

Cornish, D. B. and Clarke, R. V. (1986) *The Reasoning Criminal: Rational Choice Perspectives on Offending*, New York: Springer-Verlag.

Courts and Tribunals Judiciary (2020) 'Coronavirus (COVID-19): Jury Trials, Message from the Lord Chief Justice', 17 March, available at: https://www.judiciary.uk/announcements/coronavirus-jury-trials-message-from-the-lord-chief-justice/, accessed: 10 February 2021.

Cree, V. E., Clapton G. and Smith, M. (2014) 'The Presentation of Child Trafficking in the UK: An Old and New Moral Panic?', *British Journal of Social Work*, 44: 418–33.

Crenzel, E. (2008) 'Argentina's National Commission on the Disappearance of Persons: Contributions to Transitional Justice', *International Journal of Transitional Justice*, 2(2): 173–91.

Crenzel, E. (2017) *Memory of the Argentina Disappearances: The Political History of the Nunca Más*, New York: Routledge.

Criminal Law Revision Committee, Evidence (General) 11th Report (Command 4991), London: HMSO.

Crown Prosecution Service (2018) 'The Code for Crown Prosecutors', available at: https://www.cps.gov.uk/sites/default/files/documents/publications/Code-for-Crown-Prosecutors-October-2018.pdf, accessed: 10 February 2021.

Daly, K. (2016) 'What Is Restorative Justice? Fresh Answers to a Vexed Question', *Victims & Offenders*, 11(1): 9–29.

Dame Janet Smith Review (2016) *The Jimmy Savile Investigation Report*, available at: http://downloads.bbci.co.uk/bbctrust/assets/files/pdf/our_work/dame_janet_smith_review/savile/jimmy_savile_investigation.pdf, accessed: 29 March 2021.

Davis, R. C. and Smith, B. E. (1994) 'Victim Impact Statements and Victim Satisfaction: An Unfulfilled Promise?', *Journal of Criminal Justice*, 22(1): 1–12.

Department of Health (2013) 'A Promise to Learn – A Commitment to Act: Improving the Safety of Patients in England: National Report of the Advisory Group on the Safety of Patients in England', available at: https://assets.publishing.service.gov.uk/government/uploads/system/uploads/attachment_data/file/226703/Berwick_Report.pdf, accessed: 10 February 2021.

Dervan, L. E. and Edkins, V. A. (2013) 'The Innocent Defendant's Dilemma: An Innovative Empirical Study of Plea Bargaining's Innocence Problem', *Journal of Criminal Law & Criminology*, 103(1): 1–48.

Descartes, R. [1639] (1991) 'Letter to Mersenne: 16 October 1639', in *The Philosophical Writings of Descartes: Volume 3*, Cambridge: Cambridge University Press.

Dhami, M. K., Mantle, G. and Fox, D. (2009) 'Restorative Justice in Prisons', *Contemporary Justice Review*, 12(4): 433–48.

Dholakia, Lord (2013) 'Second Reading of the Age of Criminal Responsibility Bill (HL)', Hansard, 8 November, column 476.

Dignan, J. (2007) 'The Victim in Restorative Justice' in Walklate, S. (ed) *Handbook of Victims and Victimology*, Cullompton: Willan Publishing, pp 309–31.

Dignan, J. and Cavadino, M. (1996) 'Towards a Framework for Conceptualising and Evaluating Models of Criminal Justice from a Victim's Perspective', *International Review of Victimology*, 4(3): 153–82.

Dingwall, G. (2008) 'Deserting Desert? Locating the Present Role of Retributivism in the Sentencing of Adult Offenders', *Howard Journal of Criminal Justice*, 47(4): 400–10.

Dingwall, G. and Harding, C. (1998) *Diversion in the Criminal Process*, London: Sweet & Maxwell.

Dingwall, G. and Hillier, T. (2010) 'The Banality of Punishment: Context-Specificity and Justifying Punishment of Extraordinary Crimes', *International Journal of Punishment and Sentencing*, 6(1): 6–18.

Dingwall, G. and Hillier, T. (2016) *Blamestorming, Blamemongers and Scapegoats: Allocating Blame in the Criminal Justice Process*, Bristol: Policy Press.

Driscoll, C. (2015) *In Pursuit of Truth: A Life in the Met*, London: Ebury Press.

Drizin, S. A. and Colgan, B. A. (2004) 'Tales from the Juvenile Confessions Front' in Lassiter, G. D. (ed) *Interrogations, Confessions, and Entrapment*, New York: Kluwer, pp 127–62.

Drizin, S. A. and Leo, R. A. (2004) 'The Problem of False Confessions in the Post-DNA World', *North Carolina Law Review*, 82: 891–1007.

Duff, A., Farmer, L., Marshall, S. and Tadros, V. (2007) *The Trial on Trial: Volume 3: Towards a Normative Theory of the Criminal Trial*, Oxford: Hart Publishing.

Easton, S. and Piper, C. (2016) *Sentencing and Punishment: The Quest for Justice* (4th edn), Oxford: Oxford University Press.

Edwards, H. T. (1986) 'Alternative Dispute Resolution: Panacea or Anathema?', *Harvard Law Review*, 99(3): 668–84.

Eisenberg, T. and Hans, V. P. (2009) 'Taking a Stand on Taking the Stand: The Effect of a Prior Criminal Record on the Decision to Testify and on Trial Outcomes', *Cornell Law Review*, 90: 1356–57.

Ekman, P. and O'Sullivan, M. (1991) 'Who Can Catch a Liar?', *American Psychologist*, 46(9): 913–20.

Ekman, P., O'Sullivan, M. and Frank, M. G. (1999) 'A Few Can Catch a Liar', *Psychological Science*, 10(3): 263–6.

Ellington, J. W. (trans) [1785] (1993) Kant, I., *Grounding for the Metaphysics of Morals* (3rd edn), Indianapolis: Hackett.

Fair Trials (2019) 'The Disappearing Trial Report: A Global Study into the Spread and Growth in Trial Waiver Systems', available at: https://www.fairtrials.org/sites/default/files/publication_pdf/Report-The-Disappearing-Trial.pdf, accessed: 10 February 2021.

Fichte, J. G. (1869) *The Science of Rights*, Philadelphia, PA: Lippincott.

Field, J. (1934) *A Life of One's Own*, London: Chatto and Windus.

Fireman, G. D., McVay, T. E. and Flanagan, O. J. (eds) (2003) *Narrative and Consciousness: Literature, Psychology and the Brain*, Oxford: Oxford University Press.

Frankel, M. E. (1975) 'Search for Truth: An Umpireal View', *University of Pennsylvania Law Review*: 1031–59.

Franklin, J. (2009) 'Evidence Gained from Torture: Wishful Thinking, Checkability and Extreme Circumstances', *Cardozo Journal of International and Comparative Law*, 17: 281–90.

Galoob, S. R. (2017) 'Retributivism and Criminal Procedure', *New Criminal Law Review*, 20(3): 465–505.

Gardner, D. (2009) *Risk: The Science and Politics of Fear*, London: Virgin Publishing.

Garrett, B. L. (2011) *Convicting the Innocent: Where Criminal Prosecutions Go Wrong*, Cambridge: Harvard University Press.

Gavrielides, T. (2014) 'Reconciling the Notions of Restorative Justice and Imprisonment', *The Prison Journal*, 94(4): 479–505.

Gazzaniga, M. S. (1998) *The Mind's Past*, Berkeley: University of California Press.

Gibson, J. L. (2009) 'On Legitimacy Theory and the Effectiveness of Truth Commissions', *Law and Contemporary Problems*, 72(2): 123–41.

Gilchrist, G. M. (2011) 'Plea Bargains, Convictions and Legitimacy', *American Criminal Law Review*, 48(1): 143–83.

Goldstein, A. G., Chance, J. E. and Schneller, G. R. (1989) 'Frequency of Eyewitness Identification in Criminal Cases: A Survey of Prosecutors,' *Bulletin of the Psychonomic Society*, 27(1): 71–4.

Gottfredson, M. R. and Gottfredson, D. M. (1988) *Decision Making in Criminal Justice: Toward the Rational Exercise of Discretion* (2nd edn), New York: Plenum.

Granhag, P. A. and Stromwall, L. A. (2001) 'Deception detection based on repeated interrogations', *Legal and Criminological Psychology*, 6(1): 85–101.

Graycar, R. (1991) 'The Gender of Judgments: An Introduction' in Thornton, M. (ed) *Public and Private Feminist Legal Debates*, Melbourne: Oxford University Press.

Greene, E. and Dodge, M. (1995) 'The Influence of Prior Record Evidence on Juror Decision Making', *Law and Human Behavior*, 19(1): 67–76.

Greer, D. D. (1971) 'Anything But the Truth: The Reliability of Testimony in Criminal Trials', *British Journal of Criminology*, 11(2): 131–54.

Gudjonsson, G. H. (2003) *The Psychology of Interrogations and Confessions*, Chichester: John Wiley & Sons.

Hajjar, L. (2009) 'Does Torture Work? A Sociolegal Assessment of the Practice in Historical and Global Perspective', *Annual Review of Law and Social Science*, 5: 311–45.

Hamilton, M. (2015) 'Back to the Future: The Influence of Criminal History on Risk Assessments', *Berkeley Journal of Criminal Law*, 20(1): 75–133.

Hansard (2012) House of Commons Debates, 24 October, Vol 551, column 923.

Hansard (2017) 'Age of Criminal Responsibility Bill (HL)', 8 September, column 2187.

Helm, R. K. (2019) 'Conviction by Consent? Vulnerability, Autonomy and Conviction by Guilty Plea', *Journal of Criminal Law*, 83(2): 161–72.

Henriques Review (2016) *The Independent Review of the Metropolitan Police Service's Handling of Non-recent Sexual Offence Investigations Alleged Against Persons of Public Prominence*, available at: https://www.met.police.uk/SysSiteAssets/foi-media/metropolitan-police/other_information/corporate/mps-publication-chapters-1---3-sir-richard-henriques-report.pdf, accessed: 29 March 2021.

Henriques, R. (2020) ' "Even Now, When I See a Toddler I Think of James Bulger": Top Lawyer Richard Henriques Was the Prosecutor in Britain's Most Notorious Child Killing Case; Here He Reveals How There Was Only One Possible Verdict', *Daily Mail*, 25 May, available at: https://www.dailymail.co.uk/news/article-8355675/richard-henriques-reveals-one-possible-verdict-Britains-notorious-child-killing-case.html, accessed: 10 March 2021.

Hester, R., Frase, R. S., Roberts, J. V. and Mitchell, K. L. (2018) 'Prior Record Enhancements at Sentencing: Unsettled Justifications and Unsettling Consequences', *Crime and Justice*, 47(1): 209–54.

Higgens, D. (2012) 'Family of Jimmy Savile Hit Back at Child Abuse Claims', *The Scotsman*, 1 October, available at: https://www.scotsman.com/news/uk-news/family-jimmy-savile-hit-back-child-abuse-claims-1605999, accessed: 29 March 2021.

Holdsworth, W. S. (1922) *A History of English Law: Volume 1* (3rd edn), Boston: Little, Brown and Company.

Home Office (2020a) *Crime Outcomes in England and Wales 2018 to 2019: Data Tables*, London: Home Office.

Home Office (2020b) Vision and Purpose Statements for Crime Recording (NCRS and HOCR), available at: https://assets.publishing.service.gov.uk/government/uploads/system/uploads/attachment_data/file/387762/count-vision-december-2014.pdf, accessed: 10 February 2021.

Hope, C. (2019) 'Boris Johnson to End Early Release of Prisoners as He Demands Tougher Sentencing', *The Daily Telegraph*, 10 August, available at: https://www.telegraph.co.uk/politics/2019/08/10/boris-johnson-take-tough-stance-stop-criminals-let-automatically/, accessed: 10 March 2021.

House of Commons (1882) *Report from the Select Committee on Contagious Diseases Acts*, with the proceedings of the committee, minutes of evidence and appendix.

Hudson, B. (1998) 'Restorative Justice: The Challenge of Sexual and Racial Violence', *Journal of Law and Society*, 25(2): 237–56.

Hudson, B. (2002) 'Restorative Justice and Gendered Violence: Diversion or Effective Justice?', *British Journal of Criminology*, 42(3): 616–34.

Huhn, W. (2018) 'Foreword: Shall These Bones Live? Resurrecting Truth in American Law and Discourse', *Duquesne Law Review*, 56: 1–6.

Hulsman, L. (1986) 'Critical Criminology and the Concept of Crime', *Contemporary Crises*, 10(1): 63–80.

Hunt, J. (2013) 'Mid-Staffordshire NHS Trust', Hansard: House of Commons debates, 19 November, column 1096, available at: https://publications.parliament.uk/pa/cm201314/cmhansrd/cm131119/debtext/131119-0001.htm, accessed: 10 February 2021.

IICSA (Independent Inquiry Child Sexual Abuse) (2015) Independent Inquiry Child Sexual Abuse: Terms of Reference, available at: https://www.iicsa.org.uk/terms-reference, accessed: 9 February 2021.

IICSA (2020) *"People Don't Talk About It": Child Sexual Abuse in Ethnic Minority Communities*, available at: https://www.iicsa.org.uk/publications/research/child-sexual-abuse-ethnic-minority-communities, accessed: 29 March 2021.

Immigration and Nationality Directorate (1998) *Assessing the Claim*, London: Home Office.

Independent Asylum Commission (2008) 'Fit for Purpose Yet?: The Independent Asylum Commission's Interim Findings', available at: http://www.citizensforsanctuary.org.uk/pages/reports/InterimFindings.pdf, accessed: 10 February 2021.

Innes, M. (2014) *Signal Crimes: Social Reactions to Crime, Disorder, and Control*, Oxford: Oxford University Press.

Innocence Project (2020) 'DNA Exonerations in the United States', available at: https://innocenceproject.org/dna-exonerations-in-the-united-states/, accessed: 10 February 2021.

ITV (2012a) 'Exposure: The Other Side of Jimmy Savile', ITV television broadcast, 3 October (dir. Lesley Gardner).

ITV (2012b) 'Exposure Update: The Jimmy Savile Investigation', ITV television broadcast, 21 November (dir. Brian Stanley and Tom Stone).

Jacobs, B. A. (2010) 'Deterrence and Deterrability', *Criminology*, 48(2): 417–41.

James, W. (1907) *Pragmatism's Conception of Truth: Lecture 6: Pragmatism: A New Name for Some Old Ways of Thinking*, New York: Longman Green and Co.

Johnson, B. D., King, R. D. and Spohn, C. (2016) 'Sociolegal Approaches to the Study of Guilty Pleas and Prosecution', *Annual Review of Law and Social Science*, 12: 479–95.

Joyce-Wojtas, N. and Keenan, M. (2016) 'Is Restorative Justice for Sexual Crime Compatible with Various Criminal Justice Systems?', *Contemporary Justice Review*, 19(1): 43–68.

Judicial College (2018) *The Crown Court Compendium*, London: Judicial College.

Justice Inspectorates (2020) 'Crime Recording Process', available at: https://www.justiceinspectorates.gov.uk/hmicfrs/our-work/article/crime-data-integrity/crime-recording-process, accessed: 29 March 2021.

Kafka, F. (1953) *The Trial*, Harmondsworth: Penguin Books.

Kahneman, D. and Tversky, A. (1979) 'Prospect Theory: An Analysis of Decision Under Risk', *Econometrica*, 47(2): 263–291.

Kant, I. (1998) 'The Critique of Pure Reason' in Guyet, P. and Wood, A. W. (eds), *The Cambridge Edition of the Works of Immanuel Kant*, Cambridge: Cambridge University Press.

Kaplan, J. (1968) 'Decision Theory and the Factfinding Process', *Stanford Law Review*, 20(6): 1065–1092.

Kaptein, H., Prakken, H. and Verheij, B. (eds) (2009) *Legal Evidence and Proof: Statistics, Stories, Logic*, Farnham: Ashgate Publishing.

Kassim, S. M. (2017) 'False Confessions: How Can Psychology So Basic Be So Counterintuitive?', *American Psychologist*, 72(9): 951–64.

King, S. and Brähler, V. (2019) *Truth Project Research Methods*, London: IICSA.

Knight, C. (2014) *Emotional Literacy in Criminal Justice: Professional Practice with Offenders*, Basingstoke: Palgrave Macmillan.

Koss, M. P. (2014) 'The RESTORE Program of Restorative Justice for Sex Crimes: Vision, Process, and Outcomes', *Journal of Interpersonal Violence*, 29(9): 1623–60.

Kramer, M. H. (2014) *Torture and Moral Integrity: A Philosophical Enquiry*, Oxford: Oxford University Press.

Laudan, I. (2006) *Truth, Error and Criminal Law: An Essay in Legal Epistemology*, Cambridge: Cambridge University Press.

Lemonne, A. (2003) 'Alternative Conflict Resolution and Restorative Justice: A Discussion' in Walgrave, L. (ed) *Repositioning Restorative Justice*, Cullompton: Willan Publishing, pp 43–63.

Leon, C. and Ward, T. (2015) 'The Irish Exclusionary Rule after *DPP v JC*', *Legal Studies*, 35(4): 590–3.

Leubsdorf, J. (1991) 'Stories and Numbers', *Cardozo Law Review*, 13: 455–63.

Lippke, R. L. (2014) 'The Prosecutor and the Presumption of Innocence', *Criminal Law and Philosophy*, 8(2): 337–52.

Liptak, A. (2011) '34 Years Later, Supreme Court Will Revisit Eyewitness IDs', *The New York Times*, 22 August, available at: https://www.nytimes.com/2011/08/23/us/23bar.html#:~:text=washington%20%E2%80%94%20Every%20year%2C%20more%20than,identifications%20lead%20to%20wrongful%20convictions, accessed: 10 March 2021.

Loftus, E. F. (1979) *Eyewitness Testimony*, Cambridge: Harvard University Press.

Loftus, E. F. (2019) 'Eyewitness Testimony', *Applied Cognitive Psychology*, 33(4): 498–503.

Loftus, E. F. and Palmer, J. (1974) 'Reconstruction of Automobile Destruction: An Example of the Interaction Between Language and Memory', *Journal of Verbal Learning and Verbal Behavior*, 13(5): 585–9.

Ludwig, A. M. (1997) *How Do We Know Who We Are? A Biography of the Self*, Oxford: Oxford University Press.

Luna, E. (2003) 'Punishment Theory, Holism, and the Procedural Conception of Restorative Justice', *Utah Law Review*, 2003(1): 205–302.

MacIntyre, A. (2007) *After Virtue*, London: Bloomsbury.

Marshall, T. (1996) 'The Evolution of Restorative Justice in Britain', *European Journal of Criminal Policy and Research*, 4(4): 21–43.

May, T. (2014) 'Oral Statement on Child Abuse', available at: https://www.gov.uk/government/news/home-secretary-oral-statement-on-child-abuse, accessed: 29 March 2021.

May, T. (2015) 'Statement to the House of Commons on the Child Sexual Abuse (Independent Panel Inquiry)', available at: http://www.publications.parliament.uk/pa/cm201415/cmhansrd/cm150204/debtext/150204-0001.htm#15020467000001, accessed: 9 February 2021.

McAuley, A. (2006) 'Canon Law and the End of the Ordeal', *Oxford Journal of Legal Studies*, 26(3): 473–513.

McConville, M. and Marsh, L. (2016) 'Factory Farming and State-Induced Pleas' in Hunter, J., Roberts, P., Young, S. N. M. and Dixon, D. (eds) *The Integrity of Criminal Process from Theory into Practice*, Oxford: Hart Publishing.

McEvoy, K. and Mika, H. (2002) 'Restorative Justice and the Critique of Informalism in Northern Ireland', *British Journal of Criminology*, 42(3): 534–62.

McGlynn, C., Westmarland, N. and Godden, N. (2012) '"I Just Wanted Him to Hear Me": Sexual Violence and the Possibilities of Restorative Justice', *Journal of Law and Society*, 39(2): 213–40.

Meretoja, H. (2014) *The Narrative Turn in Fiction and Theory: The Crisis and Return of Storytelling from Robbe-Grillet to Tournier*, London: Palgrave Macmillan.

Meyer, P. N. (2014) *Storytelling for Lawyers*, New York: Oxford University Press.

Milhauser, S. (1972) *Edwin Mullhouse: The Life and Death of an American Writer 1943–1954*, New York: Alfred A. Knopf.

Mindthoff, A., Evans, J. R., Perez, G., Woestehoff, S. A., Oluguez, A. P., Klemfuss, J. Z., Normile, C. J., Scherr, K. C., Carlucci, M. E., Carol, R. N., Meissner, C. A., Michael, S. W., Russano, M. B., Stock, E. L., Vallano, J. P. and Woody, W. D. (2018) 'A Survey of Potential Jurors' Perceptions of Interrogations and Confessions', *Psychology, Public Policy, and Law*, 24(4): 430–48.

Ministry of Justice (2019) *Proven Reoffending Statistics Quarterly Bulletin, July 2017 to September 2017*, London: Office for National Statistics.

Ministry of Justice (2020) *Proven Reoffending Statistics Quarterly Bulletin, January 2018 to March 2018*, London: Office for National Statistics.

Mink, L. (1970) 'History and Fiction as Modes of Comprehension', *New Literary History*, 1(3): 557–58.

Mitchell, O., Cochran, J. C., Mears, D. P. and Bales, W. D. (2017) 'Examining Prison Effects on Recidivism: A Regression Discontinuity Approach', *Justice Quarterly*, 34(4): 571–96.

Morrison Piehl, A. and Bushway, S. D. (2007) 'Measuring and Explaining Charge Bargaining', *Journal of Quantitative Criminology*, 23(2): 105–25.

Moston, S. and Stephenson, G. M. (1993) 'The Changing Face of Police Interrogation', *Community & Applied Social Psychology*, 3(2): 101–15.

Mumm, S. (2006) 'Josephine Butler and the International Traffic of Women' in Daggers, J. and Neal, D. (eds) *Sex, Gender and Religion: Josephine Butler Revisited*, New York: Peter Lang Publishing, pp 55–72.

Munby, J. L. (2017) 'Children Across the Justice Systems', *Parmoor Lecture to the Howard League for Penal Reform*, 30 October.

Münsterberg, H. (1908) *On the Witness Stand: Essays on Psychology and Crime*, New York: McClure Co.

Nagin, D. S. (2013a) 'Deterrence: A Review of the Evidence by a Criminologist for Economists', *Annual Review of Economics*, 5(1): 83–105.

Nagin, D. S. (2013b) 'Deterrence in the Twenty-First Century', *Crime and Justice*, 42(1): 199–263.

Nagin, D. S., Cullen, F. T. and Lero Jonson, C. (2009) 'Imprisonment and Reoffending', *Crime and Justice*, 38(1): 115–200.

National Association for People Abused in Childhood (2020) 'Key Facts and Figures', available at: https://napac.org.uk/key-facts-figures/, accessed: 29 March 2021.

National Research Council (2014) *Identifying the Culprit: Assessing Eyewitness Identification*, Washington, DC: The National Academies Press.

Naughton, M. (ed) (2009) *The Criminal Cases Review Commission: Hope for the Innocent?*, Basingstoke: Palgrave Macmillan.

Naylor, B. (2010) 'Effective Justice for Victims of Sexual Assault: Taking Up the Debate on Alternative Pathways', *University of New South Wales Law Journal*, 33(3): 662–83.

Newman, D. (2013) *Legal Aid Lawyers and the Quest for Justice*, Oxford: Hart Publishing.

NSPCC (National Society for the Prevention of Cruelty to Children) (2013) *Giving Victims a Voice*, London: NSPCC, available at: https://www.nspcc.org.uk/globalassets/documents/research-reports/yewtree-report-giving-victims-voice-jimmy-savile.pdf, accessed: 18 June 2020.

ONS (Office for National Statistics) (2016) 'Abuse During Childhood: Findings from the Crime Survey for England and Wales', year ending March 2016, available at: https://www.ons.gov.uk/peoplepopulationandcommunity/crimeandjustice/articles/abuseduringchildhood/findingsfromtheyearendingmarch2016crimesurveyforenglandandwales, accessed: 9 February 2021.

ONS (2019) *Criminal Justice Statistics Quarterly: June 2019*, London: ONS.

ONS (2020) 'Child abuse in England and Wales: January 2020', available at: https://www.ons.gov.uk/peoplepopulationandcommunity/crimeandjustice/bulletins/childabuseinenglandandwales/january2020, accessed: 9 February 2021.

Ofsche, R. (1989) 'Coerced Confessions: The Logic of Seemingly Irrational Action', *Cultic Studies Journal*, 6: 1–15.

Oldenquist, A. (1988) 'An Explanation of Retribution', *The Journal of Philosophy*, 85(9): 464–76.

Ormerod, D. and Perry, D. (eds) (2018) *Blackstone's Criminal Practice 2019*, Oxford: Oxford University Press.

Owens, N. (2012) 'BBC Axe Investigation into Sir Jimmy Savile and Schoolgirls', *The Sunday Mirror*, 8 January, available at: https://www.mirror.co.uk/news/uk-news/bbc-axe-investigation-sir-jimmy-157675, accessed: 18 June 2020.

Pali, B. and Pelikan, C. (2014) 'Con-Texting Restorative Justice and Abolitionism: Exploring the Potential and Limits of Restorative Justice as an Alternative Discourse to Criminal Justice', *Restorative Justice: An International Journal*, 2(2): 142–64.

Parole Board (2019) *Parole Board for England and Wales Annual Report and Accounts 2018/19*, London: Parole Board.

Pavlich, G. (2017) 'Restorative Justice and the Rights of the Accused', *Restorative Justice: An International Journal*, 5(3): 396–407.

Pennington, N. and Hastie, R. (1991) 'A Cognitive Theory of Juror Decision Making: The Story Model', *Cardozo Law Review*, 13: 519–57.

Phillipps, M. S. and Arnold, T. J. (1859) *A Treatise on the Law of Evidence* (10th edn), New York: Banks and Brothers.

Pinard, M. (2005–06) 'Offender Reentry and the Collateral Consequences of Criminal Convictions: An Introduction', *New York University Review of Law and Social Change*, 30(4): 585–620.

Pinto, N. (2015) 'The Bail Trap', *The New York Times Magazine*, 13 August, available at: https://www.nytimes.com/2015/08/16/magazine/the-bail-trap.html?_r=0See, accessed: 10 February 2021.

Pollock, F. and Maitland, F. W. (1895) *The History of English Law Before the Time of Edward I vol 2*, available at: http://oll.libertyfund.org/title/2314, accessed: 4 November 2019.

Presser, L. (2004) 'Violent Offenders, Moral Selves: Constructing Identities and Accounts in the Research Interview', *Social Problems*, 51(1): 82–101.

Rayner, G. (2015) 'Operation Midland: Who Are the Nine People Accused of Being Part of a "VIP Paedophile Ring"?', *Daily Telegraph*, 12 October, p 1.

Reason, J. (2000) 'Human Error: Models and Management', *British Medical Journal*, 320(7237): 768–70.

Redlich, A., Wilford, M. and Bushway, S. (2017) 'Understanding Guilty Pleas Through the Lens of Social Science', *Psychology, Public Policy, and Law*, 23(4): 458–71.

Richards, K. (2014) 'A Promise and a Possibility: The Limitations of the Traditional Criminal Justice System as an Explanation for the Emergence of Restorative Justice', *Restorative Justice: An International Journal*, 2(2): 124–41.

Ricoeur, P. (1984) *Time and Narrative (Temps et Récit)*, vol. 2 (trans Kathleen McLaughlin and David Pellauer), Chicago: University of Chicago Press.

Roberts, J. V. (2008) 'Punishing Persistence: Explaining the Enduring Appeal of the Recidivist Sentencing Premium', *British Journal of Criminology*, 48(4): 468–81.

Roberts, P. (2002) 'The Presumption of Innocence Brought Home? Kebilene Deconstructed', 118(1) *Law Quarterly Review* 41–71.

Roberts, P. and Zuckerman, A. (2010) *Criminal Evidence* (2nd edn), Oxford: Oxford University Press.

Roche, D. (2003) *Accountability in Restorative Justice*, Oxford: Clarendon Press.

Romilly, S. (1810) *Observations on the Criminal Law of England: As it Relates to Capital Punishments, and on the Mode in which it is Administered*, London: T. Cadell and W. Davies.

Rossner, M. (2018) 'Restorative Justice and Victims of Crime' in Shapland, J. (ed) *Handbook of Victims and Victimology* (2nd edn), London: Routledge, pp 229–46.

Ruggiero, V. (2010) *Penal Abolitionism*, Oxford: Oxford University Press.

Ruggiero, V. (2011) 'An Abolitionist View of Restorative Justice', *International Journal of Law, Crime and Justice*, 39(2): 100–10.

Rushton, B. (2006) 'Truth and Reconciliation? The Experience of Truth Commissions', *Australian Journal of International Affairs*, 60(1): 125–41.

Sanders, A. and Young, R. (1994) *Criminal Justice*, London: Butterworths.

Sartre, J. P. (1965) *Nausea*, Harmondsworth: Penguin Books.

Saunders, C. L. (2012) 'The Truth, The Half-Truth, and Nothing Like the Truth: Reconceptualising False Allegations of Rape', *British Journal of Criminology*, 52(6): 1152–71.

Sayers, D. L. (1937) *Busman's Honeymoon*, London: Victor Gollancz.

Schacter, S. and Singer, J. E. (1962) 'Cognitive, Social and Emotional State', *Psychological Review*, 69(5): 379–99.

Scherr, K. C., Redlich, A. D. and Kassin, S. M. (2020) 'Cumulative Disadvantage: A Psychological Framework for Understanding how Innocence can Lead to Confession, Wrongful Conviction, and Beyond', *Perspectives on Psychological Science*, 15(2): 353–83.

Schiemann, J. W. (2012) 'Interrogational Torture: Or How Good Guys Get Bad Information with Ugly Methods', *Political Research Quarterly*, 65(1): 3–19.

Sentencing Council (2011a) *Causing Grievous Bodily Harm with Intent to Do Grievous Bodily Harm/Wounding with Intent to do GBH*, London: SC.

Sentencing Council (2011b) *Inflicting Grievous Bodily Harm/Unlawful Wounding/Racially or Religiously Aggravated GBH/Unlawful Wounding*, London: SC.

Sentencing Council (2011c) *Assault Occasioning Actual Bodily Harm/Racially or Religiously Aggravated ABH*, London: SC.

Sentencing Council (2014) *Fraud*, London: SC.

Sentencing Council (2017a) *Reduction in Sentence for a Guilty Plea*, London: SC.

Sentencing Council (2017b) *Sentencing Children and Young People*, London: SC.

Sentencing Council (2019) *General Guideline: Overarching Principles*, London: SC.

Shapland, J., Atkinson, A., Atkinson, H., Chapman, B., Dignan, J., Howes, M., Johnstone, J., Robinson, G. and Sorsby, A. (2007) *Restorative Justice: The Views of Victims and Offenders: The Third Report from the Evaluation of Three Schemes*, London: Ministry of Justice.

Shargel, G. L. (2007) 'Federal Evidence Rule 608(b): Gateway to the Minefield of Witness Preparation', *Fordham Law Review*, 76(3): 1263–94.

Shaw, J. (2016) *The Memory Illusion: Remembering, Forgetting and the Science of False Memory*, London: Random House.

Silving, H. (1959a) 'The Oath: I', *Yale Law Journal*, 68: 1329–90.

Silving, H. (1959b) 'The Oath: II', *Yale Law Journal*, 68: 1527–77.

Silving, H. (1988) *Helen Silving Memoirs*, New York: Vantage Press.

Simons, D. J. and Chabris, C. F. (2011) 'What People Believe about How Memory Works: A Representative Survey of the U.S. Population', *PLoS ONE*, 6(8): e22757.

Spence D. P. (1982) 'On Some Clinical Implications of Action Language', *Journal of the American Psychoanalytic Association*, 30(1):169–184.

Sporer, S. L. (2001) 'Recognizing Faces of Other Ethnic Groups: An Integration of Theories', *Psychology, Public Policy, and Law*, 7(1): 36–97.

Starmer, K. (2014) 'Human Rights, Victims and the Prosecution of Crimes in the 21st Century', *Criminal Law Review*, 11: 777–87.

Sykes, G. and Matza, D. (1957) 'Techniques of Neutralization: A Theory of Delinquency', *American Sociological Review*, 22(6): 664–70.

Taslitz, A. (2013) 'Hypocrisy, Corruption, and Illegitimacy: Why Judicial Integrity Justifies the Exclusionary Rule', *Ohio State Journal of Criminal Law*, 10(2): 419–76.

Tesich, S. (1992) 'Government of Lies', *The Nation*, 6 January.

Thaler, M. (2016) 'A Pragmatist Defence of the Ban on Torture: From Moral Absolutes to Constitutive Rules of Reasoning', *Political Studies*, 64(3): 765–81.

Thayer, J. B. (1890–91) 'Law and Fact in Jury Trials', *Harvard Law Review*, 4(4): 147–75.

The Pollard Review (2012) *Report, 18 December 2012*, available at: http://downloads.bbc.co.uk/bbctrust/assets/files/pdf/our_work/pollard_review/pollard_review.pdf, accessed: 29 March 2021.

Thommen, M. and Samadi, M. (2016) 'The Bigger the Crime, the Smaller the Chance of a Fair Trial? Evidence Exclusion in Serious Crime Cases under Swiss, Dutch and European Human Rights Law', *European Journal of Crime, Criminal Law and Criminal Justice*, 24(1): 65–86.

Tillers, P. (1991) 'Decision and Inference', *Cardozo Law Review*, 13(2–3): 253–56.

Travis, C. (2013) 'As a Matter of Fact' in *Proceedings of the Aristotelian Society: Truth: The Virtual Issue 1*, London: The Aristotelian Society, available at: https://www.aristoteliansociety.org.uk/pdf/2013%20AS%20Virtual%20Issue.pdf, accessed: 29 March 2021.

Turner, J. I. and Weigend, T. (2019) 'Do Exclusionary Rules Ensure a Fair Trial?' in Gless, S. and Richter, T. (eds) *Do Exclusionary Rules Ensure a Fair Trial?*, Cham: Springer, pp 255–282.

Twiss, S. B. (2007) 'Torture, Justification and Human Rights: Toward an Absolute Proscription', *Human Rights Quarterly*, 29(2): 346–67.

Van Gelder, J.-L., Elffers, H., Reynald, D. and Nagin, D. (2014) *Affect and Cognition in Criminal Decision Making*, London: Taylor & Francis.

Von Hirsch, A. and Ashworth, A. (2005) *Proportionate Sentencing: Exploring the Principles*, Oxford: Oxford University Press.

von Neumann, J. and Morgenstern, O. (1944) *Theory of Games and Economic Theory*, Princeton: Princeton University Press.

Walsh, D. and Bull, R. (2012) 'How Do Interviewers Attempt to Overcome Suspects' Denials?', *Psychiatry, Psychology and Law*, 19(2): 151–68.

Watney, S. (1987) *Policing Desire*, London: Methuen.

Watson, C., Weiss, K. J. and Pouncey, C. (2010) 'False Confessions, Expert Testimony, and Admissibility', *The Journal of the American Academy of Psychiatry and the Law*, 38(2): 174–86.

Webster, R. (1998) *The Great Children's Home Panic*, Oxford: The Orwell Press.

Wells, G. L. (1978) 'Applied Eyewitness-Testimony Research: System Variables and Estimator Variables', *Journal of Personality and Social Psychology*, 36(12): 1546–57.

White, H. (1981) 'The Value of Narrativity in the Representation of Reality', in W. J. T. Mitchell (ed) *On Narrative*, Chicago: University of Chicago Press, 238–39.

Wigmore, J. H. (1937) *The Science of Judicial Proof, As Given by Logic, Psychology, and General Experience, and Illustrated in Judicial Trials*, Boston: Little, Brown.

Wigmore, J. H., Reiser, W. A., Chadbourn, J. H. and McNaughton, J. T. (1940) *A Treatise on the Anglo-American System of Evidence in Trials at Common Law: Including the Statutes and Judicial Decisions of All Jurisdictions of the United States and Canada*, Boston: Little, Brown.

Willemsens, J. (2003) 'Restorative Justice: A Discussion of Punishment' in Walgrave, L. (ed) *Repositioning Restorative Justice*, Cullompton: Willan Publishing, pp 24–42.

Winterbottom, A., Bekker, H. L., Conner, M. and Mooney, A. (2008) 'Does Narrative Information Bias Individual's Decision Making? A Systematic Review', *Social Science & Medicine*, 67(12): 2079–88.

Wood, W. R. and Suzuki, M. (2016) 'Four Challenges in the Future of Restorative Justice', *Victims & Offenders*, 11(1): 149–72.

Wright, M. (2003) 'Is it Time to Question the Concept of Punishment?' in Walgrave, L. (ed) *Repositioning Restorative Justice*, Cullompton: Willan Publishing, pp 3–23.

Youth Justice Board (2020) *Youth Justice Statistics 2018/19 England and Wales*, London: Ministry of Justice/Youth Justice Board.

Zehr, H. (1985) *Retributive Justice, Restorative Justice: New Perspectives on Crime and Justice*, Akron: Mennonite Central Committee Office of Criminal Justice.

Index